John H. Ingram, H. Ingram John

Elizabeth Barrett Browning

John H. Ingram, H. Ingram John

Elizabeth Barrett Browning

ISBN/EAN: 9783348009355

Printed in Europe, USA, Canada, Australia, Japan

Cover: Foto ©ninafisch / pixelio.de

More available books at **www.hansebooks.com**

ELIZABETH
BARRETT BROWNING

BY

JOHN H. INGRAM

SECOND EDITION.

LONDON:
W. H. ALLEN & CO., 13 WATERLOO PLACE, S.W.

1889.

LONDON:
PRINTED BY W. H. ALLEN AND CO., 13 WATERLOO PLACE, PALL MALL.   S.W.

INTRODUCTORY.

No writer approaching the eminence of Elizabeth Barrett Browning has been so little written about. Hitherto, nothing even claiming to be a biography of her has been published in her native land, whilst her works, which reveal so much of her inner self, have only been attainable in costly editions. It would almost appear as if it had been desired to retard, rather than promote, the popularity of one of England's purest as well as greatest poets.

All critical persons who have read the correspondence of Elizabeth Barrett Browning assign it a pre-eminent place in epistolary literature ; yet it is only allowed to appear in fragments, without proper or responsible editorship. It is to be hoped that this injustice to the memory of a great writer will not continue much longer, because, as Mr. Browning has himself said of another great poet, " letters and poems are obviously an act of the same mind, produced by the same law, only differing in the application to the individual. . . . Letters and poems may be used indifferently as the basement of our opinion upon the writer's character; the finished expression of a sentiment in the poems giving light and significance to the rudiments of the same in the letters, and these, again, in their incipiency and unripeness, authenticating the exalted mood and re-attaching it to the personality of the writer."

Notwithstanding these pregnant words, as, also, Mr Browning's uttered opinion that "it is advisable to lose no opportunity of strengthening and completing the chain of biographical testimony," the testimony to the goodness and greatness of our poetess, which the publication of her literary correspondence would afford, is still withheld. Those letters of Mrs. Browning which have been published, it should be observed, do not express any repugnance to afford biographical information, but rather the reverse.

The mystery which has hitherto shrouded Mrs. Browning's personal career, has caused quite a mythology to spring up around her name, and this fictitious lore the publications of those assuming to speak with authority has only increased. Miss Mitford, who saw Mrs. Browning frequently, knew her relatives intimately, and claimed to have received two letters a week from her, is utterly wrong in her biographical statements about her ; Richard H. Horne, who published two volumes of Mrs. Browning's correspondence, muddles the dates almost beyond elucidation; whilst Mrs. Richmond Ritchie, who has contributed to the *Dictionary of National Biography* the most copious and authoritative memoir of Mrs. Browning extant, has, so far as biographical *data* are concerned, made " confusion worse confounded."

With examples so misleading, and material so restricted, neither accuracy nor substance sufficient for a volume might have been hoped for ; but some past success in the paths of biography has encouraged me to place before the public what, with all its shortcomings, is the initial biography of Elizabeth Barrett Browning.

JOHN H. INGRAM.

LIST OF AUTHORITIES.

The Works of E. B. Browning. 1826–1863.

A New Spirit of the Age. Edited by R. H. Horne. 1844.

Letters of E. B. Browning to R. H. Horne. 1877.

Life of M. R. Mitford. Edited by A. G. L'Estrange. 1870.

Letters of M. R. Mitford. Edited by Henry Chorley. 1872.

The Friendships of M. R. Mitford. Edited by A. G. L'Estrange. 1882.

Dictionary of National Biography, vol. vii. pp. 78–82. 1886.

Passages from the Note-Books of Nathaniel Hawthorne. 1883.

Notes in England and Italy. By Mrs. Hawthorne. 1870.

Memoirs of Anna Jameson. By G. Macpherson. 1878.

Edgar Allan Poe. His Life and Letters. By John H. Ingram. 1886.

H. F. Chorley. Memoir, &c. Compiled by H. G. Hewlett. 1873.

Living Authors of Britain. By Thomas Powell. 1851.

"Notes on Slips connected with Devonshire," by W. Pengelly, F.R.S. (In *Devonshire Association Report*, vol. ix. pp. 354–360). 1877.

The Atlantic Monthly. Letter from W. W. Story. 1861.

The Athenæum. 1825–84.

Walter Savage Landor. Biography by John Forster. 1879.

The Correspondence of Leigh Hunt, vol. ii. 1862.

Yesterdays with Authors. Article on "M. R. Mitford." By J. T. Fields. 1873.

The Quarterly Review. "Modern English Poetesses." 1840.

At Home and Abroad. By Bayard Taylor. 1880.

Browning Society Papers. 1881, &c.

Six Months in Italy. By G. S. Hillard. 1853.

Recollections of a Literary Life. By M. R. Mitford. 1859.

Benjamin Robert Haydon. Correspondence. 1876.

Notes and Queries, Magazines, Newspapers, Wills, &c.

CONTENTS.

CONTENTS.

ELIZABETH BARRETT BROWNING.

---◆---

CHAPTER I.

HOPE END.

THE Barretts were wealthy West Indian land-owners. Edward Barrett Moulton, a member of the family, assumed the additional surname of Barrett in accordance with his grandfather's will. Edward Moulton-Barrett, as he now styled himself, had not attained his majority when he married Mary, daughter of J. Graham Clarke, at that time residing at Fenham Hall, Newcastle-on-Tyne. Of Mrs. Moulton-Barrett our records are scanty; it is known that she was several years older than her husband and that, despite their disparity in age, she was tenderly loved by him.

In 1809 the Barretts were residing in London; and in that city, on Saturday, the 4th of March, their daughter, Elizabeth Barrett Barrett, is believed to have been born.*

Soon after the birth of their daughter the Barretts removed to Hope End, near Ledbury, Herefordshire. Hope End, an estate recently acquired by Mr.

* See Appendix.

1

Barrett, had previously been the country seat of Sir Henry Vane Tempest, and was not unnoted for the beauty of its situation. It was located in a retired valley, a few miles distant from the Malvern Hills, and the Rev. J. Barrett, in a description he gave of the place some years previous to the birth of Elizabeth, says : "It is nearly surrounded by small eminences, and therefore does not command any distant prospect, except to the southward, nor is that very extensive ; but this defect is compensated by the various and beautiful scenery that immediately surrounds this secluded residence. In front of the house are some fine pieces of water; on their banks are planted a variety of shrubs and evergreens, which, in conjunction with the water, look very ornamental. The Deer Park," says the reverend gentleman in the pedantic phraseology of the period, "lies on the ascent of the contiguous eminences, whose projecting parts and bending declivities, modelled by nature, display much beauty. It contains an elegant profusion of wood, disposed in the most careless yet pleasing order. Much of the Park and its scenery is in view from the house, where it presents a very agreeable appearance."

The residence belonging to this charming estate was modern, and in keeping with the grounds ; but it was not of sufficient grandeur to suit the semi-tropical tastes of its new proprietor. Mr. Barrett had the house pulled down and on its sight erected an oriental-looking structure, bedecked with " Turkish " windows and turrets.

A large family of sons and daughters sprang up rapidly around the wealthy West Indian, and the quaint residence and its pleasant environments re-

echoed daily to the prattle of little tongues and the
.patter of little feet. Foremost of the band was
~~Elizabeth~~. She was her father's favourite child, and
he, who was proud of her intelligence, spared no pains
to cultivate it. Although one of a large family, and
presumably the sharer in the sports of her brothers
and sisters, she appears to have been fond of solitude
and solitary amusements. She was allowed a little
room to herself, and thus describes it :—

> I had a little chamber in the house
> As green as any privet-hedge a bird
> Might choose to build in. . . .
> The walls
> Were green, the carpet was pure green, the straight
> Small bed was curtained greenly, and the folds
> Hung green about the window, which let in
> The out-door world with all its greenery.
> You could not push your head out and escape
> A dash of dawn-dew from the honeysuckle.

A member of Mr. Barrett's family, who is said to
remember Hope End as it was in those days, speaks
of "Elizabeth's room" as a lofty chamber with a stained
glass window casting lights across the floor, and upon
little Elizabeth as she used to sit propped against the
wall, with her hair falling all about her face, a child-
like fairy figure. "Aurora Leigh's" recollections,
however, are probably accurate, and it may be assumed
that her record of childish rambles in the early sum-
mer mornings when she would—

> Slip down-stairs through all the sleepy house
> As mute as any dream then, and escape
> As a soul from the body, out of doors,
> Glide through the shrubberies, drop into the lane
> And wander on the hills an hour or two,
> Then back again before the house should stir,—

faithfully represents little Elizabeth's own doings.

1 *

Of Hope End and the surrounding scenery "Aurora Leigh" furnishes many glimpses, but whether the. heroine's father, "who was an austere Englishman" who taught his little daughter Latin and Greek himself, is intended for Mr. Barrett, is more than doubtful. Indulgent as her father was in some things, he was sternly despotic in others, and although, as she grew up, Elizabeth evidently revered him, it is certain that he would never allow himself to be thwarted. There is evidence that the gentle wife, who flits like a colourless spirit across the early life-track of her celebrated child, had often to soothe the anger of the wealthy West Indian slave-owner against his own offspring.

Although little Elizabeth found some things "as dull as grammar on an eve of holiday," as a rule she took more kindly to grammars than children of her age generally do. At nine—she herself is the authority—the only thing the mystic number nine suggested to the little girl was that the Greeks had spent nine years in besieging Ilium! Pity for her lost childhood's pleasures rather than admiration for her precocity would arise were it not palpable that infant necessity for play caused her to mingle frolic with her classical endowments. In the poem of "Hector in the Garden," Elizabeth Barrett tells that a device for amusement she invented when she was only nine years old was to cut out with a spade a huge giant of turf and, laying it down prostrate in the garden, style the creation of her childish fancy "Hector, son of Priam." Then, she says,—

With my rake I smoothed his brow,
Both his cheeks I weeded through.

Then she made her plaything—

> Eyes of gentianellas azure,
>   Staring, winking at the skies :
>   Nose of gillyflowers and box;
>   Scented grasses put for locks,
> Which a little breeze at pleasure
>   Set a waving round his eyes.
>
> Brazen helm of daffodillies,
>   With a glitter toward the light ;
>   Purple violets for the mouth,
>   Breathing perfumes west and south;
> And a sword of flashing lilies,
>   Holden ready for the fight.
>
> And a breastplate made of daisies,
>   Closely fitting, leaf on leaf ;
>   Periwinkles interlaced,
>   Drawn for belt about the waist ;
> While the brown bees, humming praises,
>   Shot their arrows round the chief.

Even at this tender age the little girl began to write verses, and dream of becoming a poet. "I wrote verses," she said, "as I daresay many have done who never wrote any poems, very early; at eight years old and earlier. . . . I could make you laugh by the narrative of nascent odes, epics, and didactics, crying aloud on obsolete Muses from childish lips. The Greeks were my demi-gods, and haunted me out of Pope's Homer, until I dreamt more of Agamemnon than of 'Moses,' the black pony."

The result of this was an "epic" on *The Battle of Marathon.* The composition was completed before its author was eleven, and Mr. Barrett was so proud of the production that he had fifty copies of it printed and distributed. The little booklet, consisting of seventy-two pages, was dedicated to her

father, from " Hope End, 1819." *The Battle of
Marathon* is divided into four books, and is truly
described by its author as " Pope's Homer done over
again, or rather undone; for, although a curious pro-
duction for à child, it gives evidence only of an imi-
tative faculty and an ear, and a good deal of reading in
a peculiar direction."

" The love of Pope's Homer threw me into Pope on
one side, and Greek on the other, and into Latin as
a help to Greek," is her own record of this period
of her life, contradicting the legend of her reading
Homer in the original at eight years old. About
the time of the grand epic, a cousin of Elizabeth
was wont to pay visits to Hope End, where their
grandmother, says Mrs. Ritchie, "would also come
and stay. The old lady did not approve of these read-
ings and writings, and used to say she would rather
see Elizabeth's hemming more carefully finished off
than hear of all this Greek."

Mr. Barrett evidently differed from the old lady in
this respect, and encouraged his daughter both in her
studies and her writings. In some of her earliest
known verses, inscribed to him, Elizabeth says :—

> 'Neath thy gentleness of praise,
> My Father! rose my early lays!
> And when the lyre was scarce awake,
> I lov'd its strings for *thy* lov'd sake ;
> Woo'd the kind Muses—but the while
> Thought only how to win thy smile—
> My proudest fame—my dearest pride—
> *More* dear than all the world beside!

Mrs. Barrett, who was still living when these lines
were written, doubtless divided her affections more
equally among her many little sons and daughters

than did her husband ; what with continuous ill-health
and a constant succession of children, she had some-
thing else to think of than *The Battle of Marathon*, or
" Hector, son of Priam." In those days it was the
father's praise that sounded sweet to the little author's
ears ; in after life, when too late, a lost mother's love
were more often the first thought of her verse.

The principal sharer of Elizabeth's childish amuse-
ments was her brother Edward. There was little
more than a year's difference in age between them,
and as he was, by all accounts, a suitable companion for
her in both study and frolic, it was but natural that
they should regard each other with intense affection.
Alluding to the pet-name by which she was known
in the family circle, she says :—

> My brother gave that name to me
> When we were children twain,
> When names acquired baptismally
> Were hard to utter, as to see
> That life had any pain.

In her earliest volume of poems, published in 1826,
Elizabeth included " Verses to my Brother," intro-
duced by the quotation from *Lycidas*, " For we were
nurs'd upon the self-same hill." She addressed him
as " Belov'd and best . . . my Brother ! dearest,
kindest as thou art ! " adding :—

> Together have we past our infant hours,
> Together sported childhood's spring away,
> Together cull'd young Hope's fast budding flowers,
> To wreathe the forehead of each coming day !

> And when the laughing mood was nearly o'er,
> Together, many a minute did we wile
> On Horace' page, or Maro's sweeter lore ;
> While one young critic, on the classic style,
> Would sagely try to frown, and make the other smile.

Surrounded by happy children, companioned by a beloved brother, encouraged in her pursuits by a proud father, supplied by all that wealth could procure, it is easy to imagine that Elizabeth's early life was a happy one. Her greatest pleasure was, apparently, derived from reading. "I read," she said, "books bad and good," anything, in fact, in the shape of a book that could be got hold of.

Neither her indiscriminate and extensive reading nor her close application to study prevented her joining in pursuits suitable to her age and position. Riding and driving were among her amusements; and Mrs. Ritchie relates :—"One day, when Elizabeth was about fifteen, the young girl, impatient for her ride, tried to saddle her pony alone, in a field, and fell with the saddle upon her, in some way injuring her spine so seriously that she was for years upon her back."

That Elizabeth was an invalid for many years is certain, as it also is that to the end of her life she remained in delicate health; but, although she remarked that at fifteen she nearly died, she attributed the origin of her illness to a cough; "a common cough," she said, "striking on an *insubstantial* frame, began my bodily troubles." Be the cause of her delicacy what it may, confinement and ill-health only increased her passion for reading.

About this epoch in her life came to pass an event that must be regarded as one that influenced Elizabeth's future as largely as anything in her career. Her father obtained an introduction for her to the well-known Greek scholar, Hugh Stuart Boyd. Mr. Boyd, although blind, was a profound student of Hellenic literature and an accomplished author. Under his friendly tuition the eager girl drank deep draughts of Grecian lore,· and acquired a knowledge of its less studied branches that stood her in good stead in after days. In her poem on "Wine of Cyprus," addressed by her to this dear friend, she proves, by the happiness of her allusions and the condensation of character, how thoroughly she had grasped the most salient features of Greek literature: her poem is at once a proof of her capacity to acquire, and her friend's to instruct. Some of the stanzas are charming reminiscences of these early days :—

And I think of those long mornings
  Which my thought goes far to seek,
When, betwixt the folio's turnings.
  Solemn flowed the rhythmic Greek.
Past the pane, the mountain spreading,
  Swept the sheep-bell's tinkling noise,
While a girlish voice was reading—
  Somewhat low for *ai*'s and *oi*'s!

Then what golden hours were for us!—
  While we sat together there;
How the white vests of the chorus
  Seemed to wave us a live air!
How the cothurns trod majestic
  Down the deep iambic lines;
And the rolling anapæstic
  Curled like vapour over shrines!

For we sometimes gently wrangled:
  Very gently, be it said.—
For our thoughts were disentangled
  By no breaking of the thread!
And I charged you with extortions
  On the noble fames of old—
Ay, and sometimes thought your Porsons
  Stained the purple they would fold.

*   *   *   *

> Ah, my gossip! you were older,
>   And more learned, and a man!—
> Yet that shadow,—the enfolder
>   Of your quiet eyelids—ran
> Both our spirits to one level;
>   And I turned from hill and lea
> And the summer-sun's green revel—
>   To your eyes that *could not see!*"

Elizabeth Barrett never forgot the advantages she had derived from the patient kindness and profound learning of the blind scholar, nor did he forego friendly correspondence with his apt and able pupil in after years. She deferred often to his opinion, despite her intense independence, and allowed his somewhat eccentric course of reading to influence her own studies. In later life she addressed three sonnets to this

> Steadfast friend,
> Who never didst my heart or life misknow,

on "His Blindness," "His Death, 1848," and his "Legacies" to her, which last consisted of his

> Æschylus,
> And Gregory Nazianzen, and a clock
> Chiming the gradual hours out like a flock
> Of stars, whose motion is melodious.

"The books," she says, "were those I used to read from," thus

> Assisting my dear teacher's soul to unlock
> The darkness of his eyes: now mine they mock,
> Blinded in turn, by tears: now murmurous
> Sad echoes of my young voice, years agone,
> Entoning from these leaves, the Grecian phrase,
> Return and choke my utterance.

"All this time," says Elizabeth, "we lived at Hope End, a few miles from Malvern, in a retirement scarcely broken to me except by books and my own thoughts, and it is a beautiful country, and was a retirement happy in many ways. . . . There I had my fits of Pope and Byron and Coleridge, and read Greek as hard under the trees as some of your Oxonians in the Bodleian ; gathered visions from Plato and the dramatists, and eat and drank Greek and made my head ache with it."

The young girl by practice and increasing intensity of feeling was gradually learning to become a true poet. Most of the *events* of her life, she said, had passed in her *thoughts*, and these thoughts she had continuously striven to transmute into poesy. Many youths wrote verses, but with her, "what is less common," as she remarked, "the early fancy turned into a will, and remained with me, and from that day poetry has been a distinct object with me—an object to read, think, and live for."

Already as early as 1825, Elizabeth Barrett had contributed fugitive verses to literary publications of the day, but now her ambition prompted her to more daring flights. Her childish lines on *The Battle of Marathon* can scarcely be taken into account in any chronicle of her literary deeds, but a volume which she published anonymously in 1826 marks a distinct epoch in her career. It was entitled *An Essay on Mind and Other Poems*, and the leading piece, written in heroic verse, and extending to eighty-eight pages, is produced in view, not without some doubts as to its truth, of the utterly false dictum of Byron, that " ethical poetry is the highest of all poetry, as the highest of all earthly objects is moral truth."

The lines display no originality of thought, are in the see-saw style of the Pope school, and are not very wonderful even for a girl of seventeen, but the *Essay* is remarkable, as has been pointed out, " for the precocious audacity with which she deals with the greatest names in the whole range of literature and science. Gibbon, Berkeley, Condillac, Plato, Bacon, Bolingbroke, all come in for treatment in the scope of the young girl's argument."

Some of Elizabeth's words in her preface, needlessly long and wordy as it is, offer a much better specimen of her prose than does the *Essay on Mind* of her poesy, and, as the first known example of her unrhymed writings may be cited from. With youthful modesty she says : " I wish that the sublime circuit of intellect, embraced by the plan of my Poem, had fallen to the lot of a spirit more powerful than mine. I wish it had fallen to the lot of one more familiar with the dwelling-place of mind, who could search her secret chambers, and call forth those that sleep; or of one who could enter into her temples, and cast out the iniquitous who buy and sell, profaning the sanctuary of God; or of one who could try the golden links of that chain which hangs from Heaven to earth, and show that it is not placed there for man to covet for lucre's sake, or for him to weigh his puny strength at one end against Omnipotence at the other; but that it is placed there to join, in mysterious union, the natural and the spiritual, the mortal and the eternal, the creature and the Creator. I wish the subject of my poem had fallen into such hands that the powers of the execution might have equalled the vastness of the design—and the public will wish so too. But as it is—though I desire this field to be more meritoriously occupied by others, I would mitigate the voice of censure for myself. I would endeavour to show that while I may

have often erred, I have not clung willingly to error ;
and that while I may have failed in representing, I
have never ceased to love Truth.   If there be much to
condemn in the following pages, let my narrow capacity,
as opposed to the infinite object it would embrace,
be generously considered ; if there be anything to
approve, I am ready to acknowledge the assistance
which my illustrations have received from the exalt-
ing nature of their subject—as the waters of Halys
acquire a peculiar taste from the soil over which
they flow."

Besides the *Essay on Mind*, preface, analyses, and
notes, the little book contained fourteen short pieces
pretty equally divided between Byronic and domestic
themes.   Whilst none of these verses gave cause to
believe in the advent of a great poetess, some of them,
notably those beginning " Mine is a wayward lay,"
were skilfully handled and were not barren of felicitous
turns of thought.

Reverting to the more personal history of the young
poetess, we arrive at what may be deemed the first, and
probably the greatest, real trouble she ever had to
endure.   For some time past Mrs. Barrett had had a
continuance of ill-health, and eventually, on the 1st of
October 1828, she died, at the comparatively early
age of forty-eight.   Elizabeth, herself an invalid, was
left by her mother's death not only the chief con-
soler of her widowed father, but, to some extent,
the guardian and guide of her seven brothers and
sisters.

How Elizabeth managed to bear her grief, or what
part she took in household affairs, are mysteries which
have not been revealed, but she continued to seek
consolation for human trouble, and an outlet for her

ambition, for ambitious she was, in beloved Poesy. For a time, apparently, she was sent to France to pursue her studies, and contracted at least one strong friendship there, but neither her words nor works evince that any strong imprint was made on her mind by that stay on French soil.

Storm-clouds were gathering at home, and Elizabeth's influence was wanted to soothe, and her companionship to cheer, her father. As a West Indian proprietor, his chief wealth was, naturally, derived from slave labour. The voice of the British people had gradually been growing louder and stronger against slavery, and finally, guided by Wilberforce and his compatriots, demanded its abolition. Emancipation, after a long and weary fight, was at last obtained, and though still shackled by certain galling restrictions, the fiat went forth that, henceforth, unpaid compulsory labour should cease. Liberty for slaves in many instances meant ruin or, at the best, heavy pecuniary loss for their late owners. On Jamaica the blow fell with peculiar force, and the Barretts naturally felt the shock. Mr. Edward Moulton Barrett's fortune appears to have been very largely affected by Emancipation, and one of the chief results of his diminished income would appear to have been the relinquishment of the Hope End establishment.

• The place where so many happy days had been spent, so many fond dreams born and nourished, so many loving ties formed, had to be left. " Do you know the Malvern Hills ?—the hills of *Piers Plowman's Visions* ? " wrote Elizabeth in later years ; " they ' seem to me my native hills, for I was an infant when I went first into their neighbourhood, and lived there until I had passed twenty by several years. Beautiful, beautiful hills they are; and yet not for the whole world's beauty would I stand in the sunshine and shadow of them any more. It would be a mockery, like the taking back of a broken flower to its stalk."

CHAPTER II.

WOMANHOOD.

From Hope End the Barretts removed to Sidmouth, and resided there for two years. Nothing is known of the family doings during that time, save the publication, in 1833, of Elizabeth's second volume. This book was entitled *Prometheus Bound, translated from the Greek of Æschylus, and Miscellaneous Poems,* and was issued as by the author of *An Essay on Mind.* That author's own account is that her translation " was written in twelve days, and should have been thrown in the fire afterwards—the only means of giving it a little warmth."

Miss Barrett's judgment on her own work is perhaps somewhat too sweeping, but as she not only replaced it in after life by a more mature version, but desired the earlier attempt should be consigned to oblivion, there can be no incentive to drag it into daylight again. All the copies not issued, she says, " are safely locked up in the wardrobe of papa's bedroom, entombed as safely as Œdipus among the olives." " A few of the fugitive poems connected with that translation," she added, " may be worth a little, perhaps;

but they have not so much goodness as to overcome the badness of the blasphemy of Æschylus."

Some of the fugitive pieces thus carelessly referred to are, indeed, worth something more than a little. The initial poem, styled "The Tempest: A Fragment," not only suggests a tale of intense horror, but contains lines as grand, sonorous, and truly poetic as any blank verse Elizabeth Barrett ever published.

Several other short pieces in the 1833 volume are well worthy republication; as a reviewer has said they are, " for the most part, in no sense immature, or unworthy of the genius of the writer," and certainly are equally good with many of those poems given in her collected works. There are some grand thoughts in " A Sea-side Meditation," " A Vision of Life and Death," " Earth"; and others in the volume are well worthy their author's name, and very different from the general *juvenilia* of even eminent poets. There is sustained pathos, albeit bitter irony, in the lines, " To a Poet's Child "—presumably Ada Byron—whilst none of the pieces are common-place or devoid of some traces of their author's peculiar originality and genius. The lines " To Victoire, on her Marriage," unless totally different from all Elizabeth Barrett's personal poems, in being pure imagination instead of a record of real life, refer to a certain period of her life spent in France. There are not wanting proofs that Elizabeth Barrett proposed to republish, with revision, some of the poems, at least, of this volume of her early womanhood, as she did, indeed, still earlier but less meritorious pieces.

After two years' residence in Devonshire, the Barretts removed to London, where Mr. Barrett took a house at 74, Gloucester Place. After the pure country air and invigorating sea-breezes, the change was naturally a trying one for all the household, but more especially did it affect Elizabeth. Her health for years past had been delicate—as she said herself, at fifteen she nearly died—and now it gave way entirely. Instead of rambling about Devonshire lanes, or gazing upon the varying ocean, she sat and watched the sun,

> Push out through fog with his dilated disk,
> And startle the slant roofs and chimney pots
> With splashes of fierce colour. Or I saw
> Fog only, the great tawny weltering fog,
> Involve the passive city, strangle it
> Alive, and draw it off into the void,
> Spires, bridges, streets and squares, as if a sponge
> Had wiped out London.

Notwithstanding, or rather because of, her want of health, Elizabeth devoted herself more and more to poesy. She no longer contented herself with the composition of poems, but began to send them for publication to contemporary periodicals. Chief among the friends outside her own immediate family circle whom she saw was John Kenyon, a distant relative. Mr. Kenyon, West Indian by birth, but European by education and choice, being in possession of ample means, was enabled to select his own method of living. Fond of literary and artistic society, and a dabbler in verse himself, he devoted his time to entertaining and being entertained by the makers of pictures and poems. Crabb Robinson, who knew everybody of his time worth knowing, describes Kenyon as having the face of a Benedictine monk and the joyous talk of a good fellow. He delights, he says, in seeing at his hospitable table every variety of literary notabilities, and was popularly styled the " feeder of lions." Coleridge,

Wordsworth, and most of the best, as well as best known, literary folk of the day were among Kenyon's most intimate associates, and it was one among the many pleasant traits of his character to seek to introduce and make acquainted with each other such celebrities as he knew himself. Such was Kenyon, whom it delighted Elizabeth Barrett to call "cousin," and to whom she naturally turned for advice in literary matters.

It was Kenyon who introduced the young poetess to most of her earliest literary friends, and he was the means of getting her poems accepted and works noticed by the chief literary journals of the day. Many of her earlier poems have, doubtless, been lost sight of altogether, not so much on account of their unworthiness as through their author's carelessness or forgetfulness of their existence.

"The Romaunt of Margret," which appeared in the July part of the *New Monthly Magazine*, was a great advance upon everything the poetess had as yet published, and was well calculated to enhance her reputation, not only among those few literary acquaintances who began to proclaim her as a rising star, but also with the outside public. This fine ballad is based upon the idea which permeates so many literatures, and has excited the imagination of so many great poets, of the possibility of man's dual nature; upon the possibility of a mortal being enabled, generally just before death, to behold the double or duplicate of himself.

Although here and there somewhat misty in the filling up, as are, indeed, many of her later poems, the "Romaunt" is worthy of its author's most matured powers. It has that weird, pathetic, indescribable glamour often found pervading the older

2

ballads, but rarely discoverable in those of modern date, and is noteworthy as being the earliest known specimen of Miss Barrett's use of the *refrain,* a metrical, euphonic adornment which Elizabeth Barrett, as well as her contemporary Edgar Poe, doubtless adopted from, or rather had suggested to them by, Tennyson's resuscitation of it.

During May of this year, Miss Barrett formed the acquaintance of Mary Russell Mitford, whose friendship and advice had no little influence on her future literary career. Miss Mitford being up in London on a visit, was taken by her friend Kenyon sight-seeing; on the way they called at Gloucester Place, and, after much persuasion, induced Miss Barrett to go out with them. Miss Mitford described her as " a sweet young woman who reads Greek as I do French, and has published some translations from Æschylus, and some most striking poems. She is a delightful young creature, shy and timid and modest."

The day following Miss Mitford dined at Kenyon's, and there met several notabilities, including Wordsworth, described as "an adorable old man," Landor, " as splendid a person as Mr. Kenyon, but not so full of sweetness and sympathy," and chief of all, "the charming Miss Barrett," who, so Miss Mitford wrote home, " has translated the most difficult of the Greek plays—the *Prometheus Bound*—and written most exquisite poems in almost every style. She is so sweet and gentle, and so pretty, that one looks at her as if she were some bright flower." Again, Miss Mitford describes her as being at this time " of a slight, delicate figure, with a shower of dark curls falling on either side of a most expressive face, large tender eyes, richly fringed by dark eye-lashes, a smile like a sunbeam, and such a look of youthfulness that I had some difficulty in persuading a friend that the translatress of Æschylus, the author of the *Essay on Mind*, was, in technical language, ' out.' "

To another friend, Miss Mitford described Miss Barrett as " a slight, girlish figure, very delicate, with exquisite hands and feet, a round face with a most noble forehead, a large mouth, beautifully formed and full of expression, lips like parted coral, teeth large, regular, and glittering with healthy whiteness, large dark eyes, with such eye-lashes, resting on the cheek when cast down, when turned upwards touching the flexible and expressive eyebrow, a dark complexion, literally as bright as the dark china rose, a profusion of silky, dark curls, and a look of youth and of modesty hardly to be expressed. This, added to the very simple but graceful and costly dress by which all the family are distinguished, is an exact portrait of her."

Once introduced to each other, the acquaintanceship between the two authoresses grew rapidly. " I saw much of her during my stay in town," writes Miss Mitford. " We met so constantly and so familiarly that, in spite of the difference of age, intimacy ripened into friendship, and after my return into the country, we corresponded freely and frequently, her letters being just what letters ought to be—her own talk put upon paper."

No sooner had Miss Mitford returned home to the companionship of her idolized but extremely undeserving father, than she commenced a constant and voluminous correspondence with her new friend Elizabeth Barrett, confiding all her troubles to her, in return being made acquainted with the young poetess's aspirations and achievements. The first letter from the elder correspondent, soon after her return home, was entrusted for delivery, with some flowers, to Henry Chorley, an author and influential critic, " who, if he have the good luck to be let in, as I hope he may," says Miss Mitford, " will tell you all about our doings. . . . To be sure I will come and see you when next I visit London, and I shall feel to know you better when I have had the pleasure of being introduced to Mr. Barrett, to be better authorized to love you, and to take a pride in your successes—things which, at present, I take the liberty of doing without authority." Some not altogether needless advice to her young friend on the fault of obscurity wound up the epistle.

A few weeks later Miss Mitford returned to the charge saying, " You should take my venturing to criticise your verses as a proof of the perfect truth of my praise. I do not think there can be a better test of the sincerity of the applause than the venturing to blame. It is also the fault, the one single fault (obscurity) found by persons more accustomed to judge of poetry than myself ; by Mr. Dilke, for instance (proprietor of the *Athenæum*), and Mr. Chorley (one of its principal writers). Charles Kemble once said to me," says Miss Mitford, *par exemple*, " with regard to the drama, 'Think of the stupidest person of your acquaintance and, when you have made your play so clear that you are sure that he would comprehend it, then you may venture to hope that it will be understood by your audience.' And really I think the rule will hold good with regard to poetry in general." Happily Miss Barrett did not try to bring her poetry down to the level of the stupidest person's comprehension, and, although she never did free it from occasional obscurity, fortunately it never came within the category of "poetry in general."

In October, Miss Barrett contributed to the pages of the *New Monthly Magazine,* her lengthy ballad of "The Poet's Vow." It certainly justified Miss Mitford's hint that, though prepared to love ballads, she was "a little biassed in favour of great directness and simplicity." The poem, after opening with allusions to the duality of most mundane things, proceeds to recount, more or less directly, how a poet chose to forego all human intercourse. He gave away his worldly goods and spurned his bride expectant, in the hope, apparently, that by casting off the trammels of human sympathy he might escape the woes Adam had entailed upon the human race. To comprehend the nature of the vow and its result the poem must be read in its entirety.

" The Poet's Vow " is not only a beautiful poem but is also one of the most characteristic and representative Elizabeth Barrett ever wrote. It has not the grasp of character of "Aurora Leigh," nor the gush and glow of passion which flows through the melody of " Lady Geraldine's Courtship," but it has a mournful weirdness that haunts the memory long after the words of it have been forgotten. That no sane man could make such a vow, nor that making could keep it, is beside the question; the problem being one in every respect suitable for a poet to grapple with.

Poems of the mystical nature of the two last referred to were scarcely the class of writing to prove attractive to the clear-minded, somewhat conventional, kindly-hearted Miss Mitford, Miss Barrett's chief correspondent. From time to time in the course of her chatty epistles she cautions her young friend against lapses into obscurity, bidding her write " poems of human feeling and human action." Such warnings could not have hindered Elizabeth Barrett at any time from writing as she felt, but they may have caused her to feel occasionally that the human element should not be quite overshadowed by the psychological. Sometimes when she turned her thoughts to incidents of her daily life, she wrote with a simplicity and pathetic tenderness as unparalleled in their way as were her spiritualistic speculations in theirs. One such poem as these, entitled " My Doves," refers to a pair of doves recently sent to her from the tropics as a present. She wrote to Miss Mitford :—

> My little doves were ta'en away
>   From that glad nest of theirs,
> Across an ocean rolling grey,
>   And tempest-clouded airs ;
> My little doves, who lately knew
> The sky and wave by warmth and blue.
>
> And now, within the city prison,
>   In mist and chillness pent,
> With sudden upward look they listen
>   For sounds of past content,
> For lapse of water, swell of breeze,
> Or nut-fruit falling from the trees.

The doves formed quite a topic for the two authoresses to dilate upon. Miss Mitford considered that when she said that *her father* was quite charmed with Miss Barrett's account of the little brown birdies, she had, indeed, awarded high honour, and when she heard that they had so far grown accustomed to the strangeness of their new habitation as to build a nest and lay their eggs therein, she sent her love to them, with the hope that the eggs might be good. " It would be such a delight to you," she wrote, "to help the parent birds to bring up their young."

A few months after this incident Miss Barrett had a very different theme to write upon, and upon it she wrote in hot haste. William the Fourth died on June 20th, 1837, and on July 1st the *Athenæum* contained a poem on "The Young Queen," by E. B. B.

Why this poem, so characteristic of its author, should not have been included in her *Collected Works,* where several earlier and less worthy pieces are given, it is difficult to say; but it is still less easy to comprehend what principle or plan has guided the editor's selection when we find excluded from the collection Miss Barrett's next production, "Victoria's Tears," a poem even finer than "The Young Queen," published the week following in the *Athenæum*; one quatrain of this poem has become quite a standard quotation :—

> They decked her courtly halls—
> They reined her hundred steeds—
> They shouted at her palace gates
> "A noble Queen succeeds!"

About 1837, a publication entitled *Finden's Tableaux of National Character, Beauty and Costume,* was started by W. and E. Finden. It was to be issued in fifteen monthly parts, each part to contain four plates, "designed and engraved by the most eminent artists," and "original tales and poems, by some of the most distinguished authors of the day." Mrs. S. C. Hall undertook the editorship of the new publication, and obtained the assistance of several well-known writers as contributors. The illustrations were of that ultra-sentimental type which adorned fashionable annuals of fifty years ago; and, although they would not in any way satisfy the more critical taste of the present time, were thought very highly of in those days. Instead of the illustrations being made to illustrate the text, writers had to manufacture, and generally in hot haste, poetry and prose to eluci- date or accompany the illustrations. This system, unfortunately not yet abolished, was ruinous as a rule to the production of anything of permanent value, and yet, for various reasons, many truly high-class authors submitted to its tyranny. Elizabeth Barrett, strange to say, was one of those who did not deem it prostrating her talents to patch up pieces to accompany these pictorial shams, and, for *Finden's Tableaux*, wrote the introductory poem of " The Dream." The peg upon which she hung her lines was the picture of a chubby Cupid surrounded by such conventional em- blems as one would expect to see decorating a "Valen- tine." That her stanzas were unequal—that some of them were unworthy of their authoress—is not surprising, and the only matter for wonder is that she could have been persuaded into doing such hack work.

For the third number of the *Tableaux*, to accom- pany one of these commonplace pictures, Miss Bar- rett wrote her ballad, "The Romaunt of the Page." The subscribers to the five-shillings part must, if they were intellectually capable of appreciating it, have been surprised at the power, originality, and beauty of the poem thus given to them.

Notwithstanding many defects, partly due to the nature of her inspiration, "The Romaunt of the Page," although not to be included among her finest poems, will always be a favourite one with Elizabeth Barrett's readers, because it is free from metaphysical obscurity and deals directly with the " human feeling and human action " Miss Mitford had so wisely recommended her to resort to as theme for her poesy. This same experienced counsellor, who had succeeded Mrs. Hall in the editorship of the *Tableaux*, writing to her young correspondent on 28th June, says :—

My Sweet Love—I want you to write me a poem in illustration of a very charming group of Hindoo girls floating their lamps upon the Ganges—launching them, I should say. You know that pretty superstition. I want a poem in stanzas. It must be long enough for two pages, and may be as much longer as you choose. It is for *Finden's Tableaux*, of which I have undertaken the editorship; and I must entreat it within a fortnight or three weeks if possible, because I am limited to time, and have only till the end of next month to send up the whole copy cut and dry. I do entreat you, my sweet young friend, not to refuse me this favour. I could not think of going to press without your assistance, and have chosen for you the very prettiest subject, and, I think, the prettiest plate of the whole twelve. I am quite sure that, if you favour me with a poem, it will be the gem of the collection.

To these highly complimentary expressions, Miss Mitford added that the proprietor had given her thirty pounds—" That is to say, five pounds each for my six poets (I am to do all the prose and dramatic scenes myself); and with this five pounds . . . I shall have the honour of sending a copy of the work, which will be all the prettier and more valuable for your assistance. . . . If you can give me time and thought enough to write one of those ballad stories, it would give an inexpressible grace and value to my volume. Depend upon it the time will come when those verses* of yours will have a money value."

Miss Barrett agreed to write the required verses, not, it may be assumed, for the money value, whatever may have been her motive. The "prettiest plate," according to the dexterous editorial description, was as commonplace and conventional an engraving as one could meet with, even in those days, depicting a group of Hindoo girls, or rather women, following the traditional custom of testing their lovers' fidelity by launching little lamps fixed in cocoa shells down the Ganges. If the lover were faithful the symbol boat floated away safely down the river; but, if otherwise, the tiny token quickly disappeared. That "The Romance of the Ganges" was better than the usual run of such " plate " versification may be granted, but, notwithstanding the fact that it is, as was all she wrote at this period of her life, replete with Miss Barrett's idiosyncrasies, it is a poor specimen of her skill, and scarcely worthy of the warm praise lavished on it by Miss Mitford.

Whilst the editor was writing all sorts of laudatory things to and of her favourite contributor, "the most remarkable person now alive," and of her ballad, "The Romaunt of the Page," as "one of the most charming poems ever written," that contributor's life seemed hanging by a thread. At the very time that Miss Mitford was describing Elizabeth Barrett as " a young and lovely woman, who lives the life of a hermitess in Gloucester Place . . . and who passes her life in teaching her younger brothers Greek," that very person was suffering from what looked like a mortal illness. Whether she had broken a blood-vessel on the lungs, as is frequently stated, is problematical; but, at any rate, her lungs were affected, and her life, which had so long appeared waning, seemed about to flicker out. Notwithstanding the many poems she continued to write, and the long hours of study she contrived to undergo, nothing but her mind appeared to live; her body was almost helpless.

At this time, also, occurred a domestic affliction to

rack the invalid's mind. It was the death of her uncle, the only brother of Mr. Edward Moulton Barrett, and who was, says Elizabeth, "in past times more than an uncle to me." As he died childless, the whole of his considerable property devolved, it is believed, upon his brother and his brother's family.

In the letter Miss Barrett wrote to Miss Mitford, informing her of her uncle's death, alluding to her own delicate health, she remarked—"The turning to spring is always trying, I believe, to affections such as mine, and my strength flags a good deal, and the cough very little; but Dr. Chambers speaks so encouragingly of the probable effect of the coming warm weather, that I take courage and his medicines at the same time, and 'to preserve the harmonies,' and satisfy some curiosity, have been reading Garth's 'Dispensary,' a poem very worthy of its subject."

Unfortunately, the hopes which Dr. Chambers endeavoured to inspire his patient with were vain. The warm weather was so long in coming that year (1838) that even in the middle of May Miss Mitford wrote, bitterly, that it seemed as if it would never come. Shortly before that letter from Miss Mitford, Miss Barrett said to her—"Our house in Wimpole Street is not yet finished, but we hope to see the beginning of April in it. You must not think I am very bad, only not very brisk, and really feeling more comfortable than I did a fortnight since." The improvement foreshadowed, if not imaginary, was certainly not permanent. Miss Barrett continued bodily ill, although her mental vigour never faltered. In the midst of her ailments she prepared a collection of her poems, and arranged for their publication. Writing to Miss Mitford, to thank her for some encouraging words, she tells her the projected volume will include "a principal poem called the 'Seraphim,' which is rather a dramatic lyric than a lyrical drama." "I can hardly hope that you will thoroughly like it," is her comment; "but know well that you will try to do so   Other poems, longer or shorter, will make up the volume, not a word of which is yet printed."

Why Miss Barrett feared that her friend would not be altogether satisfied with the chief poem in her volume will readily be understood by those acquainted with Miss Mitford's ideas on the treatment of "sacred" themes. The preface was, in all probability, written with a view of combating just such objections as those of her way of thinking were likely to put forward. The preface states :—

The subject of the principal poem in the present collection having suggested itself to me, though very faintly and imperfectly, when I was engaged upon my translation of the "Prometheus Bound" . . . I thought that had Æschylus lived after the incarnation and cruci- fixion of our Lord Jesus Christ, he might have turned, if not in moral and intellectual, yet in poetic, faith from the solitude of Caucasus to the deeper desertness of that crowded Jerusalem, where none had any pity; from the "faded white flower" of the Titanic brow to the "withered grass" of a Heart trampled on by its own beloved; from the glorying of him who gloried that he could not die, to the sublime meekness of the taster of death for every man; from the taunt stung into being by the torment, to His more awful silence, when the agony stood dumb before the love! . . . . But if my dream be true that Æschylus might have turned to the subject before us, in poetic in- stinct, and if in such a case . . . its terror and its pathos would have shattered into weakness the strong Greek tongue, and caused the conscious chorus to tremble round the thymele, how much more may *I* turn from it, in the instinct of incompetence! . . . I have written no work, but a suggestion . . . I have felt in the midst of my own thoughts upon my own theme, like Homer's "Children in a Battle."

The agents in this poem are those mystic beings who are designated in Scripture the Seraphim. . . . I have endeavoured to mark in my two Seraphic personages, distinctly and predominantly, that shrinking from and repugnance to evil which, in my weaker Seraph, is expressed by *fear*, and in my stronger one by a more complex passion. . . . To recoil from evil is according to the stature of an angel; to subdue it is according to the infinitude of a God.

If the leading poem of her book failed to make the impression on her readers Miss Barrett desired, it was neither owing to her want of the requisite learning, nor the poetic power to deal with her abstruse theme, but rather that the public preferred to abstract spiritualities such poems as Miss Mitford described—" poems of human feeling and human action." With respect to the other shorter pieces in her book, the authoress claimed that though if her life were prolonged she would hope to write better verses hereafter, she could never feel more intensely than at that moment " the sublime uses of poetry and the solemn responsibilities of the poet." When it is considered that among the poems thus referred to were, besides those already spoken of, such examples of her genius as " Isabel's Child," " The Deserted Garden," " Cowper's Grave," and others equally representative of her various moods, and all now become permanent glories of our language and literature, the intensity of Elizabeth Barrett's feelings in their production will not be doubted for a moment by anyone having belief in " the sublime uses" of her art, and in " the solemn responsibilities " alluded to by their architect.

CHAPTER III.

TORQUAY.

TOWARDS the autumn of 1838 Miss Barrett's condition grew critical. Almost as a last resource Dr. Chambers, her medical adviser, recommended her removal to a warmer situation than London. Whilst on the one hand it was feared she could not survive the winter in the metropolis, on the other a long journey was hazardous. Ultimately, in preference to trying a foreign climate, it was decided to risk a move as far as Torquay, and her brother Edward, a brother, as Miss Mitford says, "in heart and in talent worthy of such a sister," constituted himself her guardian. Miss Barrett herself said that her beloved brother meant to fold her in a cloak and carry her in his arms.

The journey to Torquay was accomplished in safety. Comfortable apartments, with a fine view of the bay, were obtained at the lower end of Brecon Terrace, At first the mild breezes of the south coast appeared to exercise a beneficial effect upon the invalid, and she was enabled to continue her correspondence with literary friends, especially with Miss Mitford. That lady writes on November 5th, "My beloved Miss

Barrett is better . . . If she be spared to the world and should, as she probably will, treat of such subjects as afford room for passion and action, you will see her passing all women and most men, as a narrative or dramatic poet. After all," she adds, " she is herself in her modesty, her sweetness, and her affectionate warmth of heart, by very far more wonderful than her writings, extraordinary as *they* are." A few days after these eulogistic lines their writer received a letter from the subject of them, in which she remarks, " Whenever I forget to notice any kindness of yours, do believe, my beloved friend, that I have, notwithstanding, marked the date of it with a white stone, and also with a heart *not* of stone." Referring then to some precious seedlings which Miss Mitford, from her own luxuriant little floral realm had sent her, she adds : " You said, ' Distribute the seeds as you please,' so, mindful of 'those of my own household,' I gave Sept. and Occy. (Septimus and Octavius, her youngest brothers) leave to extract a few very carefully for their garden, composed of divers flower-pots and green boxes a-gasping for sun and air from the leads behind our house, and giving the gardeners fair excuse for an occasional coveted colloquy with a great chief gardener in the Regent's Park. Yes, and out of a certain precious packet inscribed—as Arabel (her sister Arabella) described it to me—*from Mr. Wordsworth*—I desired her to reserve some for my very own self, because, you see, if it should please God to permit my return to London, I mean (' pway don't waugh,' as Ibbit says, when she has been saying something irresistibly ridiculous)—I mean to have a garden too— a whole flower-pot to myself—in the window of my particular sitting-room ; and then it will be hard indeed if, while the flowers

3

grow from those seeds, thoughts of you and the great poet may not grow from them besides."

A page or two more of such innocent chatter follows, and would seem to imply that the invalid's case was not deemed so hopeless, at least by herself, as had been imagined. Turning to more personal affairs, Miss Barrett says :—

My beloved father has gone away ; he was obliged to go two days ago, and took away with him, I fear, almost as saddened spirits as he left with me. The degree of amendment does not, of course, keep up with the haste of his anxieties. It is not that I am not better, but that he loves me too well ; *there* was the cause of his grief in going, and it is not that I do not think myself better, but that I feel how dearly he loves me ; *there* was the cause of my grief in seeing him go. One misses so the presence of such as dearly love us. His tears fell almost as fast as mine did when we parted, but he is coming back soon—perhaps in a fortnight—so I will not think any more of *them*, but of *that*. I never told him of it, of course, but, when I was last so ill, I used to start out of fragments of dreams, broken from all parts of the universe, with the cry from my own lips, "Oh, papa! papa!" I could trace it back to the dream behind, yet there it always was very curiously, and touchingly too, to my own heart, seeming scarcely *of* me. though it came *from* me, at once waking me with, and welcoming me to, the old straight humanities. Well! but I do trust I shall not be ill again in his absence, and that it may not last longer than a fortnight.

This exposure of her inmost thoughts is thoroughly characteristic of Elizabeth Barrett: the words not only show what intense affection existed between her and her father, but are representative of that semi-mesmeric state which illness, confinement, and over-study appear to have cast her into. Her religion was so real, so intense, so much a part of her existence at this period of her life, that it coloured everything about her and caused her to regard every incident for good or ill as if it were a direct interposition of the Deity. Seraphim and Cherubim, of whom she had recently written so much, were not the purely ideal personages of her poetic fancy, but she held on to her belief in them as strongly as if they were visually knowable, and she regarded Lucifer, Adam, Eve, and other characters of the ancient scriptures as truly historical as Cæsar or Brutus, Antony or Cleopatra. Science was little more than blasphemy, and that the world had existed upwards of six thousand years the fancy at the best of over-heated imagination. Such a woman could be a poet of poets, a very woman of women, with a heart for all that suffers and exists, and yet, at times, so bigoted and so blinded by excess of faith that she could not rightly judge the motives and their main-springs of many of the best about her.

Life at Torquay passed away quietly enough. The invalid's physical state varied, yet on the whole a gradual improvement was evidently taking place in her physique. On the 3rd of December she is found writing Miss Mitford one of her usual chatty epistles, discussing with her wonted clarity their various literary and personal matters of mutual interest, not, however, without some slight allusions to her own foreboding fancies. Referring to some disputes the editress of the *Tableaux* was having with its proprietor, Miss Barrett says, " You may make whatever use of me you please, as long as I am alive, and able to write at all," and that Miss Mitford did not fail to avail herself of this permission is self-evident. After some remarks about Mr. Kenyon, Miss Barrett observes, " So he won't have anything to say to our narrative poetry in Finden ? But he is a heretic, therefore we won't mind. After all, I am *afraid* (since it displeases you) that what I myself delight in most, in narrative poetry, is NOT the *narrative*. Beaumont and Fletcher, strip them to their plots, your own Beaumont and Fletcher, and you take away their glory. Alfieri is more markedly a poet of *action* than any other poet I can think of, and how he makes you shiver ! "

Speaking of the franking of her letter, she says, with the humour so frequently displayed in those earlier days of her career: "Little thinks the Bishop, whose right reverend autograph conveys my letter to you, that he is aiding and abetting the intercourse of such very fierce radicals. Indeed, the last time I thought of politics I believe I was a republican, to say nothing of some perilous stuff of 'sectarianism,' which would freeze his ecclesiastical blood to hear of." The "fierce radicalism" of "dearest Miss Mitford" was, after all, scarcely strong enough to have disturbed his Grace's equanimity, whatever her young correspondent's would have done, had he learned aught of it.

On the 5th of January 1839, Miss Barrett writes to inform her friend that her wishes for a happy new year are already fulfilled, for "papa has come!" Then, speaking of certain family reports as to their friend Kenyon not appearing to be in such good spirits as is usual with him, she throws certain side-lights upon her own character. "It must be that the life he (Kenyon) leads," she observes, "will tell at last and at least on his *spirits*. Only the unexcitable by nature can be supposed to endure continual external occasions of excitement. As if there were not enough—too much —that is exciting *from within*. For my own part, I can't understand the craving for excitement. Mine is for *repose*. My conversion into *quietism* might be attained without much preaching; and, indeed, all my favourite passages in the Holy Scriptures are those which express and promise peace, such as 'The Lord of peace Himself give you peace always and by all means'; 'My peace I give you, not as the world giveth give I'; and 'He giveth His beloved sleep,"—all such passages. They strike upon the disquieted earth with such a *foreignness* of heavenly music. Surely the 'variety,' the *change*, is to be unexcited, to find a silence and a calm in the midst of thoughts and feelings given to be too turbulent."

In these remarks, so illustrative of her character at this period, Miss Barrett, as is not unusual with her, fails to appreciate the immense difference there is between opposite dispositions, between the bright, healthy, wealthy, much fêted man of the world, and the invalided, pious, somewhat superstitious "hermitess." "I am tolerably well just now," is her significant conclusion, "and all the better for the sight of papa. He arrived the day before yesterday."

But even all the kind care, much less the sight of dear ones, could not restore the invalid to health and strength. Her studies and her poetry, her readings and her correspondence, were carried on fitfully and during intervals of longer or shorter duration as her forces permitted. To her enthusiastic praises of some foreign poetry, sent during this period to Miss Mitford, that lady rejoins, in a letter of May 28th: "After all, to be English, with our boundless vistas in verse and in prose, is a privilege and a glory; and *you* are born amongst those who make it such, be sure of that. I do not believe, my sweetest, that the very highest poetry does sell at once. Look at Wordsworth! The hour will arrive, and all the sooner, if to poetry, unmatched in truth and beauty and feeling, you condescend to add story and a happy ending, that being among the conditions of recurrence to every book with the mass even of cultivated readers—I do not mean the few."

Much as the poetess loved and admired this experienced correspondent, she never allowed *her* ideas or advice to influence the thought or—save in the *Tableaux*—even the theme of her works, and continued to write poems in which the story, if any, was subordinated to the sentiment, and in which the ending was as far removed from happiness as possible.

The slow months dragged on at Torquay, and no great improvement took place in the invalid's condition; indeed, she went from bad to worse, and at last seemed scarcely to have any hold on life, so far as physical power was concerned. According to Miss Mitford, writing in March 1840, since the 1st of October she had not been dressed, "only lifted from her bed to the sofa, and for the last month not even taken out of bed to have it made. Yet she still writes to me," says her friend, "and the physicians still encourage hope; but her voice has not for six months been raised above a whisper." Then again, writing about the same time to another correspondent, Miss Mitford says of the invalid: "The physicians at their last consultation said it was not only possible, but probable, that she would so far recover as to live for many years in tolerable comfort. In the meanwhile she writes to me long letters at least twice a week, reads everything, from the magazines of the day to Plato and the Fathers, and has written (*vide* the *Athenæum* of three weeks ago) the most magnificent poem ever written by woman on the Queen's Marriage. Great as is her learning, her genius is still more remarkable, and it is beginning to be felt and acknowledged in those quarters where alone the recognition of high genius is desirable."

The poem thus highly praised appeared in the *Athenæum* of February 15th, 1840, as "The Crowned and Wedded Queen." Marvellous a production as it was, when the circumstances in which it was produced are considered, and abounding though it does in felicitous expressions, it scarcely realises the pre-eminence Miss Mitford claims for it. Grander poems had been produced by women, had been produced by Miss Barrett herself, who certainly surpassed it a few weeks later by her most suggestive lines on "Napoleon's Return," written on the conveyance of Napoleon's body from St. Helena to Paris for reinterment in the French metropolis.

During the whole of the winter of 1839, and the first half of 1840, a constant exchange of correspondence was carried on between the invalid at Torquay and Miss Mitford and other correspondents, in which all the leading literary and other topics of the day were discussed in a way that proves, however prostrated by illness Miss Barrett may have been, her mental powers retained all their vigour, and that she still contrived to keep in touch, either by reading or conversation, with the outer world. But a calamity was impending that almost extinguished the dim spark of vitality left in her, and, as she averred, " gave a nightmare to her life for ever."

The advent of summer and the warm breezes of the south coast had begun to effect some improvement in her constitution, and to cause her to regard the future somewhat hopefully. She had been nursed through the cold months with the utmost care and affection; of those devoting themselves to her, both in body and mind, none was more unwearied in attention and self-sacrificing for her sake than her eldest brother, Edward. Next to her father he was first in her heart and mind, and her affection for him was fully reciprocated. He seems to have been an amiable and admired young man, known and liked amongst the visitors and residents at Torquay. He joined in the general amusements of the place as often as he could leave his sister's couch, and had formed acquaintance with other young men of his own position in life at Torquay.

July came. One Saturday, it was the 11th, Edward Barrett arranged to go for a sail with two companions; they were Charles Vanneck, the only son of the Honourable Mrs. Gerard Vanneck, a young man in his twenty-first year, and Captain Carlyle Clarke, nick-named "Lion Clarke," on account of a narrow escape he had from the clutches of a lion he killed in Bengal. The three hired the *Belle Sauvage*, a small pleasure yacht noted for its great speed, and as winner of a large number of prize cups. They took with them an experienced pilot named White, and started for a few hours' trip, intending only to go as far as Teignmouth.

Saturday passed, and the boat did not return; Mr. Barrett, Senior, was not at Torquay, and Miss Barrett had to endure the agony of uncertainty and suspense uncheered by her father's presence. Sunday came and the boat did not return. The dreary agonizing hours passed and no sign of the pleasure party. At last a rumour reached Torquay, and found its way to the heartsick watchers, that a boat corresponding in appearance with the missing one had been seen to sink off Teignmouth. The terrifying intelligence wanted confirmation; and as there still remained a possibility that the young men might have gone on to Exmouth, searchers were sent to that place, as well as along the coast, to make inquiries. Their efforts were vain; nothing could be heard of the lost ones. At last full evidence of the worst was obtained; two boatmen, of Exmouth, deposed that they saw a yacht with four men on board sink off Teignmouth. In consequence of this information two boats, well manned and armed with grapnels and other appliances, were despatched to the spot where the yacht was supposed to have gone down, to search for the bodies.

How can the horror and misery of this time be told. The dreadful suspense, which all the grief of the terrible truth could scarcely intensify. A widowed mother mourning for her only son; a father and brother for a brother and son, who had survived the dangers of war and deadly climes only to sink into the deep almost in sight of home; and a sister, lying helpless on a sick bed, wasting vain tears for the beloved companion of her life, who was gone for ever, whose corse even could not be wept over, and who, horror of horrors! but for the affection which had brought him to her side, might still have been alive and happy! Thus thought Miss Barrett, as she lay utterly prostrated with anguish and suspense; thus she argued in the midst of her terrible agony.

Mr. Barrett arrived, but his arrival seemed of little value now. In conjunction with the other bereaved persons he offered heavy rewards for recovery of the bodies, but the days passed and no vestige could be obtained. At last, on the 18th instant, it was announced that Captain Clarke's body had been picked up by the trawler, about four miles from Dartmouth, and although several days had elapsed since the accident, it was not in the least disfigured, and in the button-hole of his coat were still the flowers which he had worn when he started on the pleasure trip. The days still came and went, and again the sea cast forth its dead. It was not until the 4th of August that the body of Edward Barrett was discovered; it had been seen floating near the Great Rock, Torbay, and was picked up by a boatman and taken ashore. Mr. Barrett identified his son's body, a Coroner's verdict of "Accidentally Drowned" was returned, and the remains, together with those of Captain Clarke, and subsequently of William White, the pilot, were interred in the parish church of Tormohun, Torquay. Whether Charles Vanneck's body was ever found is doubtful.

The suspense was over, and "the sharp reality now must act its part." Nor money, nor genius, nor love were now of any avail, and the poor broken-hearted invalid, lying half senseless on her couch, had neither mind nor hearing for aught save the cruel sea beating upon the shore, and sounding, as she afterwards said, like nothing but a dirge for the untimely dead. "The sound of the waves rang in her ears like the moans of one dying."

For months Elizabeth Barrett hovered between life and death: "I being weak," as she said, "was struck down as by a *bodily* blow in a moment, without having time for tears." Everything that love and wealth could do for her was done, and time and nature both soothed and strengthened her in her affliction. Some slight reflex of her feelings may be gained from a perusal of her poem "De Profundis," published only after death had claimed her also. The earlier stanzas express the depth of her despair when she was first enabled to comprehend the certainty of her loss. After the full heart has given vent to its wild passionate cry of utter hopelessness a ray of light breaks in, the consolation of religion is sought and found, and the weary heart, as expressed in the remainder of the poem, is soothed to rest by faith in Divine goodness.

During these months of misery, whilst the invalid's life was hanging by a thread, there appeared the most influential notice of her poetic efforts that had as yet been published. In the September number of the *Quarterly Review* a criticism was given of the various volumes of poetry she owned. The reviewer was not altogether unjust nor unappreciative, although Miss Barrett subsequently took an opportunity of controverting his animadversions upon some of her mannerisms. Attention was called to her extraordinary acquaintance with ancient classic literature, as also to the daring nature of her themes. Her beautiful lines on " Cowper's Grave " were selected for especial commendation, and an extract from " Isobel's Child," a poem the reviewer did not appear to recognise the full value of, was given as a " specimen of her general manner and power."

The Seraphim was noticed by the reviewer as a subject " Miss Barrett would not have attempted, if she had more seriously considered its absolute unapproachableness," whilst her translation of *Prometheus*, although pronounced "a remarkable performance for a young lady," was deemed uncouth, unfaithful to the original, and devoid of fire. Altogether the review was calculated to improve Miss Barrett's position in the world of letters, classing her, as it did, among " modern English poetesses," and manifestly to the disadvantage of those ladies whose names and works were coupled with hers. It was this classification, however, that annoyed our poetess more than aught else in the review.

Towards the end of November Miss Mitford was enabled to report that her friend was somewhat better, but I fear, she added, "we dare not expect more than a few months of lingering life." But the vital spark did not flutter out, and the improvement in the invalid's condition, if slow, was, with some fluctuations, continuous. "I did not think," she wrote some few months later, "to be better any more, but I have quite rallied now, except as to strength, and they say that on essential points I shall not suffer permanently—and this is a comfort to poor papa." To another correspondent Miss Barrett wrote, as an excuse for not following up some literary labour :—

No—no; the headache is no excuse. I have not frequent headaches, and if just now I am rather more feverish and uncomfortable than usual, the cause is in the dreadful weather—the snow and east wind. . . . These extreme causes do, however, affect me as little, even less, my physician says, than might have been feared; and I think steadily—hope steadily—for London at the end of May, so to attain a removal from this place, which has been so eminently fatal to my happiness.

The only gladness associated with the banishment here has been your offered sympathy and friendship. Otherwise, bitterness has dropped on bitterness like the snows more than I can tell, and independent of that last most overwhelming affliction of my life, from the edge of the chasm of which I may struggle, but never can escape.

Writing on the 17th of May 1841, to Richard H. Horne, the author of *Orion* and *Cosmo de' Medici*, with whom she had already been a correspondent for some time past, she says :—

I shall be more at ease when I have thanked you, dear Mr. Horne, for your assurance of sympathy, which, in its feeling and considerate

expression a few days since, touched me so nearly and deeply. With-
out it I should have written when I was able—I mean physically able
—for in the exhaustion consequent upon fever, I have been too weak
to hold a pen. As to reluctancy of feeling, believe me that I must
change more than illness or grief can change me, before it becomes a
painful effort to communicate with one so very kind as you have been
to me. . . . Besides the appreciated sympathy. I have to acknow-
ledge four proofs of your remembrance, the seals of which lay
unbroken for a fortnight or more after their removal here. . . .
You have been in the fields—I know by the flowers—and found there,
I suppose, between the flowers and the life and dear Mrs Orme, that
pleasant dream (for me!) about my going to London at Easter. *I*
never dreamt it. And while you wrote, what a mournful contrary
was going on here! It was a heavy blow (may God keep you from
such!). I knew you would be sorry for me when you heard.

A few days later she resumed her correspondence
with Horne, chiefly with respect to his fine drama of
Gregory the Seventh, to which was prefixed an " Essay
on Tragic Influence " :—

I have read but little lately, and not at all until very lately; but
two or three days ago papa held up *Gregory* before my eyes as some-
thing sure to bring pleasure into them. " Ah! I knew that would
move you." After all, I have scarcely been long enough face to face
with him to apprehend the full grandeur of his countenance. There
are very grand things, and expounded in your characteristic massive-
ness of diction. But it does so far appear to me that for the tragic
heights, and for that passionate singleness of purpose in which you
surpass the poets of our time, we shall revert to *Cosmo* and *Marlowe*.
Well, it may be very wrong—I must think over my thoughts. And
at any rate the " Essay on Tragic Influence " is full of noble philo-
sophy and poetry—perhaps the highest—and absolutely independent,
in its own essence, of stages; which involve, to my mind, little more
than its translation into a grosser form, in order to its apprehension
by the vulgar. What Macready can touch *Lear?* In brief, if the
union between tragedy and the gaslights be less incongruous and
absurd than the union between Church and State, is it less desecra-
tive of the Divine theory? In the clashing of my *No* against your
Yes, I must write good-bye.

Soon afterwards Miss Barrett commenced a series
of most interesting letters to Horne in connection with

dramatic subjects.   He had solicited her signature for
a memorial to Parliament, petitioning the abolition of
the theatrical monopoly, and praying that " every
theatre should be permitted to enact the best dramas
it could obtain."   In the most delicate yet determined
way possible, the invalid recluse declined to comply
with the request.   "I tremble to do it," she says;
"take a long breath before I begin, and then beg
you to excuse me about the signature."   Alluding
to his belief that as soon as the monopoly was
abolished a career of glory would commence at
once for the best drama and the best dramatists, and
that the public would immediately flock to those
houses where good plays and good actors only were
to be seen, Miss Barrett says, " As to the petition
. . . you are sure to gain the immediate object,
and you ought to do so, even although the ultimate
object remain as far off as ever, and more evidently
far.   There is a deeper evil than licences or the want
of licences—the base and blind public taste.   Multiply
your theatres and licence everyone.   Do it to-day, and
the day after to-morrow (you may have one night)
there will come Mr. Bunn, and turn out you and
Shakespeare with a great roar of lions.   Well! we
shall see."

Reverting to more personal matters, this determined
and not to be persuaded invalid is found once more
looking with eager eyes to her home in the distant
metropolis.   " When do you go to Italy?" she asks;
"for *me*, I can't answer.   I am longing to go to
London, and hoping to the last.   For the present—
certainly the window has been opened twice, an inch—
but I can't be lifted even to the sofa without fainting.
And my physician shakes his head, or changes the

conversation, which is worse, whenever London is
mentioned. But I do grow stronger; and if it become
possible I shall go—*will go!* That sounds better,
doesn't it? Putting it off to another summer is like
a 'never.' "

In her next letter, early in June, she informs Horne
that she is

Revived just now—pleased, anxious, excited altogether, in the hope
of touching at last upon my last days at this place. I have been up,
and bore it excellently—up an hour at a time, without fainting, and
on several days without injury; and now am looking forward to the
journey. My physician has been open with me, and is of opinion that
there is a good deal of risk to be run in attempting it. But my mind
is made up to go; and if the power remains to me I *will* go. To be
at home, and relieved from the sense of doing evil where I would
soonest bring a blessing—of breaking up poor papa's domestic peace
into fragments by keeping my sisters here (and he won't let them
leave me)—would urge me into any possible " risk "—to say nothing
of the continual repulsion, night and day, of the sights and sounds of
this dreary place. There will be no opposition. So papa promised
me at the beginning of last winter that I should go when it became
" possible." Then Dr. Scully did not talk of " risk," but of *certain*
consequences. He said I should die on the road. I know how to
understand the change of phrase. There is only a " risk " now—and
the journey is " possible." So I go.

We are to have one of the patent carriages, with a thousand springs,
from London, and I am afraid of nothing. I shall set out, I *hope*, in a
fortnight. Ah! but not directly for London. There is to be some
intermediate place where we all must meet, papa says, and stay for a
month or two before the final settlement in Wimpole Street—and he
names " Clifton," and I pray for the neighbourhood of London, because
I look far (too far, perhaps, for me), and fear being left an exile again at
those Hot Wells during the winter. I don't know what " the finality
measure " may be. The only thing fixed is a journey from hence.

Considering the condition Miss Barrett was in, and
that she had even to recline on her back whilst writing,
it is marvellous that she was enabled to write the
quantity, apart from the quality, of matter that she did
at this time. Besides her lengthy communications to

Horne, Miss Mitford, and others, she was busy assisting the first-named correspondent in sketching out and writing a lyrical drama.

Psyche Apocalypté, the name finally adopted by the two poets as the title of their joint drama, was to be modelled on " Greek instead of modern tragedy." The correspondence which the suggestions and dual labour on this drama gave rise to was most voluminous, and although the work was never completed, there was quite enough of it put together to justify Horne publishing the fair-sized pamphlet on it he eventually did.

Miss Barrett's original conception of the work is shadowed forth in these words :—

My idea, the terror attending spiritual consciousness—the man's soul to the man—is something which has not, I think, been worked hitherto, and seems to admit of a certain grandeur and wildness in the execution. The awe of this soul-consciousness breaking into occasional lurid heats through the chasm of our conventionalities has struck me, in my own self-observation, as a mystery of nature very grand in itself, and is quite a distinct mystery from *conscience.* Conscience has to do with action (every thought being spiritual action), and not with abstract existence. There are moments when we are startled at the footsteps of our own being, more than at the thunders of God.

Horne accepted this psychological problem as the basis for the drama, taking good care, however, in his own practical way, to make it more comprehensible, and humanising it by a fairly readable plot and the introduction of numerous supernumerary personages, human and otherwise. Much of it was already written when Miss Barrett's removal from Torquay and journey to London caused a lengthy interregnum in the work, and subsequent events intervened to prevent its continuation and completion.

In her charming literary correspondence with Horne Miss Barrett furnishes many interesting little pieces o personal history. She does not refrain from jesting about her own invalided condition, and, in the communication just cited from, says : " How you would smile sarcasms and epigrams out of the ' hood ' if you could see from it what I have been doing, or rather suffering, lately ! Having my picture taken by a lady miniature-painter, who wandered here to put an old view of mine to proof. For it wasn't ' the ruling passion strong in death,' ' though by your smiling you may seem to say so,' but a sacrifice to papa."

A month later, and she, still a prisoned sprite, writes :—

What made me write was, indeed, impatience—there is no denying it—only not about the drama. Do you know what it is to be shut up in a room by oneself, to multiply one's thoughts by one's thoughts—how hard it is to know what " one's thought is like "—how it grows and grows, and spreads and spreads, and ends in taking some supernatural colour—just like mustard and cress sown on flannel in a dark closet? . . . I was very sorry about the cough. Do not neglect it, lest it end as mine did ; for a common cough striking on an *insubstantial* frame began my bodily troubles ; and I know well what that suffering is, though nearly quite free from it now.

The fortnight within which the invalid was to risk a remove came and went, and still her letters bear the post-mark of hated Torquay. On the 4th August she writes :—" I am gasping still for permission to move too; but papa has gone suddenly into Herefordshire, and I am almost sure not to hear for a week. Something, however, must soon be determined ; and in the meantime, being tied hand and foot, and gagged, I am wonderfully patient." Ten days later and still the Barretts did not risk removal. On the 14th Elizabeth wrote a characteristic letter to Horne, wherein was much playful badinage, and the remark, in reference to her childish epic—" Ah ! when I was ten years old, I beat you all—you and Napoleon and all—in ambition; but now I only want to get home."

"I only want to get home!" such had been the burden of Elizabeth Barrett's wishes from month to month; and at last, late in the summer of 1841, she was conveyed to her father's residence in Wimpole Street in safety. All that is known of the journey is told by Miss Mitford—a very imaginative person, be it remembered, in some things. "My beloved Miss Barrett," she says, "accomplished the journey by stages of twenty-five miles a-day in one of the *invalide* carriages, where the bed is drawn out like a drawer from a table." She had not been home many days before Miss Mitford travelled up to London to visit her, and remarks—" I found her better than I dared to hope."

CHAPTER IV.

HOME.

MISS MITFORD found Elizabeth Barrett better than
she had dared to hope, yet still an utter invalid.
Speaking of her appearance now as contrasted with
what it was when she first met her, she says :—

She has totally lost the rich, bright colouring, which certainly made
the greater part of her beauty. She is dark and pallid; the hair
is almost entirely hidden; the look of youth gone (I think she now
looks as much beyond her actual age as formerly she looked behind
it), nothing remaining but the noble forehead, the matchless eyes, and
the fine form of her mouth and teeth—even now their whiteness is
healthy. . . . The expression, too, is completely changed; the sweet-
ness remains, but it is accompanied with more shrewdness, more
gaiety, the look not merely of the woman of genius—that she always
had—but of the superlatively clever woman. An odd effect of
absence from general society, that the talent for conversation should
have ripened, and the shyness have disappeared—but so it is. When
I first saw her, her talk, delightful as it was, had something too much
of the lamp—she spoke too well—and her letters were rather too
much like the very best books. Now all that is gone; the fine
thoughts come gushing and sparkling like water from a spring, but
flow as naturally as water down a hillside, clear, bright, and sparkling
in the sunshine. All this, besides its great delightfulness, looks like
life, does it not? Even in this weather—very trying to her—she has
been translating some hymns of Gregory Nazianzen . . . and is
talking of a series of articles for the *Athenæum*, comprising critiques
on the Greek poets of the early Christian centuries, with poetical

translations. I had rather she wrote more "Cloud Houses," and have told her so; and, above all, I had rather see a great narrative poem, of an interest purely human (for one can't trust her with the mystical).

"The House of Clouds," alluded to by Miss Mitford, had appeared in the *Athenæum* of August 21st. It was alone sufficient to have made a poetic reputation; no poet ever penned a purer or more poetic piece, or one in which the music is wedded to the metre in more ethereal beauty. A sample stanza is sufficient to show what an artist in words Elizabeth Barrett could be at her best—

> Cloud-walls of the morning's grey.
>   Faced with amber column
> Crowned with crimson cupola,
>   From a sunset solemn!
> May-mists, for the casements, fetch,
>   Pale and glimmering;
> With a sunbeam hid in each,
>   And a smell of spring!

Who but will agree with Miss Mitford in her wish that a poet who could indite such lovely lines should continue so to write, instead of squandering her genius over the hopeless task of trying to resuscitate the dry bones of those irretrievably dead Greek Fathers of the Church. But what Elizabeth Barrett willed she did, and having made her mind up that the early Greek Christians kept the torch of Hellenic poesy from utterly fluttering out, she wrote a series of papers, and translated a lot of mouldering verse, to prove it to the public. These translations from, and articles on "The Greek Christian Poets," duly appeared in the *Athenæum* of the following year. They are now chiefly memorable and valuable for their author's sake, and as a specimen of her magnificent diction; the opening sentence of the first essay is a splendid example of the

richness and verbal picturesqueness of English prose
in competent hands.

In the preceding October, Miss Barrett had pub-
lished in the *Athenæum*, to which she was a frequent
contributor, some charming, characteristic lines, en-
titled, " Lessons from the Gorse," and in many ways
displayed increased literary activity. With reviving
health her energies appeared to revive; and although
she suffered much during the short frost which ushered
in the early winter of 1841, she recovered quickly.
Her correspondence with literary people increased and,
at rare intervals, friends were admitted into the darkened
chamber in which she passed her time. She was,
indeed, much better now that she had left behind the
terrible, suggestive sound of the never-silent sea, and
had regained the calm seclusion of home. She wrote
continually, and read and studied unceasingly. With-
out these occupations for her mind, it has been sug-
gested, she never could have lived. Her medical
attendant did not comprehend this phase of her con-
stitution, and remonstrated with her on her close
application to her favourite Greek authors. To save
herself from his diatribes she had a small edition of
Plato bound up to resemble a novel.

Writing to Horne on the subject of her varied read-
ing, Elizabeth Barrett says :—

So you think I never read Fonblanque or Sydney Smith—or Junius,
perhaps? Mr. Kenyon calls me his " omnivorous cousin." I read
without principle. I have a sort of unity, indeed, but it amalgamates
instead of selecting—do you understand? When I had read the
Hebrew Bible, from Genesis to Malachi, right through, and was never
stopped by the Chaldean—and the Greek poets, and Plato, right through
from end to end—I passed as thoroughly through the flood of all
possible and impossible British and foreign novels and romances, with
slices of metaphysics laid thick between the sorrows of the multitu-

dinous Celestinas. It is only useful knowledge and the multiplication
table I have never tried hard at. And now—what now? Is this
matter of exultation? Alas, no! Do I boast of my omnivorousness of·
reading, even apart from the romances? Certainly no! never, except
in joke. It's against my theories and ratiocinations, which take upon
themselves to assert that we *all* generally err by *reading too much*, and
out of proportion to what we *think*. I should be wiser, I am per-
suaded, if I had not read half as much—should have had stronger
and better exercised faculties, and should stand higher in my own
appreciation. The fact is, that the *ne plus ultra* of intellectual in-
dolence is this reading of books. It comes next to what the Ameri-
cans call "whittling."

These wise and pregnant sentences are well worth
reproduction and pondering over, although it must be
confessed that Elizabeth Barrett, even if her reading
were so varied as she humorously asserts, is an appa-
rent exception to the theory she propounds. Her
large range of reading continually supplies her with
apt allusions and appropriate similes. Her letters, as
Miss Mitford exclaims, "are such letters!"

Writing early in December 1841, that lady says she
has just been reading a favourite book of Miss Barrett,
lent her by that dear friend. It is Stilling's *Theory of
Pneumatology*, and Miss Mitford faithfully describes it as
"a most remarkable collection of ghost stories, dreams,
&c., very interesting for its singular mixture of credulity,
simplicity, shrewdness, and good faith." This letter
contains the first intimation of Miss Barrett's leaning
to a belief in apparitions, a belief which doubtless laid
the foundation of her future credulity in matters con-
nected with that modern imposture, Spiritualism.

Miss Mitford, in her voluminous correspondence
with Elizabeth Barrett, continued to make remarks
anent her spiritual theories. At first the elder lady
appeared to somewhat sympathise with her friend's
views; but as they became more pronounced, and

credence was given to the more *outré* forms of modern superstition, Miss Mitford retreated from the field.

In the following February one learns that Miss Barrett is much better in health, and that she can even walk from the bed to the sofa, quite a grand deed for her. The report for the next month shows maintained improvement, and her friends are now quite hopeful for her. Her reading continues to be as varied and large as ever, and her letters to be filled with her clever comments upon what she reads. Her chief correspondent was Miss Mitford, who encouraged her to her utmost by praises of her great and growing powers. She writes—

My love and ambition for you often seems to be more like that of a mother for a son, or a father for a daughter (the two fondest of natural emotions), than the common bond of even a close friendship between two women of different ages and similar pursuits. I sit and think of you, and of the poems that you will write, and of that strange, brief rainbow crown called Fame, until the vision is before me as vividly as ever a mother's heart hailed the eloquence of a patriotic son. Do you understand this? And do you pardon it? You must, my precious, for there is no chance that I should unbuild *that* house of clouds; and the position that I long to see you fill is higher, firmer, prouder than ever has been filled by a woman.

Great as was Miss Barrett's improvement, and well as she had borne the winter, we find that even by April she is unable to do more than move into the next room at the most, and that she is still unable to receive any new visitors. Her interchange of letters with Miss Mitford, however, becomes more incessant than ever, and from them one is enabled to learn what books the two ladies are reading, what their opinions upon them and upon the leading literary topics of the day are, and what each is doing as regards literature. As for Miss Barrett, little save literature seemed to her worth living for. Books, books, books, were almost the sole object of her life, and to read or write them her only occupation. Almost the only unliterary subject introduced is "Flush," a favourite spaniel presented to the poetess by Miss Mitford.

The year 1842 passed away quietly for Elizabeth Barrett. Her health's improvement—slow, very slow, if sure—was the chief and most important event for her. If she wrote much, she published little or nothing beyond a few poems, and "The Greek Christian Poets," already spoken of. But during this time she was steadily preparing a new collection of poetry, of priceless value, for the press. Writing to Horne at the end of December, she says, in her jesting way, "The world is better than I imagined, and since I wrote to you about booksellers, I have had an inkling of a reason for believing what I had not faith for previously, that in the case of my resolving to deliver up a volume of poems to my own former publisher, he would print it without being paid for it."

The first few months of 1843, like the last few of its predecessor, are almost a blank as far as any records of Miss Barrett's career are available. In April, Miss Mitford says she has a letter from her, "more cheerful and healthy than any I have received for a very long time." And on the 14th of June, the poetess sends a more than usually humorous letter to Horne, in reference to the distribution of his grand epic of *Orion*, published originally at the price of One Farthing. This nominal price, Horne says, was fixed in order to save the author the trouble and expense of sending copies to his numerous friends. Miss Barrett's first letter on the subject, which reads as if she were *pretending* to be piqued with the poet, shows that, after all, he did not escape either gratuitous distribution or literary correspondence in consequence. Certainly, if all his correspondents had possessed the epistolary talent of this one, he would have had nothing to regret at the failure of his plan. She writes :—

I have read and forwarded your letter to Miss Mitford, who tells me in a letter yesterday (a cross stitch) that, in spite of all I can say, she is glad of having written to you, because you " *will be obliged to say something in your answer.*" Well ! I also am glad that somebody is curious besides myself; and I am not sorry that the somebody should be herself, being jealous of her, " with Styx nine times round me," in natural proportion to her degree of glory and victory and twenty-five promised copies !

Very well, Mr. Horne !

" It is quite useless," said I to Miss Mitford, " that you should make *your* application ! *Have I not asked for six copies, and been refused ?* " Now carry the result of the application historically downwards -and me with it !

As to your suggestion about the compromise of her and my struggling heroically for these *spolia opima*—really you can know little of what heroes, female heroes, are made, to suggest such a thing ! I have told Miss Mitford (to disabuse you at once) that not if she and you asked me on your four knees to touch a page of the twenty-five would I consent to such a thing. I make feminine oaths against it. I DON'T CHOOSE TO DO IT. . . . Not in the least do I approve of your distributing the second edition in the manner of the first. The cause of it, and the object in it, are inscrutable to me, particularly as I don't hold to the common opinion that much poetry has made the author mad. Papa says, " Perhaps he is going to shoot the Queen, and is preparing evidence of monomania "—an ingenious conjecture, but not altogether satisfactory.

The letter from which these extracts are taken had not been written long before the writer began to fear that their humorous banter might be taken too seriously, so she indited another epistle about *Orion*, saying, " I am more sorry . . . at having written a very silly note to you. That it was simply silly—meaning that it wasn't *seriously* silly—I beg you to believe. I am apt to write, the thought or the jest as it may be, which is uppermost—and sometimes, too, when it is not uppermost. I struggle against a sadness which is strong, by putting a levity in the place of it. Now you will wonder what I have been writing if you have not received the note yet, and so I will explain to you that it was only some foolishness about the twenty-five copies—about Miss Mitford's victory and my defeat. κ. τ. λ."

The tone of this and other letters written by Elizabeth Barrett is explained by what she writes in a following communication to Horne. Referring to her great shyness in meeting strangers, she says, " But *that* you won't believe, because, as Mr. Kenyon says, I grow insolent when I have a pen in my hand, and you know me only ' by that sign.' I sometimes doubt to myself (do you know, besides) whether if I should ever be face to face with you, the shame and the shyness would not annihilate the pleasure of it to me !"

That this shyness was real, no student of Elizabeth Barrett's life and letters can doubt, and that that it was which ofttimes forced her into writing somewhat over-strained and bold epistles—so different to her retiring nature—just as very bashful people often blurt out more forcible and more courageous things than really brave but more self-possessed persons would dare to.

As the year advanced, and there were no signs of the invalid's falling back into her former sad condition, Miss Mitford, assisted by Mr. Kenyon, endeavoured to impress upon Mr. Barrett the advantages likely to accrue to his daughter by her being got out of town; but either he or the invalid herself feared the risk, and nothing was done. Her collection of poems, which it was arranged Moxon should publish, was rapidly approaching completion. It was to be in two volumes,

and not to contain anything included in the previous,
the 1838, collection. One important piece to be in
this new work had appeared in *Blackwood* for August,
under the title of "The Cry of the Children." It
had been suggested by the *Report* of Horne on "The
Employment of Children in Mines and Manufactories."
He had been appointed by the Government an Assis-
tant Commissioner to the Commission appointed to
inquire into the subject, and his evidence, says Miss
Barrett, excited her to write the poem named "The
Cry of the Children." This poem, which Edgar Poe
well characterised as "full of a nervous unflinching
energy—a horror sublime in its simplicity—of which
Dante himself might have been proud "—created quite
a sensation on its appearance, and has been deemed,
with much show of probability, to have hastened and
helped the passing of the initial Act of Parliament
restricting the employment of children of tender
years. The poem is grand in its pathos and passion,
in the simplicity of its suffering children, and the
hardly restrained and lofty anger at their treatment.
Some stanzas should be cited, if only to show what a
lofty position their author had now achieved in the
realms of poetry :—

> Do you hear the children weeping, O my brothers,
>   Ere the sorrow comes with years ?
> They are leaning their young heads against their mothers' ·
>   And *that* cannot stop their tears.
> The young lambs are bleating in the meadows ;
>   The young birds are chirping in the nest;
> The young fawns are playing with the shadows ;
>   The young flowers are blowing towards the west—
> But the young, young children, O my brothers.
>   They are weeping bitterly !—
> They are weeping in the playtime of the others,
>   In the country of the free.

Do you question the young children in their sorrow,
     Why their tears are falling so ?—
The old man may weep for his to-morrow,
     Which is lost in Long Ago—
The old tree is leafless in the forest—
     The old year is ending in the frost—
The old wound, if stricken, is the sorest—
     The old hope is hardest to be lost:
But the young, young children, O my brothers,
     Do you ask them why they stand
Weeping sore before the bosoms of their mothers
     In our happy Fatherland ?
    *   *   *   *   *

' For all day the wheels are droning, turning,
     Their wind comes in our faces,—
Till our hearts turn,—our heads with pulses burning,
     And the walls turn in their places—
Turns the sky in the high window blank and reeling—
     Turns the long light that droppeth down the wall—
Turn the black flies that crawl along the ceiling—
     All are turning, all the day, and we with all !
And all day, the iron wheels are droning ;
     And sometimes we could pray :
' O ye wheels ' (breaking out in a mad moaning),
     ' Stop ! be silent for to-day ! ' "
    *   *   *   *   *

Now tell the poor young children, O my brothers,
     That they look to Him and pray—
So the blessed One who blesseth all the others,
     Will bless them another day.
They answer, " Who is God that He should hear us,
     While the rushing of the iron wheels is stirred ?
When we sob aloud, the human creatures near us
     Pass by, hearing not, or answer not a word !
And *we* hear not (for the wheels in their resounding)
     Strangers speaking at the door ;
Is it likely God, with angels singing round Him,
     Hears our weeping any more ?

" Two words, indeed, of praying we remember,
     And at midnight's hour of harm,—
' Our Father,' looking upward in the chamber,
     We say softly for a charm.*

---

  * A fact rendered pathetically historical by Mr. Horne's Report
of his Commission

We know no other words except ' Our Father,'
And we think that in some pause of angels' song
God may pluck them with the silence sweet to gather,
And hold both within His right hand which is strong.
' Our Father ! ' If He heard us, He would surely
(For they call him good and mild)
Answer, smiling down the steep world very purely,
' Come and rest with me my child.' "

*   *   *   *   *

Another piece included in the collection, "To Flush, my Dog," is of a very different calibre, although replete with excellence in its way. "Flush," the many years canine companion and four-footed friend of the poetess, was a gift from Miss Mitford and, says Elizabeth Barrett, "belongs to the beautiful race she has rendered celebrated among English and American readers. The Flushes have their laurels as well as the Cæsars, the chief difference (at least the very head and front of it) consisting, according to my perception, in the bald head." If Miss Mitford made "Flush' celebrated by her prose, Miss Barrett immortalised it by her poesy. "Loving friend," she writes—

Loving friend, the gift of one,
Who, her own true faith hath run,
  Through thy lower nature ;
Be my benediction said
With my hand upon thy head,
  Gentle fellow creature !

Like a lady's ringlets brown,
Flow thy silken ears adown
  Either side demurely,
Of thy silver-suited breast
Shining out from all the rest
  Of thy body purely.

Darkly brown thy body is,
Till the sunshine, striking this,
  Alchemise its dulness,—

When the sleek curls manifold
Flash all over into gold,
　　With a burnished fulness.

Underneath my stroking hand,
Startled eyes of hazel bland
　　Kindling, growing larger,—
Up thou leapest with a spring,
Full of prank and curvetting,
　　Leaping like a chargor.

Yet, my pretty sportive friend,
Little is 't to such an end
　　That I praise thy rareness !
Other dogs may be thy peers
Haply in these drooping ears.
　　And this glossy fairness.

But of *thee* it shall be said,
This dog watched beside a bed
　　Day and night unweary,—
Watched within a curtained room,
Where no sunbeam brake the gloom
　　Round the sick and dreary.

Other dogs in thymy dew
Tracked the hares and followed through
　　Sunny moor or meadow—
This dog only, crept and crept
Next a languid cheek that slept,
　　Sharing in the shadow.

＊　　＊　　＊　　＊　　＊

And if one or two quick tears
Dropped upon his glossy ears,
　　Or a sigh came double,—
Up he sprang in eager haste,
Fawning, fondling, breathing fast,
　　In a tender trouble.

And this dog was satisfied,
If a pale thin hand would glide
　　Down his dewlaps sloping,—
Which he pushed his nose within,
After,—platforming his chin
　　On the palm left open.

＊　　＊　　＊　　＊　　＊

Therefore to this dog will I,
Tenderly not scornfully,
  Render praise and favour !
With my hand upon his head,
Is my benediction said
  Therefore, and for ever.

The allusion to the "other dogs in thymy dew" who "tracked the hare," is suggested by an incident told the poetess by Miss Mitford in one of her chatty letters. This lady's spaniel, the sire of the second "Flush," does not appear to have been, at all times, so sedate as his daughter. One evening, when his mistress was taking her wonted walk, the one daily walk which she said kept her alive, her Flush found a hare and quested it for two miles. She says—

I heard him the whole time, and could follow by the ear every step that they took, and called in desperate fear lest some keeper should kill my pet. To be sure, as Ben (her servant) and my father said when I returned and told my fright, "Flush is too well known for that." But you can comprehend my alarm at finding that the more I called, the more Flushie would not come; whilst he was making the welkin ring with a tongue unrivalled amongst all spaniels that ever followed game. Instead of pitying me, both my father and Ben were charmed at the adventure. The most provoking part of it was that when, after following the hare to a copse on the other side of the avenue, he had at length come back to me, he actually, upon crossing the scent again, as we were returning homeward, retraced his steps and followed the game back to cover again. This, which was the most trying circumstance of all to me, was exactly what, as proving the fineness of his nose, Ben and his master gloried in. Indeed, Ben caught him up in his arms, and declared that he would back him against any spaniel in England for all that he was worth in the world So, I suppose, to-morrow he'll run away again.

In further proof of the value of the Flush family, Miss Mitford, on another occasion, recounts how a half sister of Miss Barrett's Flush "is so much admired in Reading that she has already been stolen four times— a tribute to her merit which might be dispensed with

—and her master, having upon every occasion offered ten pounds reward, it seems likely enough that she will be stolen four times more."

The dog-stealers were also the bane of Miss Barrett. Writing to Horne in October of this year, she says :—

Yes, I have recovered my pet. No, I have "idealised" none of the dog-stealing. I had no time. I was crying while he was away, and I was accused so loudly of "silliness and childishness" afterwards, that I was glad to dry my eyes, and forgot my misfortunes by way of rescuing my reputation. After all, it was excusable that I cried. Flushie is my friend, my companion, and loves me better than he loves the sunshine without. Oh, and if you had seen him when he came home and threw himself into my arms, palpitating with joy, in that dumb inarticulate ecstasy which is so affecting—love without speech! "You had better give your dog something to eat," said the thief to my brother when he yielded up his prize for a bribe, "for he has tasted nothing since he has been with us." *And he had been with them for three days,* and yet his heart was so full when he came home that he could not eat, but shrank away from the plate and laid down his head on my shoulder. The spirit of love conquered the animal appetite even in that dog. He is worth loving. Is he not?

In the letter containing the foregoing account of Flushie's return home from his unlawful detention, his fond mistress had placed a very neat and characteristic pen-and-ink portrait of little Flush, humorously made to resemble herself. This sketch was jocularly sent in lieu of her own portrait, which Horne had solicited for insertion in his forthcoming work, *A New Spirit of the Age,* and was introduced by these words : " Here I send you one of the ' Spirits of the Age,' strongly recommending it to a place on your frontispiece. It is Flush's portrait, I need scarcely say ; and only fails of being an excellent substitute for mine through being more worthy than I can be counted." Later on, she writes : " Mr. Kenyon was with me yesterday, and praised *Orion* most admir-

ingly. He accused me of the *Athenæum* paper,* and
convicted me against my will; and when I could no
longer deny, and began to explain and ' pique myself
upon my diplomacy,' he threw himself back into his
chair and laughed me to scorn as the least diplomatic
of his acquaintance. ' *You* diplomatic!' "

In her correspondence with Horne generally the
topics discussed were literary, and frequently referred
to projects in which one or both were co-operating.
The following letter from her, dated August 31st, is,
however, more relative to her personal affairs than
usual :—

Ah, my dear Mr. Horne, while you are praising the weather—
stroking the sleek sunshine—it has been, not exactly killing me, but
striking me vigorously with intent to kill. It was intensely hot, and
I went out in the chair, and was over excited and over tired, I sup-
pose; at least, the next day I was ill, shivering in the sun, and
lapsing into a weariness it is not easy for me to rally from. Yet
everybody has been ill, which—in the way of pure benevolence—
ought to be a comfort to me; and now I am well again. And the
weather is certainly lovely and bright by fits, and I join you in
praising the beauty and glory of it; but then, you must admit that
the *fits*, the spasmodic changes of the temperature from sixty-one
degrees to eighty-one, and back again, are trying to mortal frames,
more especially to those conscious of the frailty of the "native mud,"
in them If I had the wings of a dove, and could flee away to the
south of France, I should be cooing, peradventure, instead of moan-
ing. Only I could not *leave everything*, even then! I must stay, as
well as go, under any circumstances, dove or woman.

By the way, two of my brothers are on the Rhine at this moment.
They have gone, to my pain and pleasure, to see Genova, and come
home at the end of six weeks, by Paris, to re-plunge (one of them)
into law.

It pleases me to think of dear Miss Mitford reading my " House
of Clouds" to you, with her " melodious feeling " for poetry, and the
sweeter melody of her kindliness; and it moreover pleased me to
know that you liked it in any measure. Mr. Boyd told me that " He
had read my papers on the Greek Fathers with the more satisfaction

* Miss Barrett's review of *Orion* in the *Athenæum.*

beoause he had inferred from my 'House of Clouds' that illness had *impaired my faculties.*" Ah! but I hope to do something yet, better than the past. I hope, and shall struggle to it.

I have had a great pleasure lately in some correspondence with Miss Martineau, the noblest female intelligence between the seas, "as sweet as spring, as ocean deep." She is in a hopeless anguish of body, and serene triumph of spirit, with at once no hope and all hope! To hear from her was both a pleasure and honour for me.

It is a gratification to know that this high appreciation of one great-souled woman for another—another, too, in many things so different!—was fully reciprocated, and that shortly after the opinion just cited was given, Harriet Martineau told Edward Moxon she deemed "Miss Barrett the woman of women," and that there was nothing to be likened to her recent two volumes of poems.

Not long after the publication of *Chaucer Modernized,* in which he was greatly assisted by our poetess, Horne projected a work to be entitled *A New Spirit of the Age.* The title, if not the theme, was suggested by Hazlitt's well-known work, and, like that, it was to be a work of criticism, but literary criticism only. "As in the case of *Chaucer,*" says Horne, "the work was to be edited and partly written by myself, and the principal and most valuable of my coadjutors was Miss Barrett. The critique entitled "William Wordsworth and Leigh Hunt," he proceeds to tell us, "was written in about equal proportions by Miss Barrett and myself." This was done at first in separate manuscripts, and then each interpolated the work of the other "as the spirit moved." It was written in letters, and some of them of considerable length.

"I believe I am making public for the first time," says Horne, "the fact that the mottoes, which are singularly happy and appropriate, were for the most part supplied by Miss Barrett and Robert Browning, then unknown to each other."

The article on the merits of "Walter Savage Landor," Horne is our authority for saying, was mainly the work of Miss Barrett. "It was forwarded in two letters, which were carefully transcribed. What she had done was preceded by a few biographical and other remarks, founded upon communications forwarded to me by Mr. Landor." That Miss Barrett's observations on Landor are noteworthy needs no confirmation; but that a portion, at least, of the autobiographical information in the article—such as the marvellous anecdote of its hero's connection with the First Napoleon, related by the man himself as an instance of his "great hatred and yet greater forbearance"—was palpably evolved from pure imagination, is self-evident.

The classicism of Walter Savage Landor's style was calculated to inspire Miss Barrett with admiration for his undeniable genius, and, perhaps, to some extent, to blind her to his many eccentricities. Her critique on his writings, and the cause of their slow growth into popular favour, is not only a valuable example of her marvellous clear insight into the real nature of such things, but is a wonderful specimen of her terse and trenchant prose.

The following lines written to Horne by Miss Barrett during the progress of his *New Spirit*, and with reference to it, are very interesting as proving, what our readers may have already discovered, that there was a light and humorous side to her personality :—

You will conclude, from certain facts, that I am very like a *broom*!— not Lord Brougham, who only does a little of everything ; and not a wheeled brougham, which will stop when it is bidden; and not a

new broom, which sweeps clean and then has done with it; but that be-
witched broom in the story, which, being sent to draw water, drew bucket
after bucket, until the whole house was in a flood.   Montaigne says
somewhere that to stop gracefully is a sure proof of high race in a
horse.   I wonder what not to stop at all is proof of—in horse, man, or
woman?   After all, I am not improving my case by this additional
loquacity; and the case is bad enough . . . You asked me to write
four or five pages for your work, and I have written what you see! . . .
Indeed, I did not mean to write so much—I didn't think of writing
your whole book for you !

Miss Barrett's correspondence with Horne, ranges
rapidly from grave to gay in its treatment of literary
and other themes, during the latter months of 1843
and the first quarter of 1844.   Her letters, furnish
almost the only knowledge we have of their writer's
existence during the period named, and are chiefly due
to her co-operation in the *New Spirit of the Age.*   As
an embodiment of Miss Barrett's untrammelled and
real opinion of her contemporaries they are replete
with interest; frequently with a few vitalizing words
furnishing a more vivid portrait of a celebrity or
notoriety of the day than an ordinary bookmaker will
in a volume.   She possessed power of insight that
enabled her to penetrate through the mere action of
individuals and behold clearly their motives.   With no
one, apparently, was she on more friendly terms than
with Miss Mitford, and yet frequently does she give proof
that she refrains from showing her heart to that ami-
able but extremely indiscreet lady, as, also, that she
comprehended thoroughly the limited range of that
correspondent's literary qualifications.   Nevertheless,
Miss Barrett fought nobly on behalf of Miss Mitford
whenever she had the opportunity.   It would be
difficult to cull from any man's essay, however much
an experienced literary man of the world he might

be, a clearer, more condensed, and more impartially worded critique on a fellow author than one on Miss Mitford by Elizabeth Barrett, sent to the editor of *The New Spirit of the Age.*

In the course of their correspondence anent the various personages to be introduced in the projected work Horne had desired his fair contributor to write on one side only of her paper and to leave wide margins to her manuscript, in order, evidently, to permit of his alterations and annotations. She replied : " Very well ! I will be good as I am fair—*i.e.* by courtesy. And I will be very courteous to your right honourable printers, who can't be at the trouble to turn over a leaf or read from anything except large paper, and an inch of margin on each side ! Very well, they shall have their will—although, to be sure, I have been in the habit of writing for the press on the ordinary long note paper, and on both sides the page, and never heard a printer's murmur."

In her *postscript* she says, " ' How I do go on in the dark ! ' To be sure I do. The dark, you know, is my particular province—even *without* the political economy. *That* would have made me a Princess of Darkness."

Miss Barrett's allusion to the darkness will be more readily comprehended, when it is known that after the return to London she lived in a large darkened chamber whence, for some years, she never went further than the bed-room adjoining. She makes frequent allusions to this solitary confinement in her poems and, occasionally, in her correspondence, as in the following letter to a fellow poet :—

I am thinking—lifting up my pen—what I can write which is likely to be interesting to you. After all I come to chaos and silence, and

even old Night, it is growing so dark.   I live in London, to be sure,
and except for the glory of it, I might live in a desert—so profound
is my solitude, and so complete my isolation from things and persons
without.   I lie all day, and day after day, on this sofa, and my windows
do not even look into the street.   To abuse myself with a vain deceit
of rural life, I have had ivy planted in a box—and it has flourished
and spread over one window, and strikes against the glass, with a
little stroke from the thicker leaves, when the wind blows at all
briskly.   *Then* I think of forests and groves . . . It is my triumph.
when the leaves strike the window pane.   And this is not to sound like
a lament.   Books and thoughts and dreams (too consciously *dreamed*,
however, for me—the illusion of them has almost passed) and
domestic tenderness can and ought to leave nobody lamenting.

To Horne—in reply to his request that she would
furnish him with some biographical particulars of
herself, for use in his article on her in the *New Spirit
of the Age*—she says :—

So you think that I am in the habit of keeping biographical sketches
in my table drawer for the use of hypothetical editors?

Once, indeed, for one year. I kept a diary in detail and largely ; and
at the end of the twelve months was in such a crisis of self-disgust
that there was nothing for me but to leave off the diary.   Did you
ever try the effect of a diary upon your own mind? It is curious,
especially where elastic spirits and fancies are at work upon a fixity of
character and situation . . . .

My dear Mr. Horne, the public do not care for me enough to care at
all for my biography.   If you say anything of me (and I am not
affected enough to pretend to wish you to be absolutely silent, if you
see any occasion to speak), it must be as a writer of rhymes, and not
as the heroine of a biography : you must not allow your kindness
for me to place me in a prominency which I have to deserve—and do
not yet deserve.   And then as to stories, my story amounts to the
knife-grinder's, with nothing at all for a catastrophe.   A bird in a
cage could have as good a story.   Most of my events, and nearly all
my intense pleasures, have passed in *thoughts*

" For the rest," she adds, " you see that there is
nothing to say : it is a blank "; and, considering that
up to this time, how little she had done to startle the
world, that how few even of her better poems were

before it, it must be confessed that Horne's request for particulars of her life seems to have been rather premature. Still she could not dismiss the idea from her mind, and resuming the subject, says, " Yet I could write an autobiography, but not now, and not for an indifferent public ; of whom, by the way, I never did and do not complain, seeing that they received my 'Seraphim' with some kindness, and that everything published previously by me I reject myself, and cast upon the ground as unworthy. The 'Seraphim' has faults enough—and weaknesses, besides—but my voice is in it, in its individual tones, and not inarticulately."

Miss Barrett's projected paper on " Wordsworth and Leigh Hunt " for *A New Spirit*, aroused a controversy between the editor and contributor : they were fully agreed as to the treatment of Wordsworth, but over Leigh Hunt held a somewhat excited discussion. Hunt's theological ideas did not come up to the standard of Miss Barrett's faith, but, upon the assurance of Horne that the man was really " a religious man," only not quite orthodox, she relented towards him, adding to her remarks upon the tone of his poetry—" May I say of myself that I hope there is nobody in the world with a stronger will and aspiration to escape from *sectarianism* in any sort or sense, when I have eyes to discern it, and that the sectarianism of the National Churches, to which I do not belong, and of the Dissenting bodies, to which I do—stand together before me on a pretty just level of detestation."

In a subsequent note, referring to the projected paper on herself, after protesting that she will be neither surprised nor disconcerted if the remarks are not of the pleasantest, she says :—" For the rest, or rather under the whole, if I myself am not *tame* about the ' Seraphim,' it is because I am the person interested. I wonder to myself sometimes, in a climax of dissatisfaction, how I came to publish it.   It is a failure, in my own eyes; and if it were not for the poems of less pretension in its company, would have fallen, both probably and deservedly, a dead weight from the press."

In a further epistle, dated in December, she confesses curiosity to know whom it is Mr. Horne now, with some mystery, is wishing her to write on.   "Not Dr. Pusey!" she exclaims.   "Thank you for the 'not.' And not a political economist, I hope—not a mathematician, nor a man of science—such a one as Babbage, for instance, to undo me."   "I am a little beset with business just now," she continues, " being on the verge of getting another volume into print—with one or two long poems struggling for completion at my hands, in order to a subsequent falling upon the printer's."

Later letters continue to discuss the merits and demerits of various authors omitted from, or commented upon, in *A New Spirit of the Age.*   Several female contemporary writers are passed in review, and then the novelists come under notice.   Here, as everywhere, Miss Barrett does not hesitate to express her own opinions, although they may differ widely from her editor's.   "It appears to me," she remarks, "that you cultivate scorn for the novel-readers, or else have no comprehension for them, dividing them into classes of Godwin-readers, Fielding-readers, Richardson-readers, James-readers, and so forth.   You have no sympathy for persons who, when they were children, beset everybody in the house, from the proprietor to the second housemaid, to ' tell them a story,' and retain so much of their childhood—green as grass—as that love of stories."

Oh, that love for story-telling! It may be foolish, to be sure; it leads one into waste of time and strong excitements, to be sure; still, how pleasant it is! How full of enchantment and dream-time gladnesses! What a pleasant accompaniment to one's lonely coffee-cup in the morning or evening, to hold a little volume in the left hand and read softly along how Lindoro saw Monimia over the hedge, and what he said to her! After breakfast we have other matters to do—grave " business matters," poems to write upon Eden, or essays on Carlyle, or literature in various shapes to be employed seriously on. But everybody must attend to a certain proportion of practical affairs of life, and Lindoro and Monimia bring us ours. And then, if Monimia behaves pretty well, what rational satisfaction we have in settling her at the end of the book. No woman who speculates and practises " on her own account " has half the satisfaction in securing an establishment that we have with our Monimias, nor *should* have, let it be said boldly. Did we not divine it would end so—albeit, ourselves and Monimia were weeping together at the end of the second volume? Even to the middle of the third, when Lindoro was sworn at for a traitor by everybody in the book, may it not be testified gloriously of *us* that *we* saw through him, and relied implicitly upon an exculpating fidelity which should be "in" at the finis, to glorify him finally? What, have you known nothing, Mr. Editor, of these exaltations? Indeed your note looks like it.

The correspondence with Horne, in respect to matters connected with the *New Spirit,* ran on into the new year. One note in January contained some very appropriate and truthful words on Byron, one of Elizabeth Barrett's childish idols, to whom, with her usual unswerving tenacity, she held true in her maturity. "Horne!" she exclaims, "do *you*, too, call Byron vindictive? I do not. If he turned upon the dart, it was by the instinct of passion, not by the theory of vengeance, I believe and am assured. Poor, poor Lord Byron! Now would I lay the sun and moon against a tennis-ball that he had more tenderness in one section of his heart than * * * * has in all hers, though a

tenderness misunderstood and crushed, ignorantly, pro-
fanely, and vilely, by false friends and a pattern wife.
His blood is on our heads—on us in England."

Many contemporaries included in or suggested for
A New Spirit of the Age are criticised by Miss Barrett
with that independence of expression, that vigour—
absurdly styled " masculine vigour "—of thought ; but
enough has been said to prove that her mastery of
language was not confined to poesy only, and that her
thoughts could be told as fluently, yet as condensedly,
in prose.   With some few words from her letters on
Horne's paper about herself, a paper of which she saw
nothing until it appeared in print, we can take leave of
A New Spirit of the Age.   To write about herself was,
as Horne points out, a nice and delicate thing, but,
as he adds, " she gets through it with the ease of
any truthful person who believes in the truthfulness
of another."

It has been haunting me all this morning that you may be drawing
the very last inference I should wish you to draw from my silence.
But I have been so unwell that I could not even read. and the writing
has been impossible, and people cry out even now, " Why, surely you
are not going to write ! "

I *must* write.   It is on my mind and must be off it.

First to thank you for the books, which it was such unnecessary
kindness for you to send—and then for the abundant kindness in
another way which will, at the earliest thought. occur to you.   My
only objection to the paper is, that the personal kindness is too
evident.   My objection, you will see, leaves me full of gratitude to
you, and fills to the brim that Venetian goblet of former obligations,
which never held any poison.

You are guilty of certain exaggerations, however, in speaking of me,
against which I shall oppose my *dele* as you allow me.   For instance,
I have not been shut up in one room for six or seven years—four or
five would be nearer ; and then, except on one occasion, I have not
been for "several weeks together in the dark" during the course of
them.   And then there is not a single " elegant Latin verse" extant
from my hand.   I never cultivated Latin verses. . . .

There is nothing to alter—that is. nothing to add—in relation to myself; but there are some inaccuracies, as I have explained to you.

In a later letter Miss Barrett returns to the subject of Horne's paper on herself, saying—

Bear in your mind, then, with regard to me, that I thoroughly understand the fulness both of your kindness and your integrity. You are my friend, I hope, but you do not on that account lose the faculty of judging me, or the right of judging me frankly. I do loathe the whole system of personal compliment as a consequence of a personal interest, and I beseech you not to suffer yourself *ever* by any sort of kind impulse from within, or extraneous influence otherwise, to say or modify a word relating to me. The notice as it stands can be called " inadequate " only in one way—that you enter on no analysis of my poetical claims in it. In every other respect you know it is *extravagantly laudatory.* You have rouged me up to the eyes. . . .

In any case of your approaching the subject of my poetry, you will please me best by speaking out the truth as it occurs to you, broadly, roughly, coarsely, in its whole dimensions. I set more price on your sincerity than on your praise, and consider it more closely connected with the quality called kindness. Recollect that these people who offer a pin to me that they may prick you with it in passing, do not care a pin for me. . . . I want kindness the rarest of all nearly—which is truth.

CHAPTER V.

FAME.

As early as February 1843, Elizabeth Barrett had pre-
pared another volume of poems for the press, but was
unable to find a publisher willing to undertake the
risk of publication.   Moxon, when applied to, declared
that Tennyson was the only poet he did not lose by.

In the spring of 1844 she tells Horne: "I hope my
book will be out in a few weeks now.   It fags me and
over-excites me too much.   Perhaps you will think
me improved?   Perhaps—I seem to myself to have
more strength.   I only wish that bodies and souls
would draw together."

Her hope notwithstanding, the poems remained un-
published all through the summer, and when at last
the collection appeared, it had grown into two well-
filled volumes which, after all, were issued by Moxon.
The work was inscribed to her father in as affec-
tionate terms as was her childhood's poetry, and the
Dedication is interesting as showing, apart from other
reasons, on what a footing she still lived with her sur-
viving parent.   "My father," she writes—

When your eyes fall upon this page of dedication, and you start to
see to whom it is inscribed, your first thought will be of the time far
off when I was a child and wrote verses, and when I dedicated them
to you who were my public and my critic.   Of all that such a recollec-

tion implies of saddest and sweetest to both of us, it would become neither of us to speak before the world; nor would it be possible for us to speak of it to one another with voices that did not falter. Enough that what is in my heart when I write thus will be fully known to yours.

And my desire is that you, who are a witness how if this art of poetry had been a less earnest object to me, it must have fallen from exhausted hands before this day—that you, who have shared with me in things bitter and sweet, softening or enhancing them, every day— that you, who hold with me over all sense of loss and transiency, one hope by one name—may accept from me the inscription of these volumes, the exponents of a few years of an existence which has been sustained and comforted by you as well as given. Somewhat more faint-hearted than I used to be, it is my fancy thus to seem to return to a visible personal dependence on you, as if indeed I were a child again; to conjure your beloved image between myself and the public, so as to be sure of one smile—and to satisfy my heart while I satisfy my ambition, by associating with the great pursuit of my life its tenderest and holiest affection.

Her Dedication was followed by a lengthy Preface, which was to no small extent a criticism on her own collection, especially on the chief poem in it. After stating that the collection now offered to the public consisted of poems written since the publication of the *Seraphim* volume, and which were now, with a few exceptions, printed for the first time, she refers to the "Drama of Exile," the initial piece, " as the longest and most important work (to *me !*) which I have ever trusted into the current of publication."

The theme of the " Drama of Exile " is so daring, and the execution, despite innumerable faults, so excellent, that either condemnation or praise is hard to award. The great defect in what the poetess intended should be her masterpiece is that—notwithstanding the introduction of Adam and Eve, and the self-sacrificing love of the latter for her partner in sorrow—it is almost entirely devoid of human interest. Admiration is frequently compelled by bursts of true lyrical beauty, but the heart never throbs with hope nor thrills with terror for the poetic phantasmata whose weeping and wailing fill so many pages of the drama. There are, it is true, some magnificent passages of poetry in the work, notably Lucifer's description of the effect of the curse upon animal creation. Reminding Adam of " when the curse took us in Eden," he says—

On a mountain peak,
Half sheathed in primal woods. and glittering
In spasms of awful sunshine, at that hour
A lion couched—part raised upon his paws,
With his calm, massive face turned full on thine,
And his mane listening.   When the ended curse
Left silence in the world—right suddenly
He sprang up rampant. and stood straight and stiff
As if the new reality of death
Were dashed against his eyes—and roared so fierce,
(Such thick carnivorous passion in his throat
Tearing a passage through the wrath and fear)—
And roared so wild, and smote from all the hills
Such fast, keen echoes crumbling down the vales
Precipitately—that the forest beasts,
One after one, did mutter a response
In savage and in sorrowful complaint,
Which trailed along the gorges.   Then, at once,
He fell back, and rolled crashing from the height.

This is a magnificent picture most grandiloquently portrayed, but it is the finest passage in the *Drama.* Its author appears to have felt that there was something wanting in her work, and, therefore, strives to explain away what might be objected to, and to deprecate criticism, by a lengthy Preface.

" The Vision of Poets," the second longest poem in the collection, is referred to by her as an attempt to express her view of the poet's mission, " of the self-abnegation implied in it, of the great work involved in it, of the duty and glory of what Balzac has beau-

tifully and truly called *la patience angélique du génie;*
and of the obvious truth, above all, that if knowledge
is power, suffering should be acceptable as a part of
power." Without in any way endorsing Miss Barrett's
theory, and, indeed, feeling that it is radically false to
nature and genius, and that no poet should humiliate
himself to the "world's use," or suffer unresistingly
the humiliation of the "world's cruelty," it must at
once be acknowledged that the grandeur and power of
the poem is likely to blind readers to its perverse doc-
trine. Apart from Dante and Shakespeare, it would
be difficult to meet with so great a condensation of
thought, such abridged yet complete characterisation,
as is frequently met with in this marvellous poem,
and yet, all things considered, it is not perhaps very
strange that the "Vision of Poets" has failed to elicit
the applause of critics, and indeed to find that many
of them have refrained from speaking of it at all. In
the whole range of literature it would be difficult to
parallel, in prose or verse, such concise yet descriptive
portraiture as the poem contains. It is replete with com-
pound words and epigrammatic sentences, but it must
be confessed that the "Conclusion" is out of tone
with the rest of the poem, and uncalled for. Every
poem should, as Elizabeth Barrett says herself, have
"an object and a significance"; but her propensity to
drag in a moral, or to tag on a didactic dissertation
of some kind, even from an artistic point of view, dis-
figures her most beautiful work.

Her Preface to the collection concludes with the
hope that some of the faults which she had formerly
been reproached with may have been outgrown :—

.Because some progress in mind and in art every active thinker
and honest writer must consciously or unconsciously make, with the

progress of existence and experience; and, in some sort—since "we learn in suffering what we teach in song"—my songs may be fitter to teach. But if it were not presumptuous language on the lips of one to whom life is more than usually uncertain, my favourite wish for this work would be, that it be received by the public as a step in the right track, towards a future indication of more value and acceptability. I would fain do better—and I feel as if I might do better: I aspire to do better . . . In any case, while my poems are full of faults—as I go forward to my critics and confess—they have my heart and life in them—they are not empty shells. . . . Poetry has been as serious a thing to me as life itself; and life has been a very serious thing: there has been no playing at skittles for me in either I never mistook pleasure for the final cause of poetry; nor leisure, for the hour of the poet. I have done my work, so far, as work—not as mere hand and head work, apart from the personal being—but as the completest expression of that being, to which I could attain—and as work I offer it to the public—feeling its shortcomings more deeply than any of my readers, because measured from the height of my aspiration—but feeling also that the reverence and sincerity with which the work was done should give it some protection with the reverent and sincere.

The collection was received by quite an outburst of applause. Although the critics, with their usual dread of committing themselves too deeply, all found something to object to in the work, one admiring what another disliked, and the other disliking what the former admired, they all arrived at the conclusion that another true and great poet had arisen. "The critics," says Miss Barrett, "have all, according to their measure, been kind and generous to me. For the newspapers, besides those I mentioned, the *Examiner* sounded a clarion for me. I am well pleased altogether." To Horne she says,—

I have had a long and most kind letter from Harriet Martineau, and from Mrs. Jameson, and a kind note from Mr. Landor, and others. Now I do beseech you, by whatever regard you may feel for me (in which I am ambitious to believe), to write to me a kind letter too—that is, a *sincere* letter. Do not fancy yourself obliged to write compliments to me—surely our friendship has outgrown such mere green wood. I promise not to enact the Archbishop of Granada if you speak the truth to me. . . "The Drama of Exile," the longest poem, has been thrown aside by nearly all the official critics as inferior to the rest—and perhaps, as a whole, is unsuccessful. "Lady Geraldine's Courtship" appears to be the popular favourite. Oh, for life and strength to do something better and worthier than any of them! I feel as if I could do it.

In this instance all must now agree that the popular voice was the voice of justice. The "Drama of Exile," evidently the author's favourite, her most ambitious performance, and the work on which she had relied for fame, is a failure; a grand failure it is true, but from the very nature of its theme, bound to be more or less a failure, notwithstanding the fact that it contains passages of extraordinary grandeur and is replete with others of lyrical sweetness.

"Lady Geraldine's Courtship" is, deservedly, one of the most popular poems of the age. The best-known legend connected with its composition was, doubtless, originally promulgated by Miss Mitford to account for its wonderful rush of glowing language, and to enhance the mystery of its authoress, of whose personality so few people knew anything. The poem, making forty-two octavo pages, was averred to have been written within the space of twelve hours, written off at electric speed in order to make up the number of sheets required by the American publisher of the poems. How much of truth may be contained in this myth is hard to say, but that Miss Barrett composed at times with great rapidity is a fact. Much of the rugged rhythm and apparent carelessness of construction which characterises so many of her poems is doubtless due to the speed at which they were evolved, and to the same cause may be ascribed their occasional obscurity and other defects, but that their defective or affected

6

rhyming was not due to this cause we have her own words to prove.

Of "Lady Geraldine's Courtship" Edgar Poe, no careless critic, said that, with the exception of Tennyson's "Locksley Hall," he had never perused a poem "containing so much of the fiercest passion with so much of the most ethereal fancy." "Lady Geraldine's Courtship" he somewhat too dogmatically pronounced to be "the only poem of its author which is not deficient, considered as an artistic whole. Her constructive ability," he added, "is either not very remarkable, or has never been properly brought into play. In truth, her genius is too impetuous for the minuter technicalities of that elaborate *art* so needful in the building up of pyramids for immortality."

It is but justice to Poe to tell that, after a full and frank exposition of her faults and her fancied faults, he gives ungrudging praise to her merits, not only deeming her poetic inspiration to be of the highest, the most august conceivable, but declaring it to be his deliberate opinion, "not idly entertained, nor founded on any visionary basis," that she had "surpassed all her poetical contemporaries of either sex, with a single exception," the exception being Tennyson. Poe's most enthusiastic admiration for Miss Barrett led him to do his best to spread a knowledge of her works in the United States, where, indeed, he was the pioneer of her fame. He dedicated to her—"To the noblest of her sex"—his last and most valuable volume of poems. Something of what the lady thought of him will be learned later on.

The story told in "Lady Geraldine's Courtship,"— "A Romance of the Age," as it is sub-titled — is devoid of sensational episodes or romantic incidents.

It is almost barren of plot, and is founded on the threadbare basis of being told by the chief actor in a letter to a friend. The writer of the story is supposed to be a poet named Bertram, a man of the people, who has won a place in society by his poetic talent—

And because I was a poet, and because the people praised me,
With their critical deductions for the modern writer's fault ;
I could sit at rich men's tables, though the courtesies that raised me
Still suggested clear between us the pale spectrum of the salt.

Lady Geraldine meeting him, invites him to her country residence—Wycombe Hall, in Sussex. She, an earl's daughter, is proud and noble, and being richly dowered with halls and castles, is beset by many suitors, all of whom are treated with disdain. Of course, Bertram falls passionately in love with her—

Yet I could not choose but love her—I was born to poet uses—
To love all things set above me, all of good and all of fair.

Meeting and conversing with her daily, and reading his own or other poets' writings to her, her hold upon him becomes more and more intense, until at last he cannot fly her presence, hopeless though he feels his love to be, and knowing that the longer he lingers near her the stronger grow his chains. Tangled in love's meshes, Bertram follows in the retinue of his fair hostess, wandering with her and her companions about the glorious grounds. Lady Geraldine is thus described as one day she stood :—

Thus, her foot upon the now-mown grass—bareheaded—with the flowings
Of the virginal white vesture, gathered closely to her throat ;
With the golden ringlets in her neck, just quickened by her going,
And appearing to breathe sun for air, and doubting if to float,—
With a branch of dewy maple, which her right hand held above her,
And which trembled a green shadow in betwixt her and the skies,—
As she turned her face in going, thus, she drew me on to love her,
And to study the deep meaning of the smile hid in her eyes.

Thus Bertram continues to linger, although he knows how hopeless his case must be; he lingers still, like the stag "that tries to go on grazing with the great deep gunwound in his neck." And Lady Geraldine, although she has many suitors, smiles upon them "with such a gracious coldness that they could not press their futures" upon her decision. Until one day Bertram, accidentally placed in an inner chamber, becomes the unintentional auditor of someone pleading for the lady's hand :—

> Well I knew that voice—it was an earl's, of soul that matched his
>   station—
> Of a soul complete in lordship—might and right read on his brow:
> Very finely courteous—far too noble to doubt his admiration
> Of the common people—he atones for grandeur by a bow.

The poor poet, compelled to listen against his will, hears the lady reject her noble suitor, it is true, but, in answer to an inaudible remark from the earl, hears her respond—

> And your lordship judges rightly.   Whom I marry shall be noble,
> Ay, and wealthy.   I shall never blush to think how he was born.

When Bertram heard this, and knew that whatever foolish hopings against hope he may have entertained were for ever dashed to the ground, he forbore no longer, but rushed into her presence, as her lordly suitor retreated, and "spake out wildly—fiercely" :—

> I plucked up her social fictions, bloody-rooted, though leaf verdant,—
> Trod them down with words of shaming—all the purples and the
>   gold,
> And the "landed stakes" and lordships—all that spirits pure and
>   ardent
> Are cast out of love and reverence, because chancing not to hold.

" For myself I do not argue," said I, " though I love you, Madam,—
But for better souls, that nearer to the height of yours have trod—
And this age shows, to my thinking, still more infidels to Adam,
Than directly, by profession, simple infidels to God.

　　*　　　*　　　*　　　*　　　*

But at last there came a pause. I stood all vibrating with thunder,
Which my soul had used. The silence drew her face up like a call.
Could you guess what word she uttered? She looked up as if in
　　wonder,
With tears beaded on her lashes, and said " Bertram ! " it was all.

If she had cursed me—and she might have—or if even, with queenly
　　bearing,
Which at need is used by women, she had risen up and said,
" Sir, you are my guest, and therefore, I have given you a full
　　hearing—
Now, beseech you, choose a name exacting somewhat less, in-
　　stead "—

I had borne it !—but that '' Bertram "—why, it lies there on the
　　paper
A mere word, without her accents,—and you cannot judge the weight
Of the calm which crushed my passion ! I seemed swimming in a
　　vapour,—
And her gentleness did shame me, whom her scorn made desolate.

　　*　　　*　　　*　　　*　　　*

After this what follows is not difficult to guess;
and it does not come as a surprise to learn this solu-
tion of her words :—

Softened, quickened to adore her, on his knee he fell before her—
And she whispered low in triumph—It shall be as I have sworn !
Very rich he is in virtues,—very noble—noble, certes ;
And I shall not blush in knowing, that men call him lowly born !

The poverty of the plot, the improbability of the
whole story, the author's frequent ignorance of worldly
matters, the faulty and too long deferred rhymes, lapses
in the rhythm and occasional commonplaces, all vanish
in the passionate glow of thought, in the rush of burn-
ing words, and the magnificent flood of imaginative

poetry, tearing everything along with it in a resistless torrent of glory and grandeur, that fairly overpowers and conquers the most critical reader's judgment.

Besides the more prominent pieces already alluded to, the 1844 collection contained several other pieces of supreme merit. The sonnet, a condensed and artificial form of poesy almost outside the fluent muse of Elizabeth Barrett, had several pages devoted to it, but their merits were less conspicuous, although studded with beauties, than was usual with her work. "The Soul's Expression," as an autobiographic revelation, is interesting; "Grief" contains some fine thought, such as "I tell you, hopeless grief is passionless"; and "The Prisoner" concludes with a grand idea; but, as yet, her sonnets, although vigorous, were somewhat unskilfully wrought, and uncouth in expression.

The miscellaneous poems cannot be too highly praised, nor too often perused; fresh beauties burst forth at every glance. "The Lay of the Brown Rosarie" is replete with scintillations of true poetic fervour; it is styled a ballad, but is of a purer tone and a more etherealised spirit than is generally prevalent in ballad poesy, ancient or modern. In its circumscribed space the story is complete; and although undisfigured by the "moral" so frequently and needlessly dragged in by Miss Barrett, is all through its dramatic course illuminated by an under-glow of *suggested* meaning.

"The Duchess May," another ballad, of more heroic mould, is less in sympathy with our century's way of thinking. It contains grand lines and stirring thoughts, but the narrative is improbable, the subject not in unison with the age's tendencies, and, therefore,

unsuited to its author's own practical, if passionate
mind. To "The Lost Bower," interspersed as it is
with personal allusions, reference has already been
made. It is replete with passages of the purest poesy,
and leaves an impression upon the reader's mind of
mingled melody and pathos—childish simplicity and
womanly wisdom—time will vainly try to efface. The
following lines from "The Lost Bower" will, like
petals picked from a lovely blossom, suggest how
beauteous the complete bloom may be :—

> Green the land is where my daily
> Steps in jocund childhood played—
> Dimpled close with hill and valley,
> Dappled very close with shade ;
> Summer-snow of apple-blossoms, running up from glade to
> glade.
>
> There is one hill I see nearer,
> In my vision of the rest ;
> And a little wood seems clearer,
> As it climbeth from the west,
> Sideway from the tree-locked valley, to the airy upland
> crest.
>
> Small the wood is, green with hazels,
> And, completing the ascent,
> Where the wind blows and sun dazzles
> Thrills in leafy tremblement :
> Like a heart that, after climbing, beateth quickly though
> content. . . .
>
> Yet in childhood little prized I
> That fair walk and far survey :
> 'Twas a straight walk, unadvised by
> The least mischief worth a nay—
> Up and down—as dull as grammar on an eve of holiday!
>
> But the wood, all close and clenching
> Bough in bough and root in root,—
> No more sky (for over-branching)
> At your head than at your foot,—
> Oh, the wood drew me within it, by a glamour past dis-
> pute. . .

On a day, such pastime keeping,
With a fawn's heart debonair,
Under-crawling, over-leaping
Thorns that prick and boughs that bear,
I stood suddenly astonied—I was gladdened unaware !

From the place I stood in, floated
Back the covert dim and close ;
And the open ground was suited
Carpet-smooth with grass and moss,
And the bluebell's purple presence signed it worthily across.

Here a linden tree stood, brightening
All adown its silver rind ;
For. as some trees draw the lightning,
So this tree, unto my mind,
Drew to earth the blessed sunshine, from the sky where it
was shrined. . .

Tall the linden-tree, and near it
An old hawthorn also grew ;
And wood-ivy like a spirit
Hovered dimly round the two,
Shaping thence that Bower of beauty, which I sing of thus
to you. . .

As I entered—mosses hushing
Stole all noises from my foot :
And a round elastic cushion,
Clasped within the linden's root.
Took me in a chair of silence, very rare and absolute. . .

So, young muser, I sate listening
To my Fancy's wildest word—
On a sudden, through the glistening
Leaves around, a little stirred,
Came a sound, a sense of music, which was rather felt than
heard.

Softly, finely, it inwound me—
From the world it shut me in,—
Like a fountain falling round me,
Which with silver waters thin
Clips a little marble Naiad, sitting smilingly within   . .

I rose up in exaltation
And an inward trembling heat,
And (it seemed) in geste of passion,
Dropped the music to my feet,
Like a garment rustling downwards—such a silence fol-
lowed it.   . .

In a child-abstraction lifted,
Straightway from the bower I past;
Foot and soul being dimly drifted
Through the greenwood, till, at last,
In the hill-top's open sunshine, I all consciously was cast. . . .

I affirm that, since I lost it,
Never bower has seemed so fair—
Never garden-creeper crossed it,
With so deft and brave an air—
Never bird sung in the summer, as I saw and heard them
there. . .

These stray extracts can give but a faint idea of the
pathetic beauty of the whole poem; of its gust of
melodious musical melancholy — which "resembles
sorrow only as the mist resembles rain." Haplessly,
like so many of its author's best pieces, the story is
burdened and drawn out by a lengthy, unneeded
"moral" being appended to it.

In "A Child Asleep" are to be found thoughts and
similes worthy of the highest poetic parentage; but one
idea, "Folded eyes see brighter colours than the open
ever do," is scarcely an improvement upon Coleridge's
beautiful verse, "My eyes make pictures when they
are shut." "The Cry of the Children," and some other
splendid pieces gathered into this collection have already
received notice; but amid the remainder may be spe-
cially pointed out "The Fourfold Aspect," "A Flower
in a Letter," "The Cry of the Human," with its terrible
opening—

"There is no God!" the foolish saith,
But none, "There is no sorrow";

And Nature oft, tho cry of faith
  In bitter need will borrow.
Eyes, which the preacher could not school,
  By wayside graves are raised;
And lips say " God be pitiful."
  Who ne'er said " God be praised ! "—

"A Lay of the Early Rose," despite its obtrusive moral, "Bertha in the Lane," "A Rhapsody of Life's Progress," that "most musical, most melancholy" "Catarina to Camoëns," "The Romance of the Swan's Nest," and others of various kinds of excellence, and all possessed of power and beauty sufficient for each one separately to make the reputation of any lesser poet. The peculiar pathos of " The Romance of the Swan's Nest " dowers it with some indefinable fascination, and causes it to have for us a pre-eminence of charm we have never been able to explain. It is as sweet as the aroma from new-mown hay, yet as sad as the ceaseless moan on the sea-bruised beach. It is short, and all worthy of quotation in full:—

Little Ellie sits alone
Mid the beeches of a meadow,
  By a stream-side, on the grass:
  And the trees are showering down
Doubles of their leaves in shadow,
  On her shining hair and face.

She has thrown her bonnet by;
And her feet she has been dipping
  In the shallow water's flow—
  Now she holds them nakedly
In her hands, all sleek and dripping,
  While she rocketh to and fro.

Little Ellie sits alone,—
And the smile, she softly useth,
  Fills the silence like a speech;
  While she thinks what shall be done,—
And the sweetest pleasure chooseth,
  For her future within reach!

Little Ellie in her smile
Chooseth . . . . " I will have a lover,
   Riding on a steed of steeds!
He shall love me without guile;
And to *him* I will discover
   The swan's nest among the reeds.

" And the steed shall be red-roan,
And the lover shall be noble,
   With an eye that takes the breath,—
And the lute he plays upon,
Shall strike ladies into trouble,
   As his sword stikes men to death.

" And the steed it shall be shod
All in silver, housed in azure,
   And the mane shall swim the wind
And the hoofs, along the sod,
Shall flash onward in a pleasure,
   Till the shepherds look behind.

" But my lover will not prize
All the glory that he rides in,
   When he gazes in my face!
He will say, ' O Love, thine eyes
Build the shrine my soul abides in;
   And I kneel here for thy grace.'

" Then, ay, then—he shall kneel low,·
With the red-roan steed anear him.
   Which shall seem to understand—
Till I answer, ' Rise, and go!
For the world must love and fear him
   Whom I gift with heart and hand.'

" Then he will arise so pale,
I shall feel my own lips tremble
   With a *yes* I must not say—
Nathless, maiden-brave, 'Farewell,'
I will utter and dissemble—
   ' Light to-morrow. with to-day.'

·' Then he will ride through the hills
To the wide world past the river,
   There to put away all wrong!
To make straight distorted wills,—
And to empty the broad quiver
   Which the wicked bear along.

" Three times shall a young foot-page
Swim the stream, and climb the mountain.
  And kneel down beside my feet—
' Lo ! my master sends this gage,
Lady, for thy pity's counting !
  What wilt thou exchange for it ? '

" And the first time, I will send
A white rosebud for a guerdon,—
  And the second time, a glove !
But the third time—I may bend
From my pride, and answer—' Pardon—
  If he come to take my love.'

" Then the young foot-page will run—
Then my lover will ride faster,
  Till he kneeleth at my knee !
' I am a duke's eldest son !
Thousand serfs do call me master,—
  But, O Love, I love but *thee !* '

" He will kiss me on the mouth
Then, and lead me as a lover,
  Through the crowds that praise his deeds !
And, when soul-tied by one troth,
Unto *him* I will discover
  That swan's nest among the reeds."

Little Ellie, with her smile
Not yet ended, rose up gaily,—
  Tied the bonnet, donned the shoe—
And went homeward, round a mile,
Just to see, as she did daily,
  What more eggs were with the *two.*

Pushing through the elm-tree copse
Winding by the stream, light-hearted,
  Where the osier pathway leads—
Past the boughs she stoops—and stops !
Lo ! the wild swan had deserted—
  And a rat had gnawed the reeds.

Ellie went home sad and slow !
If she found the lover ever,
  With his red-roan steed of steeds,
Sooth I know not ! but I know
She could show him never—never,
  That swan's nest among the reeds !

Another remarkable and still more powerful poem
is "The Dead Pan," with which the collection con-
cludes. In its beauties and, it must be acknowledged,
in its faults, this piece is thoroughly idiosyncratic of
its author. The poem, says Elizabeth Barrett, was
partly inspired by Schiller's *Götter Griechenlands,* and
partly by the tradition recorded by Plutarch, that at
the moment of Christ's death on the cross a cry was
heard sweeping across the sea, " Great Pan is dead ! "
and that then and forever all the oracles of heathen-
dom ceased. " It is in all veneration to the memory
of the deathless Schiller," says the poetess, "that I
oppose a doctrine still more dishonouring to poetry
than to Christianity."

To John Kenyon, whose " graceful and harmonious
paraphrase of the German poem was the first occasion
of the turning " of her thoughts towards the theme,
she inscribed " The Dead Pan." Thoroughly typical
of her style is the opening invocation :—

> Gods of Hellas, gods of Hellas,
> Can you listen in your silence?
> Can your mystic voices tell us
> Where ye hide? In floating islands,
> With a wind that evermore
> Keeps you out of sight of shore?
> Pan, Pan is dead.

Of the many peculiar rhymes which Miss Barrett—
sometimes " without rhyme or reason "—persistently
made use of in this and other of her poems, the quoted
stanza does not present an unfair example. Her
correspondence with Horne on the subject is not only
amusing, but also characteristic of her unchangeable-
ness of will when she believed in her own ideas. She
had forwarded Horne the manuscript of her poem,

and requested his opinion upon it. What was his full reply is unknown, but he remarks : "Of course, I admired its poetry and versification, but concerning her views of perfect and imperfect, or *allowable* rhymes, in that, and several of her other productions, I wished, once for all, to object, and give full reasons for it." "I took objection to many of the rhymes," says Horne. "I did not like 'tell us' as a rhyme for 'Hellas,' and still less 'islands' as a rhyme for 'silence.'" Other still less excusable examples were objected to, such as "rolls on" and "the sun"; "altars" and "welters"; "flowing" and "slow in"; "iron" and "inspiring"; "driven" and "heaving," and so forth. What little effect her brother poet's animadversions had upon Miss Barrett, the following words will show :—

"My dear Mr. Horne,—Do you know I could not help, in the midst of my horror and Panic terror, smiling outright at the *naïveté* of your doubt as to whether my rhymes were really meant for rhymes at all ? That is the *naïveté* of a right savage nature—of an Indian playing with a tomahawk, and speculating as to whether the white faces had any feeling in their skulls, *quand même !* Know, then, that my rhymes *are* really meant for rhymes, . . . and that in no spirit of care-lessness or easy writing, or desire to escape difficulties, have I run into them, but chosen them, selected them, on principle, and with the determinate purpose of doing my best. . . . What you say of a "poet's duty," no one in the world can feel more deeply in the verity of it than myself. If I fail ultimately before the public —that is, before the people—for an ephemeral popu-larity does not appear to me worth trying for—it will not be because I have shrunk from the amount of labour—where labour could do anything. I have *worked* at poetry—it has not been with me reverie, but art. As the physician and lawyer work at their several professions, so have I, and so do I, apply to mine.

" . . . With reference to the double rhyming, it has appeared to me employed with far less variety in our *serious* poetry than our language would admit of generally, and that the various employment of it would add another string to the lyre of our Terpander. . . . A great deal of attention—far more than it would take to rhyme with conventional accuracy—have I given to the subject of rhymes, and have determined in cold blood to hazard some experiments. . . .

"And now, upon all this—to prove to you that I do not set out on this question with a minority of one —I take the courage and vanity to send to you a note which a poet whom we both admire wrote to a friend of mine, who lent him the manuscript of this very "Pan." Mark! no opinion was asked about the rhymes—the satisfaction was altogether impulsive— from within. Send me the note back, and never tell anybody that I showed it to you—it would appear too vain. Also, I have no right to show it. It was sent to me as likely to please me, and pleased me so much and naturally on various accounts, and not the least from the beauty of the figure used to illustrate my *rhymatology*, that I begged to be allowed to keep it. So send it back, after reading it confidentially, and pardon me as much as you can of the self-will fostered by it."

After such a response, Horne, as will be readily imagined, dropped the subject of allowable rhymes; but, it is most interesting to learn, the poet whose opinion had proved so satisfactory to Miss Barrett was

Mr. Robert Browning, at that time personally unknown to her.

Writing on the 3rd December to Horne, Miss Barrett says : " The volumes are succeeding past any expectation or hope of mine. . . . I continue to have letters of the kindest from unknown readers. I had a letter yesterday from the remote region of Gutter Lane, beginning, ' I thank thee ! ' . . . The American publisher has printed fifteen hundred copies. If I am a means of ultimate loss to him, I shall sit in sackcloth."

There was no need to have feared for the American any more than for the English publisher—both found Miss Barrett's poems a good investment. Her reputation, indeed, was of almost as early a growth in the United States as in Great Britain. Edgar Poe, if not the first, was one of the first to introduce her to the American public, issuing some of her earlier pieces through the pages of *Graham's Magazine,* which he was then editing.

In a critique he subsequently wrote on Miss Barrett's poetry, Poe alludes to certain shortcomings in the technicalities of verse, especially bewailing her inattention to rhythm, an error that might have been fatal to her fame; but concludes with the declaration that the pen is impotent to express in detail the beauties of her work. " Her poetic inspiration," he remarks, " is the highest; we can conceive nothing more august." Nevertheless, he perceives that her sense of art, pure in itself, " has been contaminated by pedantic study of false models—a study which has the more easily led her astray, because she placed an undue value upon it as rare—as alien to her character of woman. The accident," he considers, " of her having been long secluded by ill-health from the world . . . has imparted to her . . . a comparative independence of men and opinions with which she did not come personally in contact, a happy audacity of thought and expression never before known in one of her sex "

Lofty as was Poe's opinion and exalted his praise of her, Elizabeth Barrett did not appear to care altogether for his remarks. Writing to Horne in May, 1845, she says : " Your friend, Mr. Poe, is a speaker of strong words ' in both kinds ' . . . Mr. Poe seems to me in a great mist on the subject of metre . . . But I hope you will assure him from me that I am grateful for his reviews, and in no complaining humour at all. As to *The Raven*, tell me what you shall say about it ! There is certainly a power, but it does not appear to me the natural expression of a sane intellect in whatever mood ; and I think that this should be specified in the title of the poem. There is a fantasticalness about the ' Sir or Madam,' and things of the sort, which is ludicrous, unless there is a specified insanity to justify the straws. Probably he—the author—intended it to be read in the poem, and he ought to have intended it. The rhythm, acts excellently upon the imagination, and the ' nevermore ' has a solemn chime in it . . . Just because I have been criticised, I would not criticise. And I am of opinion that there is an uncommon force and effect in the poem."

Writing subsequently to Poe on the subject of this poem, Miss Barrett says : " *The Raven* has produced a sensation—a ' fit horror ' here in England. Some of my friends are taken by the fear of it, and some by the music. I hear of persons haunted by the ' Nevermore,' and one acquaintance of mine, who has the misfortune of possessing a ' bust of Pallas,' never can bear to look at it in the twilight. Our great poet, Mr. Browning, is enthusiastic in his admiration of the rhythm."

Encouraged by her remarks, Poe sent her a copy of a selection of his *Tales*, just published, and Miss Barrett, writing to a friend, alludes to the story entitled *The Facts in the Case of M. Valdemar* thus: "There is a tale of his which I do not find in this volume, but which is going the rounds of the newspapers, about mesmerism, throwing us all into most admired disorder, or dreadful doubts as to whether it can be true, as the children say of ghost stories. The certain thing in the tale in question is the power of the writer, and the faculty he has of making horrible improbabilities seem near and familiar."

The great success of her latest literary venture naturally brought Miss Barrett a large increase of correspondence; nevertheless, she contrived to maintain epistolary chatter with such old friends as Miss Mitford and Horne. One prominent theme with her at this period was the marvellous recovery of Harriet Martineau, after several years of confirmed illness. This cure of a disease considered hopeless by orthodox medical men was ascribed to mesmerism. It naturally created a lively sensation, even beyond the boundaries of medical and literary circles, and no one appears to have been more deeply and permanently impressed by the affair than Elizabeth Barrett, who was naturally inspired with admiration and interest for the sturdy independence, in some respects akin to her own, of her friend, correspondent, and contemporary, Harriet Martineau. Writing to an American friend, Miss Barrett remarks, " Harriet Martineau's mesmeric experience . . . is making a great noise and sensation

here, and producing some vexation among her un-
believing friends.   It was, however, worthy of herself,
having, according to her own belief, received a great
benefit from means not only questionable, but questioned,
to come forward bravely and avouch the truth of it. Do
you believe at all ? *I do*, but it is in the highest degree
repulsive to me as a subject, and suggestive of horror.
It is making great way in England, and, as far as I
can understand, is disputed more by the unlearned than
the learned."

Writing to Horne in November, 1844, she says:
"As you remind me, Miss Martineau is a great
landmark to show how far a recovery can go.   She
can walk five miles a day now with ease, and is well,
she says—not comparatively well, but well in the
strict sense . . . She has an apocalyptic housemaid
(save the mark!) who, being *clairvoyante*, prophesies
concerning the anatomical structure of herself and
others, and declares ' awful spiritual dicta ' concerning
the soul and the mind and their future destination;
discriminating, says Miss Martineau, ' between what
she hears at church and what is true ' . . . I am
credulous and superstitious, naturally, and find no
difficulty in the *wonder*; only precisely because I
believe it, I would not subject myself to this mystery
at the will of another, and this induction into things
unseen.   My blood runs the wrong way to think of
it. Is it lawful, or, if lawful, expedient? Do you
believe a word of it, or are you sceptical like
papa ? "

Miss Martineau, with her usual stern idea of duty,
considered it right that her cure and its cause should
be told to the public.   Unfortunately, her medical
attendant, in order to controvert her theory, departed

7 *

from the rules of his profession, ignored the rights due to a patient, and made public particulars which he, at least, should have kept private. Alluding to these circumstances in a letter subsequent to the above, Miss Barrett says: "Miss Martineau is astonishing the world with mesmeric statements through the *medium* of the *Athenæum*—and yet, it happens so that, I believe, few converts will be made by her. The medical men have taken up her glove brutally—as dogs might do—dogs, exclusive of my Flush, who is a gentleman." Later on she writes, "I hear that Carlyle won't believe in mesmerism, and calls Harriet Martineau *mad.* 'The madness showed itself first in the refusal of a pension; next, in the resolution that, the universe being desirous of reading her letters, the universe should be disappointed; and thirdly, in this creed of mesmerism.' I wish (if he ever did use such words) somebody would tell him that the first manifestation, at least, was of a noble phrenzy, which in these latter days is not too likely to prove contagious. For my own part, I am not afraid to say that I almost believe in mesmerism, and quite believe in Harriet Martineau."

Miss Mitford's correspondence with our poetess was very voluminous during the greater part of 1844 and 1845, but little of personal incident enters into it. The elder lady was enchanted to learn that Miss Barrett intended in future " to write narrative poetry, and narrative poetry of real life," and endeavoured to arouse in her mind, but with scant success, an admiration for the first Napoleon.

That in literature, if in nothing else, woman should not only compete with man on an equal footing, but be judged by a similar measure, is a truth all right-minded men would feel, one would think, and yet it is a truth not very widely promulgated or generally recognised. Elizabeth Barrett was not the woman to feel and not assert her ideas on such a theme. " Please to recollect," she says, writing to Horne on the subject of eminent women, " that when I talk of women, I do not speak of them as many men do, . . . according to a separate, peculiar, and womanly standard, but according to the common standard of human nature."

Her fidelity to a conviction could not be shaken by any amount of popular prejudice or private influence. Her ideal of a truth once conceived nothing could destroy, or argument upset. She had formed strong opinions with regard to Leigh Hunt's theology, and, consequently, looked on his writings with suspicion. "There may be sectarianism in the very cutting off of sectarianism," she says, and instances his omission in a critical work upon poetry, " of one of the very noblest odes in the English language—that on the Nativity, because—it is not on the birth of Bacchus."

Such remarks, and they abound in her characteristic epistles, are of great biographical value, as throwing light upon her firm and thoroughly independent mind. By far the larger portion of her correspondence that has as yet come to light is purely literary. Books and their builders is her constant theme. The popularity of her works in the United States caused her to receive many letters from Americans, and sometimes drew her into discussions with them on the social and other aspects of their country. Writing to one of her New England friends, she says:—

" The cataracts and mountains you speak of have been—are—mighty dreams to me; and the great people which, proportionate to that scenery, is springing up in their midst to fill a yet vaster futurity, is dearer to me than a dream. America is our brother land, and, though a younger brother, sits already in the teacher's seat and expounds the common rights of our humanity. It would be strange if we in England did not love and exult in America. . . . It is delightful and encouraging to me to think that there, 'among the cataracts and mountains,' which I shall never see—and there is 'dream-land'—sound the voices of friends; and it shall be a constant effort with me to deserve presently, in some better measure, the kindness for which I never can be more grateful than now.

"We have one Shakespeare between us—your land and ours—have we not? And one Milton? And now we are waiting for you to give us another. Niagara ought,

> "And music born of murmuring sound
> Shall pass into his face."

In the meantime we give honour to those tuneful voices of your people, which prophesy a yet sweeter music than they utter. . . .

"You will wonder a good deal, but would do so less if you were aware of the seclusion of my life, when I tell you that I never consciously stood face to face with an American in the whole course of it. I never had any sort of personal acquaintance with an American man or woman; therefore you are all dreamed dreams to me—'gentle dreams' I may well account you."

In another characteristic letter, written about this time to her American correspondent, Miss Barrett says :—

"Poor Hood is dying, in a state of perfect preparation

and composure, among the tears of his friends. His disease has been consumption—is, in fact; but the disease is combined with water on the chest, which is expected to bring death. To a friend who asked him the other morning how it was with him, he answered with characteristic playful pathos, 'The tide is rising, and I shall soon be in port.' It is said of him that he has no regrets for his life, except for the unborn works which he feels stirring in his dying brain—a species of regret which is peculiarly affecting to me, as it must be to all who understand it. Alas! it is plain that he has genius greater than anything he has produced, and if this is plain and sad to us, how profoundly melancholy it must be to him. The only comfort is that the end of development is not here."

The light reflected on her own mental organization by these excerpts is profoundly interesting, and affords a deeper insight into her character than could possibly be obtained by the study of her works written solely for the public eye. In a lighter mood, and somewhat as a relief to the more sombre shades of thoughts lately displayed, one may revert to some of her playful but not less idiosyncratic sayings about her dog Flush. Writing to the American correspondent just referred to she says:—

"As to Flush, I thank you for him, for being glad that he has not arrived at the age of 'gravity and baldness,' and I can assure you of the fact of his not being yet four years old (the very prime of his life), and of his having lost no zest for the pleasures of the world, such as eating sponge cake and drinking coffee à la crême. He lies by me on the sofa, where I lie and write. He lies quite at ease between the velvet of my gown and the fur of my *couvre-pied*; and has no wicked dreams, I can answer for it, of a hare out of breath, or of a partridge shot through the whirring wing; if he sees a ghost at all it is of a little mouse which he killed once by accident.   He is as innocent as the first dog, when Eve patted him."

In Miss Barrett's correspondence with another literary friend of this period, the late Thomas Westwood, of poetic repute, the name of Flush frequently figures. On one occasion, says Mr. Westwood, she had expressed regret at the increasing plumpness of her pet. Apparently the gentleman had suggested starvation as a remedy, for her reply runs thus :—

"Starve Flush!   Starve Flush!   My dear Mr. Westwood, what are you thinking of ?   And besides, if the crime were lawful and possible, I deny the necessity.   He is fat, certainly ; but he has been fatter.   As I say, sometimes, with a sigh of sentiment —he has been fatter, and he may therefore become thinner.   And then, he does not eat after the manner of dogs.   I never saw a dog with such a ladylike appetite, nor knew of one by tradition.   To eat two small biscuits in succession is generally more than he is inclined to do.   When he has meat it is only once a day, and it must be so particularly well cut up and offered to him on a fork, and he is subtly discriminative as to differences between boiled mutton and roast mutton, and roast chicken and boiled chicken, that often he walks away in disdain, and 'will have none of it.'   He makes a point, indeed, of taking his share of my muffin and of my coffee, and a whole queen's cake when he can get it ; but it is a peculiar royalty of his to pretend to be indifferent even to these—to refuse them when offered to him—to refuse them once, twice,

and thrice—only to keep his eye on them, that they
should not vanish from the room by any means, as it
is his intention to have them at last.   My father is
quite vexed with me sometimes, and given to declare
that I have instructed Flush in the art of giving him-
self airs, and, otherwise, that no dog in the world
could be, of his own accord and instinct, so like a woman.
But I never did so instruct him.   The 'airs' came as
the wind blows.   He surprises me just as he surprises
other people—and more, because I see more of him.
His sensibility on the matter of vanity strikes me most
amusingly.   To be dressed up in necklaces and a turban
is an excessive pleasure to him; and to have the glory
of eating everything that he sees me eat is to be
glorious indeed.   Because I offered him cream cheese
on a bit of toast and *forgot the salt,* he refused at once.   It
was Bedreddin and the unsalted cheese-cake over
again.*   And this although he hates salt, and is con-
scious of his hatred of salt; but his honour was in
the salt, according to his view of the question, and he
insisted upon its being properly administered.   Now,
tell me if Flush's notion of honour and the modern
world's are not much on a par.   In fact, he thought
I intended by my omission to place him *below the
salt.*

"My nearest approach to starving Flush (to come
to an end of the subject) is to give general instructions
to the servant who helps him to his dinner 'not to *press*
him to eat.'   I know he ought not to be fat—I know
it too well—and his father being, according to Miss
Mitford's account, *square* at this moment, there is an

---

* The crime for which poor Bedreddin Hassan had to suffer was
leaving *pepper* out of the cheese-cakes, according to our version of the
Arabian Nights.

hereditary reason for fear. So he is not to be 'pressed'; and, in the meantime, with all the incipient fatness, he is as light at a jump, and as quick of spirits as ever, and quite well."

In a subsequent letter, she again refers to her pet, thus :—

"May I tell you that I have lost and won poor Flush again, and that I had to compound with the thieves and pay six guineas in order to recover him, much as I did last year—besides the tears, the tears! And when he came home he *began to cry*. His heart was full, like my own. Nobody knows, except you and me and those who have experienced the like affec-tions, what it is to love a dog and lose it. Grant the love, and the loss is imaginable, but I complain of the fact that people, who will not or cannot grant the love, set about wondering how one is not ashamed to make such a fuss for a dog. As if love (whether of dogs or man) must not have the same quick sense of sorrow. For my part, my eyelids have swelled and reddened both for the sake of lost dogs and birds—and I do not feel particularly ashamed of it. For Flush, who loves me to the height and depth of the capacity of his own nature, if I did not love *him*, I could love nothing. Besides, Flush has a soul to love. Do you not believe that dogs have souls? I am thinking of writing a treatise on the subject, after the manner of Plato's famous one.

"The only time almost that Flush and I quarrel seriously, is when I have, as happens sometimes, a parcel of new books to undo and look at. He likes the undoing of the parcel, being abundantly curious; but to see me absorbed in what he takes to be admira-tion for the new books is a different matter, and makes him superlatively jealous. I have two long ears flapping into my face immediately from the pillow over my head, in serious appeal. Poor Flushie! The point of this fact is, that when I read old books he does not care."

Nowhere was the name of Elizabeth Barrett now more honoured or lauded than in the United States, and many were the Americans who strove to obtain her co-operation in their schemes, philanthropic or otherwise. The Abolitionists were the most energetic and successful. There were evident reasons why the daughter of Edward, the niece of Samuel, Barrett should not take any prominent part in public questions connected with slavery, but Elizabeth could not but feel deeply for all enduring sorrow or oppression, and such, she was persuaded, were the negroes in America. Her aid was obtained, she wrote a poem on the subject, a poem intended to further the abolition of slavery, and sent it to America. She appeared to have repented subsequently of the work, and expressed a hope that the lines would not be published. They appeared however, in 1845, in *The Liberty Bell* as " A Curse for a Nation."

Her friendly tone notwithstanding, the lines appear to have created some soreness, and to one American correspondent who had remonstrated with her about them she wrote:—" Never say that I have cursed your country. I only declared the *consequences of the evil* in her, and which has since developed itself in thunder and flame. I feel, with more pain than many Americans do, the sorrow of this transition time; but I do know that it is a transition; that it *is* a crisis, and that you will come out of the fire purified, stainless, having had the angel of a great cause walking with you in the furnace." These prophetic words, referring to the result of the great conflict in America, she did not live to see verified.

During 1845, Miss Barrett continued a fitful correspondence with Miss Mitford and Horne. The latter she had not as yet seen personally, but Miss Mitford visited her from time to time, occasionally travelling up from Reading in the morning and returning home the same evening, a great fatigue for the elderly lady, as she admitted. Miss Barrett's health now seemed to have permanently improved, and there was only the English winter to fear. On the 29th September she writes to Horne :—

"My foot is in the air—balanced on the probability of a departure from England, for some land of the sun yet in the clouds. Italy perhaps, Madeira possibly ; there to finish my recovery, or rather to prevent my yearly *rechute* in the wintry cold—so let me hear from you quickly. . . . I am likely to go very soon if at all —the uncertainty is dominant—and I have been long and continue still in great vexation and perplexity from this doubtfulness. . . . If I go to Italy, it will be by sea, and high authorities among the doctors promise me an absolute restoration in consequence of it—and I myself have great courage and hope when I do not look *beyond myself.* I have been drinking life at the sun all this summer (and that is why the fountains of it have seemed so dry to you and the rest of the world), but, though in improved health and courage, I am sometimes a very Jacques for melancholy, and go moralising into a thousand similes half the uses of the day. . . . Miss Mitford proposed kindly coming to see me before I left England, but I have no spirits just now to make farewells of. When I set up my Republic against Plato's, nobody shall say good-bye in it, except the ' good haters ' one to another."

A saddening and in other ways distressing event which took place soon after the above letter was written rendered the hoped for journey still more needful. How it came about was thus. Somewhere in the autumn of 1837, Miss Mitford had forwarded Elizabeth Barrett a note introducing Haydon, the artist, remarking, " Miss Arabel will like his vivacity and good spirits." An acquaintanceship was formed, apparently by correspondence, between the poetess and the artist, and continued till the death of the latter. In 1842, Haydon forwarded to Miss Barrett, for her acceptance, a portrait he had painted of Wordsworth on Helvellyn, and her acceptance of the valuable gift ran thus :—

" My intention was to return by your messenger, when he should come for the picture, some expression of my sense of your very great kindness in trusting it with me, together with this sonnet, but having since heard from my sister (Arabel) that it may be almost as long as I wish (no ! it can't be so long) before you send such a messenger, I cannot defer thanking you beyond to-day, lest you should fancy me either struck dumb with the pleasure you conferred, or, still worse, born an ungrateful person. Nay, dear Sir, believe how different is the reality from the last supposition.

" I have indeed looked at your picture until I lost my obligation to you in my admiration of your work,' but in no other way have I been ungrateful. How could I be so ? I have seen the great poet who ' reigns over us ' twice, face to face, and by you I see him the third time. You have brought me Wordsworth and Helvellyn into this dark and solitary room. . . . You will judge the sonnet too, and will probably not acquit it.   It confesses to speaking unworthily and weakly the feeling of its writer, but *she* is none the less your obliged, ELIZABETH BARRETT."

The sonnet, which can scarcely be deemed a success, that is, a success for Miss Barrett, appeared in the *Athenæum* of October 9th.   Together with the portrait that had been the source of its inspiration, Haydon sent the poetess a sketch of his projected picture of Curtius leaping into the gulf, and several little courtesies appear to have passed between the two during the two or three succeeding years.   Haydon, who was in a chronic state of pecuniary embarrassment, appears to have occasionally troubled Miss Barrett by leaving in her charge pictures that might otherwise have passed into the possession of the law, or the law's officers.   He was also whimsical, eccentric, and often maddened by his treatment by the public.   Miss Mitford records how he had painted a portrait of her, " far bigger than life, and with equal excess of colour, but otherwise like."   Her father did not praise this production enough to please the artist, who felt that it was not considered a success.   He took it home and cut out the head, which, however, he preserved.   Some days before his melancholy death he sent this portrait to Miss Barrett, because, as he said, he knew she would value it.   The next day he called on her at Wimpole Street, to say that he could not part with the portrait, he could only lend it to her.   This was three days before his death.   The circumstances attending the unfortunate artist's fate are well known. To endeavour to attract some share of the notice the public was bestowing upon less worthy objects, he exhibited one of his most ambitious paintings in a room opposite to where " General Tom Thumb " was displaying himself. The result was disastrous ; whilst the natural phenomenon was visited by thousands, the painting was utterly deserted, and its unhappy exhibitor, in despair, put an end to his own existence. "The grotesque bitterness of the antagonism," says Miss Barrett, "was too much for Haydon—the dwarf slew the giant."

Besides the shock which the news of Haydon's suicide was to Miss Barrett, she was placed in a sad state of trouble by the information that by taking charge of his manuscripts and papers whilst he was in an insolvent state she had in some way infringed the law, and might find herself entangled in controversy with his creditors. Happily this fright proved groundless, as did also the fear that she was expected to edit or have anything to do with the twenty-six large volumes of Diary he had left in her charge. " I take it that they will be very interesting," says Miss Mitford, " not so much about art, but about poetry and literature, and the world in general, poor Haydon having been the friend of almost every eminent man for the last forty years; but he was so keen and close an observer, and so frank and bold a writer, that the publication of the *Memoirs* will be terribly dangerous, and would have killed Elizabeth Barrett."

The letter in which Miss Barrett communicated her own account of her feelings on this occasion is sufficiently explicit. She says :—

"The shock of poor Mr. Haydon's death overcame me for several days. Our correspondence had ceased a full year and a half; but the week preceding the event he wrote several notes to me; and, by his desire, I have under my care boxes and pictures of his, which he brought himself to the door.   Never did I imagine that it was other than one of the passing embarrassments so unhappily frequent with him.   Once before he had asked me to give shelter to things belonging to him, which, when the storm had blown over, he had taken back again.   I did not suppose that in this storm he was to sink—poor, noble soul!

"And be sure that the pecuniary embarrassment was not what sank him.   It was a wind still more east; it was the despair of the ambition by which he lived, and without which he could not live.   In the self-assertion which he had struggled to hold up through life he went down into death.   He could not bear the neglect, the disdain, the slur cast upon him by the age, and so he perished. . . . His love of reputation, you know, was a disease with him; and, for my part, I believe that he died of it.   That is my belief.

"In the last week he sent me his portrait of you (Miss Mitford) among the other things.   When he proposed sending it, he desired me to keep it for him; but when it came, a note also came to say that he 'could not make up his mind to part with it; he would lend it to me for a while'; a proof, among the rest, that his act was not premeditated—a moment of madness, or a few moments of madness: who knows?   I could not read the inquest, nor any of the details in the newspapers."

Beyond the shock the news of this tragedy gave Miss Barrett she suffered no other ill-effects from it. Poor Haydon's effects were handed over to his legal representatives, and the poetess released from all further trouble about them.   She was not, however, successful in getting away on her projected journey during the succeeding winter, but the dreaded relapse did not befall her. Her health continued to improve beyond all hopes, whilst the foretoken of a great coming happiness must have kept her in a fantasy of joy brighter than she could have ever, or for long past years, have looked for.

CHAPTER VI.

MARRIAGE.

THE early summer of 1846 brought Elizabeth Barrett into somewhat close communion with a new friend, Anna Jameson. Kenyon, apparently, was the medium by which these two talented women were introduced to each other. Mrs. Jameson was visiting at 51, Wimpole Street, next door to our poetess, and seems to have made more efforts than one to obtain an interview with her neighbour. Miss Barrett writes:—

"She overcame at last by sending a note to me from the next house. Do you know her? She did not exactly reflect my idea of Mrs. Jameson. And yet it would be both untrue and ungrateful to tell you that she disappointed me. In fact, she agreeably surprised me in one respect, for I had been told that she was *pedantic*, and I found her as unassuming as a woman need be—both unassuming and natural. The tone of her conversation, however, is rather analytical and critical than spontaneous and impulsive, and for this reason she appears to me a less charming companion than our friend of Three Mile Cross, who 'wears her heart upon her sleeve,' and shakes out its perfumes at every moment. She—Mrs. Jameson—is keen and calm, and reflective. She has a very light complexion —pale, lucid eyes—thin, colourless lips—fit for incisive meanings—a nose and chin projective without breadth. She was here nearly an hour, and, though on a first visit, I could perceive that a vague thought or expression she would not permit to pass either from my lips or her own. Yet nothing could be greater than her kindness to me, and I already think of her as a friend."

When once Miss Barrett had permitted anyone to gain the sanctuary of her presence she became, if the visitant satisfied her expectations, a firm friend and a trusty believer in the entire goodness of the new addition to her limited circle. Mrs. Jameson came as the authoress of several well-known works; as a woman who had suffered, and as a distinguished woman who earnestly sought her acquaintance. These qualifications bore fruit, and a close intimacy was the result. " This early period of their acquaintance," says Mrs. Jameson's biographer, "produced a multitude of tiny notes in fairy handwriting, such as Miss Barrett was wont to indite to her friends, and which are still in existence. Some of these are most charming and characteristic, and illustrate the rise and rapid increase of a friendship that never faltered or grew cool from that time up to the death of Mrs. Jameson."

One of these characteristic little notes, quoted by the biographer, alludes, in Miss Barrett's usual humorously exaggerated style, to her loss of voice, and the inconveniences resulting from it. "I am used to lose my voice and find it again," says Miss Barrett,

8 *

" until the vicissitude comes to appear as natural to me as the post itself. . . . You are not to think that I should not have been delighted to have you in a monodrama, as I heard Mr. Kenyon one morning when he came and talked for an hour, as he can talk, while the audience could only clap her hands or shake her head for the yea and nay. I should have been delighted to be just such an audience to you, but with you I was too much a stranger to propose such a thing, and the necessary silence might have struck you, I thought, as ungrateful and uncomprehending. But now I am not dumb any longer, only hoarse, and whenever I can hear *your* voice it will be better for me altogether."

In the correspondence which was now carried on between the two ladies, the same subjects which were being discussed with Miss Mitford and Horne, formed the staple themes. Mrs. Jameson, with energetic, humanitarian feelings, more akin to Miss Barrett's towards the seething humanity around us than to the optimistic contentment of Miss Mitford, felt herself stirred by the Report of the Commissioners on the Employment of Women and Children. Even as Elizabeth Barrett had been inspired to write her poem "The Cry of the Children," so Anna Jameson was moved to express her feelings on the topic in a prose article published in the columns of the *Athenæum*. Here was a subject both women could converse upon, and sympathize with; but in the marvellous recovery by mesmerism of a third friend they, apparently, had reason for differing. " I am more and more bewildered by the whole subject," said Miss Barrett. " I wish I could disbelieve it all, except that Harriet Martineau is well."

Mrs. Jameson's interest in the poetess increased with time. Her own literary engagements rendered it necessary for her to visit France and Italy, but learning that it was deemed essential for Miss Barrett's health she should winter abroad, she generously offered Mr. Barrett to take charge of his daughter and accompany her to Italy. The offer was not accepted, but the object of the elder lady's solicitude, in tendering her her thanks, said, " Not only am I grateful to you, but happy to be grateful to you : " adding, " First I was drawn to you, then I was, and am, bound to you." When Mrs. Jameson left England, she was bade farewell in another little note, in which Miss Barrett deplored her inability to call and bid good-bye in person, as she was " forced to be satisfied with the sofa and silence."

But neither the sofa nor silence was destined to be the lot of Elizabeth Barrett. The most momentous event of her life, the turning-point of her destiny was at hand. Among the few living poets of whom she was wont to speak and write with admiration was Robert Browning. He had been characteristically mentioned in "Lady Geraldine's Courtship," and from that time forward his name and reputation found frequent mention in her correspondence. Browning's father had been an old schoolfellow of Kenyon; it was, therefore, the most natural thing in the world that the wealthy man of the world should take a more than usual interest in the rising young poet.

Kenyon was wont to take all the best new books to his cousin, and to introduce to her, as far as her health and inclination allowed, the most noteworthy of their authors. Browning was so fortunate as to be included among the latter. He had travelled and had seen

personally what Elizabeth Barrett had only read of or
dreamed about.   It is no wonder that a feeling
stronger and deeper than had as yet stirred the depths
of her heart should grow up and impel the poetess
towards the poet.   With so many themes and
thoughts in common as they had, it is no matter for
surprise that the correspondence which they com-
menced, and for a long time continued, should grow
and deepen into something warmer and more sympa-
thetic than the usual interchange of literary manu-
scripts arouses.

How their friendship waxed, how their affection in-
tensified, and how, finally, they cast in their lots
together is a sweet romance the world knows not, and
never can know, the record of, beyond what they, the
two *dramatis personæ*, chose to tell themselves.   " If
you would know what she was," says a friend, " read
' One Word more.'   He made no secret of it ; why
should another ? "   In that piece, originally appended
to his collection of poems styled *Men and Women*,
Browning so far took the world into his confidence as
to tell it, as if the telling had been needed, who his
" moon of poets " was.   And, indeed, through many of
his works from that time henceforth does the thought
of one beloved wind like a golden thread through the
woof of his multi-coloured imagination.

The time has not come—can scarcely ever come—
when their story may be told fully ; but Robert
Browning has told, in his poet-speech, how his heart
had realised an ideal, and Elizabeth Barrett has contri-
buted her share towards the glorification of eternal
Love in her exquisitely beautiful *Sonnets from the
Portuguese.*   These sonnets, this delicate confession of
a pure woman's love, were written, it is averred, some

time before her marriage, and were not shown to her husband until after they were wed. Of course, they are not translations, and the fiction that they were to be found in any language but her own was but the last thin veil with which Elizabeth Barrett faintly concealed the passion she was so proud of.

Miss Barrett, although personally unacquainted with Mr. Browning until a compararatively short time before their marriage, had previously been his admirer and correspondent. Writing to an American correspondent in the spring of 1845, she had said, "Mr. Browning, with whom I have had some correspondence lately, is full of great intentions; the light of the future is on his forehead . . . he is a poet for posterity. I have a full faith in him as poet and prophet."

Their personal knowledge of each other had not, evidently, existed long before they discovered the strength of their regards for one another. To the lady, at any rate, this revelation must have been a startling discovery. Advanced into her thirty-eighth year, she had little prospect and probably little inclination to depart from the course in life she believed marked out for her. Hitherto her personal acquaintances had been so few that love and marriage can scarcely have entered into her schemes for life: as she says in the *Sonnets* :—

> I lived with visions for my company,
> Instead of men and women, years ago,
> And found them gentle mates, nor thought to know
> A sweeter music than they played to me. .
>   Then THOU didst come . .   to be,
> Belovèd, what they seemed.

Heavy griefs and precarious health had been hers, it is true; but her sorrows, saddening though they were, had been soothed by kindness and all that wealth could provide. Had she been enabled, like the majority of the world's women, to enter into the labours and struggles of the life around her, she would have placed her sorrow on one side ; but, separated as she was both from the activity and ordinary anxieties of life, she nursed her griefs as if they had been petted babes, and fed her favourite sorrows with unceasing tears. She sang—

> A heavy heart, Belovèd, have I borne
> From year to year until I saw thy face,
> And sorrow after sorrow took the place
> Of all those natural joys.

But all these long-hoarded and much-cherished griefs —truly become, through lapse of time, but ideals—now became as visionary and transient as dreams. A sudden change had taken place : "The face of all the world is changed, I think," she wrote. The ideas of Death—which she had long regarded as near—were transformed, and a restless energy took the place of her ancient langour. Most truly does she image forth, in the first of her love *Sonnets,* the change which had taken place in her whole being :—

> I saw, in gradual vision through my tears,
> The sweet, sad years, the melancholy years,
> Those of my own life, who by turns had flung
> A shadow across me. Straightway I was 'ware,
> So weeping, how a mystic shape did move
> Behind me, and drew me backward by the hair,
> And a voice said, in mastery, while I strove,
> "Guess now who holds thee?" "Death!" I said. But, there,
> The silver answer rang, "Not Death, but Love!"

Henry Chorley, a literary friend, who made the acquaintance of Miss Barrett through the medium of

Miss Mitford, said her marriage with the author of *Paracelsus* was more like a fairy-tale than anything in real life he had ever known. (Charming and appropriate as the union of the two poets seemed to many, there was one, and he the most interested and first to be consulted in the matter, who would not look upon it in such a light. To the outer world the persistent and lasting antagonism of Mr. Barrett to the marriage of his daughter with Mr. Browning may seem absurd and unnatural; yet, without prying too deeply into the private motives which inspired his dislike to the match, the few glimpses which are obtainable of his passionate yet obstinate nature render his behaviour with regard to this matter far from inexplicable. Mr. Barrett's immovable will, his determination not to falter from a resolution when once formed, was a salient trait of character inherited by his favourite and famous child. Elizabeth Barrett had been her father's idol: apparently a confirmed invalid, whom Death might claim at any time, he had lavished upon her everything love or wealth could afford. The space left vacant in his passionate heart by the death of his wife had been largely refilled by his adoration of his daughter. The fame she had created for herself was partly reflected upon him—her father and protector. The affection and pride which had prompted him to publish her childish productions must have appeared amply justified by her present success. And now, after all the long years of anxiety and affection had begun to produce their reward in improved health and widespread reputation, she, his own favourite child, proposed to leave her home and endow a stranger with all the fruits of her fame and the hours of her recovered health. No! the anger of Mr. Barrett towards his so much beloved daughter is neither unique nor singular, when his temperament is considered.)

Writing to Horne just after her marriage, our poetess states her experience that all her maladies came from without, and " the hope that if unprovoked by English winters, they would cease to come at all. The mildness of the last exceptional winter," she remarks, "had left me a different creature, and the physicians helped me to hope everything from Italy." Winter, with all its accumulative terrors, was rapidly nearing; on one hand was " the sofa and silence " of home, shared with an estranged father and a probable relapse into illness, and on the other, Hope, Italy and Love! The contest between Love and Duty, if severe, could not last long or be doubtful. " Our plans," said the lady to Horne, " were made up at the last in the utmost haste and agitation—precipitated beyond all intention."

On the 12th September, 1846, Elizabeth Barrett was married, at the Marylebone parish church, to Robert Browning, and immediately after the newly-wedded pair started for Italy, by way of Paris.

The marriage was an intense surprise for all those who only knew Elizabeth Barrett as a chronic invalid, hovering between life and death. Henry Chorley, who was selected as one of the trustees of Mrs. Browning's marriage settlement, says, " I cannot recollect when I have been more moved and excited by any surprise, beyond the circle of my immediate hopes and fears," than when " she married, after an intimacy suspected by none save a very few, under circumstances of no ordinary romance, and in marrying whom she secured for the residue of her life an emancipation from prison and an amount of happiness delightful to think of, as falling to the lot of one who, from a darkened chamber, had still exercised such a power of delighting others."

Miss Mitford, Horne, and other friends expressed equal surprise, but none of them had the wonder brought home to them so startlingly as Mrs. Jameson. She had left her friend unable to accompany her abroad—"forced to be satisfied with the sofa and silence"—and directly afterwards, almost as soon as she had reached Paris, she received a note from Mr. Browning, telling her that he had just arrived from England, and that he was on his way to Italy with his wife, the same " E.B.B." she had just taken leave of ! " My aunt's surprise," says Mrs. Macpherson, " was something almost comical, so startling and entirely unexpected was the news."

Mrs. Jameson, of course, called on the Brownings, and persuaded them to leave the hotel they were staying at for a quiet *pension* in the Rue Ville l'Evêque, where she was residing. They remained together in Paris for a fortnight, during which period Mrs. Jameson wrote to a friend: "I have also here a poet and a poetess—two celebrities who have run away and married under circumstances peculiarly interesting, and such as render imprudence the height of prudence. Both excellent; but God help them! for I know not how the two poet heads and poet hearts will get on through this prosaic world. I think it possible I may go on to Italy with them."

The possibility came about, and the whole party, Mr. and Mrs. Browning and Mrs. Jameson and niece, travelled slowly southwards to Pisa, where the newly-married couple proposed living for a while at least. How Mrs. Browning contrived to endure all the anxieties and labours of the journey seems incomprehensible. "My poor invalid friend," writes Mrs. Jameson, "suffered much from fatigue; and, considering that she had passed seven (*sic*) years without ever leaving her room, you can imagine what it was to convey her from Paris to Pisa. Luckily our journey was nearly over before the heavy rains commenced."

Miss Mitford, telling one of her correspondents of Elizabeth Barrett's marriage, adds: "Love really is the wizard the poets have called him: a fact which I always doubted till now. But never was such a miraculous proof of his power as her travelling across France by diligence, by railway, by Rhone-boat—anyhow, in fact; and, having arrived in Pisa so much improved in health that Mrs. Jameson, who travelled with them, says, 'she is not merely improved but transformed.' I do not know Mr. Browning; but this fact is enough to make me his friend."

Mrs. Macpherson, speaking of the enchanting memories of that journey from Paris to Pisa, spent in such companionship, says, "The loves of the poets could not have been put into more delightful reality before the eyes of the dazzled and enthusiastic beholder;" but she only permits herself, in the life of her aunt, to recall in print one scene among many of this wonderful journey. She says: "We rested for a couple of days at Avignon, the route to Italy being then much less direct and expeditious, though I think much more delightful, than now; and while there we made a little excursion, a poetical pilgrimage, to Vaucluse. There, at the very source of the '*chiare, fresche e dolci acque,*' Mr. Browning took his wife up in his arms, and carrying her across the shallow, curling water, seated her on a rock that rose throne-like in the middle of the stream. Thus love and poetry took a new possession of the spot immortalised by Petrarch's loving fancy." Mrs. Browning herself alluded to the pilgrimage to Vaucluse, "where the living water gushes up," she says, "into the face of the everlasting rock, and there is no green thing except Petrarch's memory. Yes there is, the water itself—that is brightly green—and there are one or two little cypresses."

Three weeks were spent by Mrs. Jameson and her niece travelling with the Brownings, and another three weeks with them in Pisa, where, says Mrs. Macpherson, "the poet pair, who were our closest associates, added all that was wanted to the happiness of this time." Well may Mrs. Macpherson, who was only sixteen then, have recalled those times and their associated memories as a golden oasis in her existence.

The Brownings settled in Pisa for several months, intending to winter there, it having been recommended as a mild, suitable residence for Mrs. Browning. In a letter to Horne, dated December 4th, she says:—"We are left to ourselves in a house built by Vasari, and within sight of the Leaning Tower and the Duomo, to enjoy a most absolute seclusion and plan the work fit for it. I am very happy and very well. . . . We have heard a mass (a musical mass for the dead) in the Campo Santo, and achieved a due pilgrimage to the Lanfranchi Palace to walk in the footsteps of Byron and Shelley. . . . A statue of your Cosmo looks down from one of the great piazzas we often pass through on purpose to remind us of you. This city is very beautiful and full of repose—'asleep in the sun,' as

Dickens said." Mr. Browning, in a note attached to his wife's letter, says, " She is getting better every day —stronger, better wonderfully, and beyond all our hopes."

The newly-married pair spent the winter in Pisa, at the Collegio Ferdinando, in a street terminated by the palace in which Cosmo the Great, Horne's hero, slew his son. The change was in every way beneficial for our poetess, a change, as she told an American correspondent in the beginning of 1847, "from the long seclusion in one room to liberty and Italy's sunshine; for a resigned life I take up a happy one." Apologising for a lengthy silence, she adds :—

" I shall behave better, you will find, for the future, and more gratefully, and I begin some four months after the greatest event of my life by telling you that I am well and happy, and meaning to get as strong in the body by the help of this divine climate as I am in the spirit—*the spirits!* So much has God granted me compensation. Do you not see already that it was not altogether the sight of the free sky which made me fail to you before. . . . My husband's name will prove to you that I have not left my vocation to the rhyming art in order to marry; on the contrary, we mean, both of us, to do a great deal of work, besides surprising the world by the spectacle of two poets coming together without quarrelling, wrangling, and calling names in lyrical measures. . . . We live here in the most secluded manner, eschewing English visitors and reading Vasari, and dreaming dreams of seeing Venice in the summer. Until the beginning of April we are tied to this perch of Pisa, as the climate is recommended for the weakness of my chest, and the repose and calmness of the place are

by no means unpleasant to those who, like ourselves,
do not look for distractions and amusements in order
to be very happy. Afterwards we go anywhere but
to England—we shall not leave Italy at present.
If I get quite strong I may cross the desert on a
camel yet, and see Jerusalem. There's a dream for
you—nothing is too high or too low for my dreams
just now."

For some time before and for a long time after her
marriage, Mrs. Browning did not publish anything of
importance. But, need it be said, neither her pen nor
brain were idle, nor, indeed, was her zest for literary
matters dormant. Poetic aspirations still swayed her
thoughts; to an American proposition to issue a selec-
tion from her poems she lent a pleased attention, only
wishing to have a voice in the selection. To the sug-
gestion of a prose volume she gave a decided negative,
for the time at least. She continued to enjoy literary
gossip about her favourite authors, and being informed
that Tennyson, then in Switzerland, was "disappointed
with the mountains," expressed her wonder that any-
one could be disappointed with anything in Nature.
" She always seems to me," was her remark, " to leap
up to the level of the heart."

In her political feelings Mrs. Browning continued to
be somewhat ahead of her contemporaries, and did
not increase her popularity by the readiness with
which she gave expression to ideas generally antagon-
istic to the views of the majority. As yet she had not
obtained a very intimate knowledge of the aspirations
for liberty with which the hearts of the Italians around
her were burning, but was greatly roused by "the
dreadful details from Ireland. Oh! when I write
against slavery," she exclaimed to an American friend,

"it is not as one free from the curse, 'the curse of Cromwell' falls upon us also! Poor, poor Ireland! But nations, like individuals, must be 'perfected by suffering,'" was her comment, to which she added the hope that "in time we shall slough off our leprosy of the pride of money and of rank, and be clean, and just, and righteous."

It is a pleasant surprise to learn that Mrs. Browning had her old friend and favourite, Flush, with her at Pisa. "He adapts himself," she says, "to the sunshine as to the shadow, and when he hears me laugh lightly, begins not to think it too strange." And whilst referring to her faithful dog, a few words may be devoted to the remainder of his history. After the marriage of his dear mistress, with her he forsook the sofa and silence to see the world. He accompanied her to France and Italy, and, as Mr. Westwood informs us, " wagged his tail in *Casa Guidi Windows*; had one or two perilous adventures—lost his coat, and became a dreadful guy in the warm climate; but he lived to an advanced old age, and was beloved and honoured to the end."

Towards the spring Pisa became unsuitable in various ways as a residence for the Brownings. Apart from climatic considerations it was, doubtless, found to be insufferably dull. To a friend Mrs. Browning wrote:—

"As to news, you will not expect news from me now; until the last few days, we had not for months even seen a newspaper, and human faces divine are quite *rococo* with me, as the French would say."

From Pisa the Brownings removed to Florence. To Horne Mrs. Browning wrote that in June they left the latter city for Ancona, in order to be cooler, and found that they were "leaping right into the cauldron. The heat was just the fiercest fire of your imagination, and I *seethe* to think of it at this distance. But we saw the whole coast, from Ravenna to Loretto, and had wonderful visions of beauty and glory in passing and re-passing the Apennines. At Ravenna we stood one morning, at four, at Dante's tomb, with its pathetic inscription, and seldom has any such sight so moved me. Ravenna is a dreary, marshy place, with a dead weight of melancholy air fading the faces of its inhabitants; and its pine-forest stands off too far to redeem it anywise."

Florence grew to be a second home and a domestic shrine to Mrs. Browning. Her first impressions of it were pleasant, and the pleasure became permanent. Writing from the Tuscan capital to Horne, she says:—

"Here we live for nothing, or next to nothing, and have great rooms, and tables and chairs thrown in; and although hearing occasionally that Florence is to be sacked on such a day, and our Grand Duke deposed on such another, I have learnt to endure meekly all such expectations, and to hold myself as safe as you in your garden through them all. One thing is certain—that the Italians won't spoil their best surtouts by venturing out in a shower of rain through whatever burst of revolutionary ardour, nor will they forget to take their ices through loading of their guns."

And later on she says: "All I complain of at Florence is the difficulty of getting sight of new books, which I, who have been used to a new 'sea-serpent' every morning, in the shape of a French romance, care still more for than my husband does. Old books we can arrive at, and besides, our own are coming over the sea." Then, lapsing from *badinage* to a more serious tone, she adds : "So used am I to be grateful to you that it scarcely can be a strange thing to read those most kind words in which you promise a welcome to my husband's poems—only you will believe that kindness in that shape must touch me nearest."

When they finally settled in Florence, the Brownings removed to a romantic old palace known as Casa Guidi, and here, with some short intervals of absence, the poetess passed the remainder of her life. She kept up her correspondence with friends in England, but rarely received any English people into her residence, her chief visitors being American and Italian. Mr. Browning being well versed, not only in Italian literature and lore, but in the political needs and wrongs of the people, his wife, also, naturally studied and mastered the whole subject and became, if possible, more Italian than the Italians themselves. With all the strength of her character, with that indomitable determination which all through life inspired her, she took up and adopted, and with heart and brain fought for, the cause of Italy. In the Casa Guidi Italian patriots found a sympathetic welcome, and a rallying place. Americans, also, found there a genial reception and an enthusiastic admirer of their country ; it is from them chiefly, indeed, almost exclusively, that we know how Mrs. Browning looked and lived and laboured in her happy Florentine home.

One American author who visited the poetess and her husband in Casa Guidi, in 1847, records of his visit that in the evening Mr. Browning presented him to his wife :—" The visitor saw seated at the tea-table

in the great room of the palace in which they were
living, a very small, very slight woman, with very long
curls drooping forward, almost across the eyes,
hanging down to the bosom, and quite concealing the
pale small face, from which the piercing, enquiring
eyes looked out sensitively at the stranger. Rising
from her chair she put out cordially the thin, white
hand of an invalid, and in a few moments they were
pleasantly chatting, while the husband strode up and
down the room, joining in the conversation with a
vigour, humour, eagerness and affluence of curious lore
which, with his trenchant thought and subtle sympathy,
made him one of the most charming and inspiring of
companions."

This same Transatlantic informant talks of having
been, a few days later, with the Brownings and one or
two others, to Vallombrosa, the whole party spending
two days there together. "Mrs. Browning was still
too much of an invalid to walk, but she sat under the
great trees upon the lawn-like hillsides near the con-
vent, or in the seats of the dusky convent chapel,
while Robert Browning at the organ chased a fugue,
or dreamed out upon the twilight keys a faint throbbing
toccata of Galuppi."

In an undated letter to Miss Mitford, Mrs. Browning
tells of a visit, doubtless the same just referred to, she
made to the monastery of Vallombrosa, and of being
dragged there in a grape basket, without wheels, drawn
by two oxen, remarking that she and her maid were
turned away by the monks "for the sin of woman-
hood."

"In all the conversation," continues the American
acquaintance of Mrs. Browning, "she was so mild,
and tender, and womanly, so true and intense and rich

9 *

with rare learning, there was a girl-like simplicity and sensitiveness and a womanly earnestness, that took the heart captive. She was deeply and most intelligently interested in America and Americans, and felt a kind of enthusiastic gratitude to them for their generous fondness of her poetry."

Another account throwing some light upon that home in the Casa Guidi, as it appeared in those days, is furnished by Mr. George Stillman Hillard. Mr. Hillard, also an American, says :—

" One of my most delightful associations with Florence arises from the fact that here I made the acquaintance of Robert and Elizabeth Browning. . . . A happier home and a more perfect union than theirs it is not easy to imagine; and this completeness arises, not only from the rare qualities which each possesses, but from their adaptation to each other. . . Mrs. Browning is in many respects the correlative of her husband. As he is full of manly power, so is she the type of the most sensitive and delicate womanhood. She has been a great sufferer from ill-health, and the marks of pain are stamped upon her person and manner. Her figure is slight, her countenance expressive of genius and sensibility, shaded by a veil of long brown locks; and her tremulous voice often flutters over her words like the flame of a dying candle over the wick. I have never seen a human frame which seemed so nearly a transparent veil for a celestial and immortal spirit. She is a soul of fire enclosed in a shell of pearl. Her rare and fine genius needs no setting forth at my hands. She is, also, what is not so generally known, a woman of uncommon, nay, profound learning, even measured by a masculine standard. Nor is she more remarkable for genius and learning than for sweetness of temper, tenderness of heart, depth of feeling, and purity of spirit. It is a privilege to know such beings singly and separately; but to see their powers quickened, and their happiness rounded, by the sacred tie of marriage, is a cause for peculiar and lasting gratitude. A union so complete as theirs—in which the mind has nothing to crave, nor the heart to sigh for—is cordial to behold and cheering to remember."

CHAPTER VII.

CASA GUIDI WINDOWS.

Thus in quiet happiness lived in their pleasant Italian home the two poets, Robert and Elizabeth Browning. They continued to write their immortal poems, cheered by each other's society, but published little or nothing, and saw little of the outer world. Few Englishmen found their way into the interior of Casa Guidi, the majority of visitors still being Americans and Italians. Mrs. Browning continued to correspond with Miss Mitford and other friends in both New and Old England, and she repeatedly alluded to her domestic happiness, the only cloud which now rested upon her life, save perhaps her chronic constitutional delicacy, being the rupture with her father. He appears never to have forgiven her for her marriage, and persistently refused to open her letters or even to allow her name to be mentioned to him.

An event was about to happen, however, to draw the poet pair still closer together and to still further wean the poetess from the painful memories of the " sofa and silence " of her old home. On the 8th February 1849, Miss Mitford received a letter from

Mrs. Browning which, besides giving her an account of the civic troubles of Florence, prepared her for the happy news shortly to be communicated. On the 9th of March 1849, Mrs. Browning's only child, a son, named after his two parents Robert Barrett Browning, was born.

Italy, Florence, above all Casa Guidi, had now stronger and unbreakable ties for the heart as well as the powerful brain of Elizabeth Browning. Was not her child, "my own young Florentine," a native of the land she had learned to love so well, the land of her married happiness! It was in that new home, where the three happiest years of her womanhood had passed, was born her

> Blue-eyed prophet; thou to whom
> The earliest world-day light that ever flowed
> Through Casa Guidi Windows, chanced to come!

The boy grew and prospered, and with its growth grew the mother's health and joy. "How earnestly I rejoice, my beloved friend," wrote Miss Mitford this year, "in your continued health! and how very, very glad I shall be to see you and your baby. Remember me to Wilson (Mrs. Browning's maid) and tell her that I am quite prepared to admire him as much as will even satisfy her appetite for praise. How beautifully you describe your beautiful country!" exclaims Miss Mitford. "Oh! that I were with you, to lose myself in the chestnut forests, and gather grapes at the vintage! If I had but Prince Hassan's carpet, I would set forth and leave Mr. May (her medical adviser) to scold and wonder, when he comes to see me to-morrow . . . Kiss baby for me, and pat Flush."

The letter just quoted from intimates a probability of Mrs. Browning's visit to England. Indeed, for all her love for Italy she could not quite forego her affection for the old country and, as she had previously told Horne in 1848, "We haven't given up England altogether—we talk of spending summers there, and have a scheme of seeing you all next year, if circumstances should permit of it." Circumstances did not, however, work together happily for this scheme, and instead of summer in England, the autumn was spent at the Baths of Lucca. An intention to winter in Rome was, also, given up, and Christmas was spent in Florence, where Mr. Browning completed for publication his poem, *Christmas-Eve and Easter Day,* and his wife wrote the first part of her poem, *Casa Guidi Windows,* although the second portion of it was not written until two years later, the complete work being published in 1851.

It is, apparently, this restful period of Mrs. Browning's life that is referred to by Mrs. Ritchie, when she remarks, "Those among us who only knew Mrs. Browning as a wife and as a mother have found it difficult to realise her life under any other condition, so vivid and complete is the image of her peaceful home, of its fire-side where the logs are burning, and the mistress established on her sofa, with her little boy curled up by her side, the door opening and shutting meanwhile to the quick step of the master of the house and to the life of the world without, coming to find her in her quiet corner. We can recall the slight figure in its black silk dress, the writing apparatus by the sofa, the tiny inkstand, the quill-nibbed penholder, the unpretentious implements of her work. 'She was a little woman; she liked little things.' Her miniature editions of the classics are, with her name written in each in her sensitive fine handwriting, and always her husband's name added above her own, for she dedicated all her books to him; it was a fancy she had."

In the spring the Brownings appear to have visited Rome, and there was again some talk of their visiting England, passing through Paris on the way, but for the present the project was abandoned. Wordsworth died in April and a suggestion was made by the *Athenæum* that the vacant laureateship should be given to Mrs. Browning. "We would urge," says the journal, "the graceful compliment to a youthful queen which would be implied in the recognition of the remarkable literary place taken by women in her reign."

A notable circumstance happened in May, and one that cannot have failed to have made a marked impression upon Mrs. Browning's highly sensitive nature. Margaret Fuller and her husband, Count d'Ossoli, spent their last evening on shore with the Brownings, previous to their departure for the United States. The vessel they sailed in was wrecked, and they never touched land again alive. Margaret Fuller was not, probably, a women with whom our poetess could ever be much in sympathy, but her tragic death and the circumstance of her last night on shore having been passed in her company must have left an indelible impression upon the mind of Mrs. Browning. Another acquaintanceship probably formed about this time was that of Isa Blagden, whose sympathy with some subjects should have drawn her towards the mistress of Casa Guidi. On Italian aspirations for liberty, on the Napoleonic myth, and upon the mysteries of mesmerism —which latter subject continued to greatly exercise Mrs. Browning's mind—they must have been in full accord. Other Florentine friends were W. W. Story, the American sculptor, and his wife. They were the most intimate friends of the Brownings, and for several summers visited and lived with them in Siena. Story's reminiscences of Mrs. Browning during the latter period of her life are among the most interesting extant of her, and will have to be largely cited from.

This 1850 passed away undisturbedly so far as the poetess was concerned. Besides her domestic ties she was busy with her pen, preparing for publication in a complete form her poem of *Casa Guidi Windows.* The poem never was and never will be popular. It contains little likely to arouse the sympathies of its author's usual readers, and to most Italians is, naturally, a sealed book. Mrs. Browning, living amid a people whom she came to regard to no little extent as fellow countrymen and friends, was naturally intensely impressed by their wrongs and moved by their aspirations for liberty. As was customary with her, her feelings found vent in song. *Casa Guidi Windows* was the result of her impressions " upon events in Tuscany of which she was a witness;" but despite its powerful passages and occasional felicities of speech, it is impossible to regard it as a success.

" It is a simple story of personal impression," says Mrs. Browning, but that is just what it strikes the reader as not being. It is full of recondite allusions, comprehensible only to those fully conversant with Florentine literary and political history. It deals with numerous political things unsuited to poesy, however worthy of prose, from which indeed, despite some outbursts of sweetest song, the work through a great portion of its length is barely discernible. As Mrs. Browning's work it will be read with interest, although interest of a somewhat languid type, but at the present day it will be difficult to discover readers who can be moved to any great amount of enthusiasm by the author's passionate and evident sincerity. She claimed for it only that it portrayed the intensity of " her warm affection for a beautiful and unfortunate country," and that the sincerity with which the feeling was manifested indicated " her own good faith and freedom from partisanship." She also considered the discrepancy which the public would see between the two parts of the poem—" the first was written nearly three years ago, while the second resumes the actual situation of 1851 "—a sufficient guarantee to her readers of the fidelity of her contemporary impressions. The causes which gave rise to her singing are no longer operative ; her prophecy of Italy's future has been fulfilled, and her poem, as of all political poems, can now only be of value for, and only judged by, its poetic worth. Unfortunately, when judged by the only standard now possible to gauge it by, *Casa Guidi Windows* cannot be regarded as one of its author's successes, any metrical music it contains being but too frequently chiefly conspicuous by the harshness of the long passages of prose by which it is overwhelmed. Probably the sweetest lines in the work are those with which the poem opens : —

> I heard last night a little child go singing
>   'Neath Casa Guidi windows, by the church,
> *O bella libertà, O bella !* stringing
>   The same words still on notes he went in search
> So high for, you concluded the upspringing
>   Of such a nimble bird to sky from perch
> Must leave the whole bush in a tremble green,
>   And that the heart of Italy must beat.
> While such a voice had leave to rise serene
>   'Twixt church and palace of a Florence street !

Of course there are many quotable lines in the poem and some grand thoughts, notably that referring to Charles Albert, who, "taking off his crown, made visible a hero's forehead."

The temporary repression of liberty in Tuscany and the neighbouring states undoubtedly had a very depressing effect upon Mrs. Browning, and rendered her more than ever desirous of leaving Florence for a time. A longing to see her native land once more, doubtless possessed her, besides which business matters necessarily rendered occasional visits to England almost unavoidable.

Accordingly, in the summer of 1851, accompanied by her husband, she left Florence for England. Among the places visited on the homeward journey was Venice, and Miss Mitford, alluding to a letter she had received from her from that city, says Mrs. Browning is so well, "she was to be found every evening at half-past eight in St. Mark's Place, drinking coffee and reading the French papers, whence they adjourned to the opera, where they had a box upon the best tier for two shillings and eight-pence English."

The Brownings took Paris in their way, finally reaching London after an absence of nearly four years. Mrs. Browning returned to England full of fame—fame not only on her own account but on account of her husband—a happy wife, a devoted mother, and apparently restored to health. What a contrast to her departure on that autumn four years ago, when, almost like a fugitive, the supposed chronic invalid had escaped from her "sofa and silence" across the waters to an unknown fate.

One of the first to call and welcome her was Miss Mitford, who says: "I have had the exquisite pleasure of seeing her once more in London, with a lovely boy at her knee, almost as well as ever, and telling tales of Italian rambles, of losing herself in chestnut forests, and scrambling on muleback up the sources of extinct volcanoes."

Not only were old friendships revived, but new friendships formed upon this pleasant return to her native land. Among those who now made her acquaintance was Bayard Taylor, the well-known American author and traveller. His reminiscences of the poetess and her surroundings are replete with interest. He says:—

"In the summer of 1851 a mutual friend offered me a letter to Browning, who was then with his wife temporarily in London. . . . Calling one afternoon in September, at their residence in Devonshire Street, I was fortunate enough to find both at home, though on the very eve of their return to Florence. In a small drawing-room on the first floor I met Browning, who received me with great cordiality. In his lively, cheerful manner, quick voice, and self-possession, he made upon me the impression of an American rather than an Englishman. He was then, I should judge, about thirty-seven years of age, but his dark hair was already streaked with gray about the temples. His complexion was fair with, perhaps, the faintest olive tinge, eyes large, clear, and gray, and nose strong and well-cut, mouth full and rather broad, and chin pointed, though not prominent. . . . He was about the medium height, strong in the shoulders, but slender at the waist, and his movements expressed a combination of vigour and elasticity."

After this graphic, if somewhat interviewer style of describing Mr. Browning, Bayard Taylor proceeds to give an equally characteristic sketch of another notable personage present—of a man, also, closely connected with the story of our poetess.

"In the room sat a very large gentleman of between fifty and sixty years of age. His large, rosy face, bald head and rotund body, would have suggested a prosperous brewer, if a livelier intelligence had not twinkled in the bright, genial eyes. This unwieldy exterior covered one of the warmest and most generous of hearts. . . . The man was John Kenyon, who, giving up his early ambition to be known as an author, devoted his life to making other authors happy. . . . His house was open to all who handled pen, brush, or chisel. . . . He had called to say good-bye to his friends, and presently took his leave. 'There,' said Browning, when the door had closed after him, 'there goes one of the most splendid men living—a man so noble in his friendships, so lavish in his hospitality, so large-hearted and benevolent, that he deserves to be known all over the world as Kenyon the Magnificent.'"

Mrs. Browning now entered the room, and the American visitor says her husband ran to meet her with boyish liveliness. He describes her as "slight and fragile in appearance, with a pale, wasted face, shaded by masses of soft chesnut curls, which fell on her cheeks, and serious eyes of bluish-gray. Her frame seemed to be altogether disproportionate to her soul. . . . Her personality, frail as it appeared, soon exercised its power, and it seemed a natural thing that she should have written *The Cry of the Children*, or *Lady Geraldine's Courtship*."

Both the husband and wife, says Taylor, expressed great satisfaction with their American reputation, adding that they had many American acquaintances in Florence and Rome. "In fact," said Mr. Browning,

" I believe that if we were to make out a list of our best and dearest friends, we should find more American than English names."

Mrs. Browning having expressed a desire to hear something from their guest as to the position of Art in America, and having, in the course of conversation, declared her belief that a Republican form of government is unfavourable to the development of the Fine Arts, Bayard Taylor dissented, and had a powerful ally in Mr. Browning, who declared that "no artist had ever before been honoured with a more splendid commission than the State of Virginia had given to Crawford." "A general historical discussion ensued," says the American, " which was carried on for some time with the greatest spirit, the two poets taking directly opposite views. It was good-humouredly closed at last, and I thought both of them seemed to enjoy it. There is no fear that two such fine intellects will rust: they will keep each other bright."

Their child, " a blue-eyed, golden-haired boy of two years old," was now brought into the room, and introduced. " He stammered Italian sentences only," says Taylor; " he knew nothing, as yet, of his native tongue."

A few days after this interview the Brownings left England. It was impossible for Mrs. Browning to think of undergoing the risk of wintering in her native land ; so, as soon as the year began to chill into autumn, she had to seek a refuge abroad. Writing to her old friend Horne, on the 24th of the month, to ask his acceptance of the new editions, recently published, of her own and her husband's poems, she says, " We leave to-morrow for Paris." They appear to have wintered in the French capital, and whilst there happened one of the most pleasant and interesting incidents in Mrs. Browning's life—her interview with George Sand.

As early as 1844 the poetess had styled her famous contemporary "the greatest female genius the world ever saw." Naturally, from her thoroughly English nature and temperament, Mrs. Browning contemned, with all the intensity of her soul, much that was innately natural to George Sand, but she fully recognised her humanity and genius, and felt urged to pay homage to both. Comparing her to Sappho, she deemed that, like her prototype, she had "suffered her senses to leaven her soul—to permeate it through and through, and make a sensual soul of it," but she indulged the hope that George Sand was "rising into a purer atmosphere by the very strength of her wing."

Inspired by such views, Mrs. Browning wrote her two sonnets on George Sand—"A Desire" and "A Recognition," and included them in the 1844 edition of her poems. Of course, she had not then met this "large-brained woman and large-hearted man," and it was not until the winter of 1851–2 that the interview—they had but one—took place between the two chief women of their age.

Introduced by a letter from Mazzini, and accompanied by her husband, Mrs. Browning called on her French contemporary, who had come to Paris in order to intercede with the President of the Republic (afterwards Napoleon the Third) for a condemned prisoner. Mrs. Browning found George Sand in quite a lowly room, with a bed in it, after a fashion common in France. Upon seeing the famous Frenchwoman, Mrs. Browning could not refrain from stooping to kiss her hand, but George Sand threw her arms round her visitor's neck, and kissed her on the lips. What passed at that interview may not be told; and although what impression our poetess may have made upon the novelist is unknown, George Sand inspired Mrs. Browning with extremely favourable ideas. She described her as not "taller than I am," and Elizabeth Browning, we know, was very short and small. George Sand's complexion appeared to her a pale olive, her hair dark, nicely parted and gathered into a knot or bunch behind. She tells of her dark glowing eyes, low voice, noble countenance, quiet simple manners, restrained rather than ardent, graceful and kind behaviour, and simple attire. Altogether a most charming person, and one well worthy the friendship even of England's pure and noble poetess. They parted, never to meet again.

The Brownings appear to have prolonged their stay in Paris for some months, and Miss Mitford received occasional letters from Mrs. Browning, as full of vivid word-painting as of yore when, as she says—" Before Mr. Browning stole her from me, we used to write to each other at least twice a week, and by dint of intimacy and frequency of communication could, I think, have found enough matter for a correspondence of twice a day. It was really talk, fireside talk, neither better nor worse, assuming necessarily a form of permanence-gossip daguerreotyped."

Notwithstanding Mrs. Browning's " terrible Republicanism," as Miss Mitford terms it, she acquired a truly marvellous belief in Louis Napoleon's goodness and genius. This belief once planted in her mind, nothing could erase or shake it; and as Miss Mitford, after having believed in an idealized First Napoleon, was fully prepared to see her ideal realised in a Third Napoleon, Mrs. Browning continued to fill her letters to her old friend with presumed evidences of the great-

ness and magnanimity of her latest hero. She endea-
voured to convert her friends to her views, and, declares
Miss Mitford, in April of this year, says that "every-
body in Paris" is coming round to an opinion similar
to that she holds of the Prince President.

Some time in the summer of 1852 the Brownings
returned to England, and stray notices of their
appearance in London are in existence. Crabb Robin-
son records in his *Diary*, under date of October 6th,
that he met them at dinner at Kenyon's. He remarks
that Mrs. Browning, whom he had never seen before,
was not the invalid he had expected. He describes
her as having "a handsome oval face, a fine eye,
and altogether a pleasing person." He suggests
that "she had no opportunity of display, and, appa-
rently, no desire, whilst her husband," he deems, "has
a very amiable expression. There is a singular
sweetness about him."

The Brownings were not able to prolong their stay
in England into the autumn, on account of the delicate
health of the poetess. The sudden setting in of cold
weather brought on a recurrence of her trying cough,
and compelled her to fly from her native land. In
company with her husband she spent a week or two in
Paris, and then they left for Italy, leaving a promise
to revisit England in the summer. Mrs. Browning
was greatly exercised in her mind as to whether the
publication of her recent work on *Casa Guidi Windows*
might not incite the Florentine authorities to exclude
her from the city, and thus keep her out of her home,
and away from her household gods. There is no
evidence, however, to hand to show that she had any
difficulty in re-entering either the city or her residence;
indeed, as Miss Mitford remarked, there was not so

much danger of her being turned away as of her being retained against her will.

In correspondence with Miss Mitford, early in 1853, Mrs. Browning, after referring to the fact that her husband's drama, *Colombe's Birthday*, was to be produced at the Haymarket in April, with Miss Helen Faucit (now Lady Martin) in the character of the heroine, recurs to her admiration for Napoleon III. Many people find it difficult to comprehend how a woman of Mrs. Browning's calibre could ever have admired and trusted the author of the *coup d'état*, but an analysis of her mental temperament renders a comprehension of her ideas on this subject comparatively easy. In the first place must be borne in mind the tenacity with which she clung to a belief when once she had accepted it. She had regarded the First Napoleon as the mighty doer of a divine mission. and the Third as his successor in that line, but as unsullied with the crimes of the first Emperor. The aid and maintenance which he gave to the cause of Italian liberty, crowned the third of the Bonapartes in her eyes with a halo of glory, and completed the subjugation of her mind; henceforth, all that he did was justified in her sight. Not unnaturally, the mist of glory in which she beheld her hero enveloped, surrounded and included his *entourage*. To Miss Mitford she says of the Emperor : " I approve altogether, none the less that he has offended Austria, in the mode of arrangement; every cut of the whip in the face of Austria being a personal compliment to me—at least, so I consider it. Let him head the democracy, and do his duty to the world, and use to the utmost his great opportunities. Mr. Cobden and the Peace Society are pleasing me infinitely just now in making head against

10 *

the immorality (that's the word) of the English press. The tone taken up towards France is immoral in the highest degree, and the invasion cry would be idiotic, if it were not something worse. The Empress, I heard the other day from the best authority, is charming and good at heart. She was educated at a respectable school at Bristol, and is very English, which does not prevent her shooting with pistols, leaping gates, driving four-in-hand, or upsetting the carriage, when the frolic demands it—as brave as a lion, and as true as a dog. Her complexion is like marble, white and pale and pure; her hair light, inclining to sandy—they say she powders it with gold-dust for effect; but her beauty is more intellectual and less physical than is commonly reported. She is a woman of very decided opinions. I like all this—don't you? and I like her letter to the Préfect, as everybody must. Ah! if the English press were in earnest in the cause of liberty, there would be something to say for our poor, trampled-down Italy—much to say, I mean. Under my eyes is a people really oppressed, really groaning its heart out; but these things are spoken of with indifference."

Another subject alluded to by Mrs. Browning in the same communication—a subject which was largely influencing her mind, and almost rivalling Italy in her thoughts—was that singular manifestation of human credulity known as "spirit-rappings." Although not altogether a modern invention or superstition, it was not until about this period that this phase of "Spiritualism" acquired any large or widely-spread popularity. The fashion or mania for this form of superstition sprang into existence in the United States of America, rapidly spread to Great Britain and, in more or less violent shapes, infected many surrounding countries.

One of the most important victims to the new epidemic was Mrs. Browning. Her letters of this period are filled with allusions to Spiritualism, and its strangest development, " spirit-rappings."

To a woman of such strong common sense as Miss Mitford, her friend's belief in such things as these " manifestations," appeared almost incomprehensible. Writing in March of this year to Fields, the American publisher, she remarks, " Mrs. Browning is most curious about your *rappings*—of which, I suppose, you believe as much as I do of the Cock Lane ghost, whose doings they so much resemble." And then again, about a month later, she writes, " Only think of Mrs. Browning giving the most unlimited credence to every ' rapping' story which anybody can tell her." Some weeks subsequent she again writes, " Mrs. Browning believes in every spirit-rapping story—all—and tells me that Robert Owen has been converted by them to a belief in a future state"; whilst directly afterwards she reiterates, " Mrs. Browning is positively crazy about the spirit-rappings. She believes every story, European or American, and says our Emperor consults the mediums, which I disbelieve."

Elizabeth Browning's strong credence in Spiritualism is not more difficult to dissect and understand than is her belief in Louis Napoleon. The great charm in Spiritualism for her was that, if true, it proved there was a life hereafter. To a woman of her intense religious cast of thought, a woman who clung with the sternest tenacity to dogmas she so often had to hear refuted and contemned, this revelation was at once a weapon and a shield. She was only too eagerly ready to accept the new doctrine and, once accepted, she was, as is already manifest, not the woman to relinquish it again. Chorley, who had long been her intimate friend, alludes to the fact that her friendship for him, though it continued through life, was interrupted by " serious differences of opinion concerning a matter which she took terribly to heart—the strange, weird questions of Mesmerism, including *clairvoyance,* —for all these things were combined and complicated with the mysteries of Spiritualism." " To the marvels of these two *phenomena* (admitting both as incomplete discoveries)," says Chorley, " she lent an ear as credulous as her trust was sincere and her heart highminded. But with women far more experienced in falsity than one so noble and one who had been so secluded from the world as herself, after they have once crossed the threshold, there is seldom chance of after retreat. Only they become bewildered by their tenacious notions of loyalty. It is over these very best and most generous of their sex that impostors have the most power."

" I have never seen one more nobly simple, more entirely guiltless of the feminine propensity of talking for effect, more earnest in her assertion, more gentle yet pertinacious in differences, than she was," pursues Chorley ; adding, " like all whose early nurture has chiefly been from books, she had a child's curiosity regarding the life beyond her books, co-existing with opinions accepted as certainties, concerning things of which (even with the intuition of genius) she could know little. She was at once forbearing and dogmatic, willing to accept differences, resolute to admit no argument ; without any more practical knowledge of social life than a nun might have when, after long years, she emerged from her cloister and her shroud."

E. D(owden?), writing with respect to Mrs. Brown-

ing's apparently inscrutable admiration for the Napo-
leonic *régime*, utters views so corroborative of Chorley,
and, save some exaggeration, coincident with our own,
that they may be cited from the article in *Macmillan's
Magazine*: " All her feelings on political subjects were
intensified not only by her woman's impetuosity, but
by the circumstances of her secluded life. To me her
judgments, both for good and bad, seemed oftentimes
like those of a dweller in some city convent. Out of
the cloister windows she could see the world moving
without, but in its active life she had neither share nor
portion. For many years past the days had been few
in number, almost to be counted upon the fingers,
throughout the long year, on which she was carried
down into the open air, to gaze upon the world from a
carriage-seat. All, indeed, that one of more than
common intellect, and who watched over her with
more than a woman's care, could bring her of glean-
ings from the outer world, she had to aid her in her
thoughts; all that books, written in almost every
modern language, could bring her of instruction, she
sought for eagerly; but still no aid of books or friends
could supply what daily contact with active life alone
can give. It was thus that the views of the world had
something of the unreality of cloister visions."

Mrs. Browning's interest in the cause of Italian
freedom continued to increase with her increase of
knowledge of the people. To her English friends she
wrote in the hopes of arousing in them something of
the sympathy she felt for her unfortunate neighbours,
but as yet with slight success. To Miss Mitford she
said, "I see daily a people who have the very life
crushed out of them, and yet of their oppressions the
English press says nothing;" and Miss Mitford's

comment to a friend on these and similar complaints was " fancy Mrs. Browning thinking Louis Napoleon ought to take up the cause of those wretched Italians ; and I hear from all quarters that they get into corners and slander each other. It is an extinct people, sending up nothing better than smoke and cinders and ashes; a mere name, like the Greeks."

Such opinions as this conservative old English lady uttered were entertained by the great majority of her country-people, and by the people of most countries, and the aspirations of Mrs. Browning and her Italian friends regarded as the idle dreams of poets. The poets' time was as yet to come.

During the hot summer of 1853 the Brownings sojourned at the Baths of Lucca. They returned to Florence in the autumn, and thence proceeded to Rome for the winter. Their stay in the latter city was somewhat prolonged, and their son, the little Robert, suffered from malaria, but seems to have rapidly recovered. During this stay in Rome Mrs. Browning became acquainted with Harriet Hosmer, the well-known American sculptor. Miss Hosmer was a favourite pupil of Gibson, and allowed to occupy a portion of the English sculptor's studio where, during work time, she might be found, " a compact little figure, five feet two in height, in cap and blouse, whose short, sunny, brown curls, broad brow, frank and resolute expression of countenance, gave one at the first glance the impression of a handsome boy." Naturally, Mrs. Browning informed Miss Mitford of the new acquaintance she had made, and that dear, prejudiced, insular-minded old lady wrote in a horrified tone to a correspondent, "Mrs. Browning has taken a fancy to an American female sculptor—a girl of 22—a pupil of Gibson, who goes with the rest of the fraterni'y of the studio to breakfast and dine at a café, *and keeps her character !*"

The Brownings returned to the quietude of their Florentine home, and during the remainder of the year mase no history to speak of. In December, Miss Mitford. speaks of having been advised by the poetess to try mesmerism for her health, which was now completely broken up, and on the 10th of the following January, 1855, the poor, kindly-hearted, if time-serving old lady, was released from her long suffering. The death of her old friend and correspondent must have been a severe blow for Mrs. Browning, but her hands and brain were now so full of her longest and most important poem that doubtless her sorrow was mitigated, if not stifled, by the excitement of the work's approaching completion.

CHAPTER VIII.

AURORA LEIGH.

THE original conception of a celebrated poem can rarely be traced. The "most mature" of her works, as Mrs. Browning terms *Aurora Leigh,* had evidently been germinating in its author's mind for several years before it was deemed fit to face the fierce glare of publication. As early as 1843, Mrs. Browning intimated to Horne the possibility that she could and, in certain circumstances might, write her own autobiography. Did not those words embody the germ idea of the "fictitious autobiography" which, after so many years and modified by so many causes, she called *Aurora Leigh?*

Years before her work saw the light or, indeed, was much beyond the embryo stage, Mrs. Browning had given intimation of her intentions with respect to it, to friends. Early in 1853 Miss Mitford had mentioned to Fields, the American publisher, that Mrs. Browning was engaged upon "a fictitious autobiography in blank verse, the heroine a woman artist, I suppose singer or actress," says the old lady, "and

the tone intensely modern." Whether Miss Mitford
had seen or heard any passages from the poem so as
to know what the *tone* was, or whether she derived her
impression from what the poetess had said, is un-
known; but at any rate she was kept advised as to its
progress, and in July, 1854, wrote to the same Mr.
Fields, saying Mrs. Browning asked her to inquire if
he would like to bring out the new poem. The pub-
lisher, with a lack of acumen not unparalleled in his
profession, let the opportunity slip, and the work was
secured by a New York rival. A few months later
Miss Mitford, after telling a correspondent that Mrs.
Browning's poem, which has been three years in hand,
and of which four thousand lines are already written,
has never been seen, not a word of it, by its authoress's
husband: " A strange reserve !" she exclaims.

During the years the work was in progress it seems
to have been written at odd moments, and when her
maternal cares were called for the manuscript was laid
down, or if a visitor came it was thrust away out of
sight. It was not until March 1856 that Mrs. Brown-
ing let her husband see any of the work, and then she
placed the first six books of it in his hands. The
remaining three books were written much more rapidly
than the others, and the whole work was completed
and transcribed in 1856 in London, in the house of
Mrs. Browning's friend and kinsman, John Kenyon,
to whom the book was dedicated as a " sign of esteem,
gratitude, and affection."

With as much of the manuscript of *Aurora Leigh* as
was ready the Brownings left Italy for England, and
at Marseilles, so Mrs. Ritchie tells us, " by some over-
sight the box was lost in which the manuscript had
been packed. In this same box were also carefully

put away certain velvet suits and lace collars in which the little son was to make his appearance among his English relatives. Mrs. Browning's chief concern was not for her manuscripts, but for the loss of her little boy's wardrobe, which had been devised with so much tender motherly care and pride. Happily one of her brothers was at Marseilles, and the box was discovered stowed away in some cellar at the Customs there."

At Paris the Brownings again met Bayard Taylor, and the American remarks about the forthcoming poem, that it is entirely new in design, and that the authoress "feels a little nervous about it." The nervousness was natural, but needless ; probably no long poem ever met with so enthusiastic a reception. The success of *Aurora Leigh* was immediate and wide, and its publication invoked a chorus of praise that time has somewhat modified the tone of. Barry Cornwall, alluding to it as " the most successful book of the season," adds, " it is, a hundred times over, the finest poem ever written by a woman." Landor, writing of it to John Forster, says, in many pages, " there is the wild imagination of Shakespeare. . . . I had no idea that anyone in this age was capable of so much poetry. I am half drunk with it." Other equally laudatory things were said by the choicest spirits of the time, and Mrs. Browning was at once and, doubtless, for ever, awarded one of the loftiest places in the fane of Poesy.

The splendour and grandeur of *Aurora Leigh* cannot be gainsaid, but at the period of its production literary England was somewhat more enthusiastic, and public taste somewhat more volcanic in its ebullitions than now-a-days, when a surfeit of sweets has somewhat blunted the appetite for such things. *Aurora Leigh* was a novelty; the rush of impassioned arguments, startling comparisons, and brilliant similes carried the reader along at fever heat, never allowing him time to linger over the improbabilities of the tale, or to criticise its faulty construction.

The plot of this autobiography—this three-volume novel in verse—is evidently founded, although probably unconsciously, upon Charlotte Brontë's *Jane Eyre*, whilst the character of Romney, the hero, frequently reminds the reader of Hollingsworth of *The Blithedale Romance.* Such coincidences of thought, however, are common among contemporaries, and only prove how really limited is man's imagination.

The mere story of *Aurora Leigh*, stripped of its poetry, is not unlike many novels in prose. It is the record of a life told by the heroine herself. Aurora, the daughter of an English father and an Italian mother, is born in Florence. At five years old a great misfortune befell her; her mother died, and the sunshine of infancy faded out of her little life, for

> Women know
> The way to rear up children (to be just).
> They know a simple, merry, tender knack
> Of tying sashes, fitting baby-shoes,
> And stringing pretty words that make no sense
> And kissing full sense into empty words;
> Which things are corals to cut life upon,
> Although such trifles; children learn by such
> Love's holy earnest in a pretty play.

Aurora's father was an "austere Englishman," but had loved his wife almost madly. When left with nothing to love but his little girl, for her sake he contrived with "his grave lips" to smile "a miserable smile." For a time he led a lonely life with his only, his child-companion, teaching her such stray scraps of learning as came into his mind: "Out of books he taught me all the ignorance of men." But after a few years, "entranced with thoughts, not aims," her father died, and Aurora, now thirteen, was doubly orphaned—

> There ended childhood: what succeeded next
> I recollect as, after fevers, men
> Thread back the passage of delirium.

When her last parent died, Aurora was conveyed from her native land to England, and placed in charge of her aunt—her father's sister. This aunt—Miss Leigh — is wonderfully well described — this prim English gentlewoman, with—

> Cheeks in which was yet a rose
> Of perished summers, like a rose in a book,
> Kept more for ruth than pleasure,—

and is, indeed, the one successful delineation of the tale. Miss Leigh

> Had lived, we'll say,
> A harmless life, she called a virtuous life,
> A quiet life, which was not life at all,
> (But that, she had not lived enough to know)
> Between the vicar and the country squires,
> The Lord-Lieutenant looking down sometimes
> From the empyreal, to assure their souls
> Against chance vulgarisms, and, in the abyss,
> The apothecary looked on once a year,
> To prove their soundness of humility.
> The poor-club exercised her Christian gifts
> Of knitting stockings, stitching petticoats,
> Because we are of one flesh after all
> And need one flannel (with a proper sense
> Of difference in the quality), and still
> The book-club, guarded from your modern trick
> Of shaking dangerous questions from the crease,
> Preserved her intellectual

The kind of life the half-wild child of the sunny south had to endure with her strait-laced English relative may be conceived : all her warmheartedness was chilled and her girlish affections suppressed, if not blighted. Thrown upon her own resources, she found solace in poetry and in dreams of artistic life. One day, in the fancied seclusion of the grounds, poetic ardour betrayed her into crowning herself, in anticipation of the world's recognition, with a wreath of ivy. Thus bedecked, she was discovered by her cousin, Romney, the heir of the Leigh estates, a calm, earnest philanthropist, who had his dreams—more extravagant even than Aurora's. His ambition was to break down the strong barriers existent between the masses and classes ; to elevate the poorest and vilest by the personal intercourse and aid of his own social order. At great personal sacrifice and toil he had commenced the crusade himself, and now, after lecturing Aurora sadly on the folly of her day-dreams, he besought her to relinguish them, and not strive to swerve from "a woman's proper sphere," concluding his harangue by asking her to become his wife.

With all the scorn of her youthful pride Aurora declined to become the wife of "a man who sees a woman as the complement of his sex merely." Romney went his way sadly, leaving Aurora still more sad, for, as the reader sees, and as her aunt saw, she really loved her cousin. Miss Leigh's wrath with her niece when she hears that she has rejected Romney, and the silent torture, a thousand times worse than words, she inflicts upon her, are ended by the sudden death of the aunt. Had not Romney, in succeeding to the Leigh property, endeavoured by a palpable stratagem to invest Aurora with a portion of his inheritance, he might perchance have won her, but her pride, wounded by his attempt to thus make her his debtor, compels her to dismiss him once more.

Aurora, whose worldly wealth consists only of a few hundreds of pounds, proceeds to London to earn fame and bread, whilst Romney busies himself more earnestly than ever in schemes for ameliorating the condition of the poor and the unfortunate. In the course of his labours Romney discovers and aids a poor outcast, Marian Erle, whose beauty and purity, if they do not altogether wean his heart from Aurora, at any rate, combined with his desire to read a lesson to the pride of caste, induces him to engage himself to her. The wedding is arranged to take place at St. James's Church, and the *élite* of London society is not only invited by the bridegroom, but actually attends to see the modern version of "King Cophetua and the Beggar Maid" enacted. Not only are these grandees present, but, at Romney's invitation, all that is foul and disreputable amongst the dregs of London life is there represented. In vain, however, is this assemblage : poor Marian has been spirited away, subjected to unutterable outrage, and Romney once more left solitary and discomforted, besides being discredited and roughly handled by the rabble he had made such sacrifices for.

Some time after this mysterious affair Aurora starts for Italy. Making a short stay in Paris, she encounters Marian Erle, or rather the wreck of she who was erstwhile the fresh and fair wearer of that name. The poor wronged girl is left with a fatherless child, which the mother shows to Aurora thus :—

                    She .   .
Approached the bed, and drew a shawl away:
You could not peel a fruit you fear to bruise

More calmly and more carefully than so—
Nor would you find within, a rosier flushed
Pomegranate.
    There he lay upon his back,
The yearling creature, warm and moist with life
To the bottom of his dimples—to the ends
Of the lovely tumbled curls about his face;
For since he had been covered over-much
To keep him from the light glare, both his cheeks
Were hot and scarlet as the first live rose
The shepherd's heart-blood ebbed away in'),
The faster for his love. And love was here
As instant! in the pretty baby mouth,
Shut close as if for dreaming that it sucked;
The little naked feet drawn up the way
Of nestled birdlings; everything so soft
And tender.—to the tiny holdfast hands,
Which, closing on a finger into sleep,
Had kept the mould of 't.
  *   *   *   *   *

The light upon his eyelids pricked them wide,
And, staring out at us with all their blue,
As half-perplexed between the angelhood
He had been away to visit in his sleep
And our most mortal presence—gradually
He saw his mother's face, accepting it
In change for heaven itself, with such a smile
As might have well been learnt there.

When Aurora learns the whole of poor Marian's tale her heart warms towards her and she takes charge of her and her baby, taking them with her to Italy. Here, in the repose of her old home, Aurora finds that rest her feverish sorrow had so much needed. She had not long dwelt in the quietude of her Italian home, however, before her cousin appears once more, and in the nobility of his heart offers to wed the poor injured Marian and to adopt her fatherless child. The unwedded mother sees that the happiness proffered her cannot now be hers, and, contented with such joy as her babe can afford her, gratefully declines the offer and leaves Romney to Aurora.

Aurora now learns that Romney's plans for succouring the wretched and the criminal had all failed; that his house, Leigh Hall, had been destroyed by the rabble; he himself, in striving to rescue one of the inmates had been irretrievably blinded, and had been driven by calumny from the neighbourhood. Her love no longer restrainable, she flings herself into the blind man's arms, and all the pent-up feelings of years find vent in a burst of acknowledged affection.

Such is a tame summary of the story which invoked so enthusiastic a reception throughout the English world of letters. Our plain prose can, of course, afford no conception of the magnificent aspirations, the glowing thoughts, the brilliant scintillations of genius, the innumerable gem-like passages of pathos, the passionate rushes of language, and the daring assaults upon time-honoured customs with which this crowning work of woman's genius is replete; nothing but citation from end to end can do justice to *Aurora Leigh.* When the glamour of perusal has passed off, however, and the reader begins to take a calm survey of the whole story, he is astounded at the extent of its shortcomings. The poem is most needlessly lengthened and hampered by continual digressions which interrupt without enriching the narrative. Nearly all the incidents are of an improbable, not to say impossible nature. None of the characters introduced, save that of the aunt, are life-like or typical. Romney Leigh's opinions and purposes, so far as they be comprehended, are something more than Quixotic, they are unnatural, and could never have been conceived by a sane, much less

a practical English philanthropist; they appear to
be introduced only to discredit the "Christian Social-
ism" of such men as Maurice, Charles Kingsley, and
their compatriots. No such rabble as that present at
the projected wedding in St. James's could have been
gathered together within an English Church, nor could
English gentlemen and gentlewomen have talked and
acted as Mrs. Browning makes her *dramatis personæ*
do. The poem leaves the impression on the mind of
having been written by a great poet, but by a great
poet whose knowledge of the world had been gained from
books and not from actual contact with its men and
women; not from personal experience of its daily toils
and troubles, its hard-earned triumphs and undeserved
defeats.

Of the artistic imperfections of *Aurora Leigh* much
has been said and much could still be said. Of its
halting metres; its long passages of pure prose; its
pedantic allusions, and needless coarsenesses; its con-
tinual introduction (in an apparent reckless way) of
names the generality of readers hold in reverential awe;
of a fondness for repeating quaint and unusual words,
and of many other blemishes the critics have already
told the tale. For ourselves, we deem that when these
imperfections—for imperfections they are—occur, they
are either wilfully introduced by the poetess, or they
are the result of hasty execution. Mrs. Browning
should not have published her great work so rapidly;
she should have retained it by her and have revised it
carefully, instead of throwing it off in haste and then
giving it to the world in still greater haste.

When all has, however, been said against *Aurora
Leigh* that can be said, how grand a monument of
genius it remains! What genuine bursts of poetry is

it not interspersed with! What utterances of truth
and of humanity are imbedded in its pages! How
few Englishmen would have uttered, even if they had
thought them, such pregnant words as these :—

> The English have a scornful, insular way
> Of calling the French light.   The levity
> Is in the judgment only, which yet stands;
> For, say a foolish thing but oft enough
> (And *here's the secret of a hundred creeds,*
> Men get opinions, as boys learn to spell,
> By reiteration chiefly) the same thing
> Shall pass at last for absolutely wise.

Another passage alluding to eminent women that has
been quoted often, and is not yet trite, is :—

> How dreary 'tis for women to sit still
> On winter nights by solitary fires,
> And hear the nations praising them far off.

It is followed by these less-known but equally
pathetic lines,—

> > To sit alone
> And think, for comfort, how, that very night,
> Affianced lovers, leaning face to face,
> With sweet half-listenings for each other's breath,
> Are reading haply from some page of ours,
> To pause with a thrill, as if their cheeks had touched,
> When such a stanza, level to their mood,
> Seems floating their own thoughts out—" So I feel
> For thee."   " And I, for thee: this poet knows
> What everlasting love is!" . . . .
> > To have our books
> Appraised by love, associated with love,
> While we sit loveless! it is hard, you think?
> At least, 'tis mournful.

Here, too, is true philosophy—

> All men are possible heroes: every age
> Heroic in proportion. . . .

Every age,
Through being beheld too close, is ill discerned
By those who have not lived past it. We'll suppose
Mount Athos carved, as Persian Xerxes schemed,
To some colossal statue of a man :
The peasants, gathering brushwood in his ear,
Had guessed as little of any human form
Up there, as would a flock of browsing goats.
They'd have, in fact, to travel ten miles off
Or ere the giant image broke on them ;
Full human profile, nose and chin distinct,
Mouth, muttering rhythms of silence up the sky,
And fed at evening with the blood of suns ;
Grand torso—hand that flung perpetually
The largesse of a silver river down
To all the country pastures. 'Tis even thus
With times we live in—evermore too great
To be apprehended near.

And, here, a truth but little recognized :—

The best men. doing their best,
Know peradventure least of what they do :
Men usefullest i' the world, are simply used.

But enough! A few lines here and there from
Aurora Leigh cannot portray what the poem is. It
is a veritable "autobiography"; a true record of the
inner life—that truest life—of a great and good woman,
and no one can expect to find so correct a portraiture
of Mrs. Browning in any book as they will in this
poem ; they must read it as the true memoir of which
our volume and any others which may be written
about her, are only the corollary.

Aurora Leigh was finished in England, whither the
Brownings came on a visit during the summer of 1856.
They were the guests of John Kenyon, at least during
a portion of their stay, the last pages of the poem
having been completed at his town house. Whilst in

London the Brownings naturally mingled in literary society, and some very interesting glimpses are obtainable of them during this visit, among others none more characteristic than that afforded by Nathaniel Hawthorne, who afterwards became so intimate with them in Italy. He describes his first meeting with them, at breakfast, in the house of Monkton Milnes, afterwards Lord Houghton. He says:—

" Mr. Milnes introduced me to Mrs. Browning, and assigned her to me to conduct into the breakfast-room. She is a small, delicate woman, with ringlets of dark hair, a pleasant, intelligent, and sensitive face, and a low, agreeable voice. She looks youthful and comely, and is very gentle and lady-like. And so we proceeded to the breakfast-room, which is hung round with pictures, and in the middle of it stood a large round table, worthy to have been King Arthur's, and here we seated ourselves without any question of precedence or ceremony. . . . Mrs. Browning and I talked a good deal during breakfast, for she is of that quickly appreciative and responsive order of women with whom I can talk more freely than with any man ; and she has, besides, her own originality wherewith to help on conversation, though I should say not of a loquacious tendency. She introduced the subject of Spiritualism, which, she says, interests her very much ; indeed, she seems to be a believer. Mr. Browning, she told me, utterly rejects the subject, and will not believe even in the outward manifestations, of which there is such overwhelming evidence. We also talked of Miss Bacon ; and I developed something of that lady's theory respecting Shakespeare, greatly to the horror of Mrs. Browning, and that of her next neighbour—a nobleman whose name I did not hear. On the whole,

I like her the better for loving the man Shakespeare with a personal love. We talked, too, of Margaret Fuller, who spent her last night in Italy with the Brownings; and of William Story, with whom they had been intimate, and who, Mrs. Browning says, is much stirred about Spiritualism. Really, I cannot help wondering that so fine a spirit as hers should not reject the matter till at least it is forced upon her. I like her very much."

After they left the breakfast-table they entered the library where, Hawthorne says, " Mr. Browning introduced himself to me—a younger man than I expected to see, handsome, with brown hair. He is very simple and agreeable in manner, gently impulsive, talking as if his heart were uppermost."

In October the Brownings returned to Italy, not waiting, apparently, for the publication of *Aurora Leigh,* which appeared simultaneously in England and America. They had not returned to their Florentine home long ere they were startled by the news of Kenyon's death. He died on the 3rd of December, at his marine residence in Cowes, Isle of Wight, and, having no near relatives, left his large property amongst his literary and other friends. Kenyon, who was known among his intimates as "the Apostle of Cheerfulness," crowned a long career of generosity and friendship by leaving handsome legacies to those who really required them, amongst those who participated being Mr. and Mrs. Browning, to whom he left the very acceptable sum of ten thousand five hundred pounds.

A few months later, and death was again busy in Mrs. Browning's family circle. On the 17th of April her father died, in the seventy-first year of his age, and was buried in Ledbury Church by the side of the wife who had predeceased him so many years. Her father's death, and the fact that he had not even alluded to her in his will, must have been a severe blow to Mrs. Browning; but comforted by the company of her husband and child, and deeply engrossed as she now was in Italian politics, the shock would naturally be far less severe than it would have been in bygone years. Nevertheless, memories of the dear old days when she had been that father's darling, must have surged across her sensitive mind, and the thought that he had passed away without remembrance of her, must have sorely wounded her feelings, and, it is not too much to suggest, have weakened her physically as well.

For some months there is little to record of Mrs. Browning's literary history. In the summer she removed with her husband and child to Bagni di Lucca in search of a few months' rest and quietude. No sooner, however, had they arrived, than a friend was attacked with gastric fever, and for six weeks they were kept in a state of anxiety and watchfulness on his behalf. Just as the friend recovered sufficiently to get back to Florence, another and a greater trial awaited them. Their little boy Robert was attacked by the fever, and for a fortnight the Brownings were in a condition of dire suspense on his account. Writing in October to Leigh Hunt, Mrs. Browning says: "We came here from Florence a few months ago to get repose and cheerfulness from the sight of the mountains, . . . instead of which . . . we have done little but sit by sick beds, and meditate on gastric fevers. So disturbed we have been—so sad! our darling precious child the last victim. To see him

lying still on his golden curls, with cheeks too scarlet
to suit the poor patient eyes, looking so frightfully like
an angel! It was very hard. But this is over, I do
thank God, and we are on the point of carrying back
our treasure with us to Florence to-morrow, quite
recovered, if a little thinner and weaker, and the young
voice as merry as ever. You are aware that that child
I am more proud of than twenty *Auroras*, even after
Leigh Hunt has praised them. He is eight years old,
and has never been 'crammed,' but reads English,
Italian, French, German, and plays the piano—then,
is the sweetest child! sweeter than he looks. When
he was ill he said to me, 'You pet! don't be unhappy
about me. Think it's a boy in the street, and be a
little sorry, but not unhappy.' Who could not be
unhappy, I wonder?"

It must have been a joy after such trials to return
to the comfort of their own home in Florence. Casa
Guidi and its inmates have been described by many,
but no more attractive picture of them has been given
than that by W. W. Story, the American sculptor. At
this period, he says, speaking of those who like him-
self were favoured visitors: "We can never forget the
square ante-room, with its great picture and piano-
forte, at which the boy Browning passed many an hour
—the little dining-room covered with tapestry, and
where hung medallions of Tennyson, Carlyle, and
Robert Browning—the long-room, filled with plaster
casts and studies, which was Mr. Browning's retreat—
and, dearest of all, the large drawing-room, where *she*
always sat. It opens upon a balcony filled with
plants, and looks out upon the iron grey church of
Santa Felice. There was something about this room
which seemed to make it a proper and especial haunt

for poets. The dark shadows and subdued light gave it a dreamy look, which was enhanced by the tapestry-covered walls, and the old pictures of saints that looked out sadly from the carved frames of black wood. Large book-cases, constructed of specimens of Florentine carving selected by Mr. Browning, were brimming over with wise-looking books. Tables were covered with more gaily-bound volumes, the gifts of brother authors. Dante's grave profile, a cast of Keats's face and brow taken after death, a pen-and-ink sketch of Tennyson, the genial face of John Kenyon, Mrs. Browning's good friend and relative, little paintings of the boy Browning—all attracted the eye in turn, and gave rise to a thousand musings. A quaint mirror, easy chairs and sofas, and a hundred nothings that always add an indescribable charm, were all massed in this room. But the glory of all, and that which sanctified all, was seated in a low arm-chair near the door. A small table, strewn with writing materials, books, and newspapers, was always by her side."

Story was so intimate a friend of the Brownings that his words about them have more than usual worth, and that his impressions were recorded at the time they were felt makes them all the more valuable. Of the lady herself, the presiding spirit of this poetry-haunted home, he says:—

"To those who loved Mrs. Browning, and to know her was to love her, she was singularly attractive. Hers was not the beauty of feature; it was the loftier beauty of expression. Her slight figure seemed hardly large enough to contain the great heart that beat so fervently within, and the soul that expanded more and more as one year gave place to another. It was

difficult to believe that such a fairy hand could pen
thoughts of such ponderous weight. . . .

" It was Mrs. Browning's face upon which one loved
to gaze—that face and head which almost lost them-
selves in the thick curls of her dark brown hair. That
jealous hair could not hide the broad, fair forehead,
' royal with truth,' as smooth as any girl's, and ' too
large for wreath of modern wont.' Her large brown
eyes were beautiful, and were in truth the windows of
her soul. . . .

" Mrs. Browning's character was well-nigh perfect.
Patient in long-suffering, she never spoke of herself,
except when the subject was forced upon her by others,
and then with no complaint. She *judged* not, saving
when great principles were imperilled, and then was ready
to sacrifice herself upon the altar of Right. . . . She
was ever ready to accord sympathy to all, taking au
earnest interest in the most insignificant and humble.
. . . Thoughtful in the smallest things for others, she
seemed to give little thought to herself, and believing
in universal goodness, her nature was free from worldly
suspicions."

Mr. Story speaks of her conversation as most
fascinating ; he remarks that it " was not characterized
by sallies of wit or brilliant repartee, nor was it of that
nature which is most welcome in society. It was
frequently intermingled with trenchant, quaint re-
marks, leavened with a quiet, graceful humour of her
own ; but it was eminently calculated for a *tête-à-tête.*
Mrs. Browning never made an insignificant remark.
All that she said was *always* worth hearing. . . . She
was a most conscientious listener, giving you her mind
and heart, as well as her magnetic eyes. Though the
latter spoke au eager language of their own, she con-

versed slowly, with a conciseness and point that, added to a matchless earnestness, which was the predominant trait of her conversation as it was of her character, made her a most delightful companion. Persons were never her theme, unless public characters were under discussion, or friends were to be praised—which kind office she frequently took upon herself. One never dreamed of frivolities in Mrs. Browning's presence; gossip felt out of place. . . . Books and humanity, great deeds, and, above all, politics, which include all the grand questions of the day, were foremost in her thoughts, and, therefore, oftenest on her lips. I speak not of religion, for with her everything was religion. Her Christianity was not confined to church or rubrics; it meant civilisation. Association with the Brownings, even though of the slightest nature, made one better in mind and soul. It was impossible to escape the influence of the magnetic fluid of love and poetry that was constantly passing between husband and wife. The unaffected devotion of one to the other wove an additional charm around the two, and the contrasts in their nature made the union a more beautiful one."

In harmonious contrast with Mr. Story's reminiscences of Mrs. Browning may be cited the more vivid and picturesque sketches of Casa Guidi's inmates made by the author of *The Scarlet Letter* and his talented wife. In the summer of 1858 Hawthorne took the Villa Montauto, just outside the walls of Florence, and he and his family became intimate with the Brownings. The story of their intercourse must be related, as nearly as possible, in the language of the Hawthornes themselves, and if in some instances it be somewhat iterative of the records made by Mr.

Story or others, it will be none the less valuable as confirmatory .of the impressions produced by the inhabitants of Casa Guidi upon other equally independent observers.

It was the 8th June 1858, records Nathaniel Hawthorne, in his *Italian Note-books :* "There was a ring at the door, and a minute after our servant brought a card. It was Mr. Robert Browning's, and on it was written in pencil an invitation for us to go to see them this evening. He had left the card and had gone away; but very soon the bell rang again, and he had come back, having forgotten to give his address.. This time he came in, and he shook hands with all of us — children and grown people — and was very vivacious and agreeable. He looked younger and even handsomer than when I saw him in London two years ago, and his gray hairs seemed fewer than those that had then strayed into his youthful head. . . .

"Mr. Browning was very kind and warm in his expressions of pleasure at seeing us; and, on our part, we were all very glad to meet him. He must be an exceeding likeable man."

The favourable impression made by the English poet upon the American romancist was evidently shared by the latter's family, as, indeed, may be learnt from Mrs. Hawthorne's note-book. Her descriptions of Mr. Browning and his domestic circle are, if possible, even more graphic and interesting than her husband's; at any rate, they supplement and complete the charming picture he conjures up to the " mind's eye " of the poet home in Casa Guidi. She says, " Mr. Browning's grasp of the hand gives a new value to life, revealing so much fervour and sincerity of nature. He invited us most cordially to go at eight and spend the evening." She continues, "At eight we went to Casa Guidi"; and Hawthorne himself says :—" After some search and inquiry we found the Casa Guidi, which is a palace in a street not very far from our own. It being dusk, I could not see the exterior, which, if I remember, Browning has celebrated in song. . . . The street is a narrow one; but on entering the palace we found a spacious staircase and ample accommodation of vestibule and hall, the latter opening on a balcony, where we could hear the chanting of priests in a church close by." " We found a little boy," proceeds Mrs. Hawthorne, "in an upper hall with a servant. I asked him if he were Pennini, and he said 'Yes.' In the dim light he looked like a waif of poetry, drifted up into the dark corner, with long, curling brown hair, and buff silk tunic embroidered with white. He took us through an ante-room, into the drawing-room, and out upon the balcony. In a brighter light he was lovelier still, with brown eyes, fair skin, and a slender, graceful figure. In a moment Mr. Browning appeared, and welcomed us cordially. In a church near by, opposite the house, a melodious choir was chanting. The balcony was full of flowers in vases, growing and blooming. In the dark blue fields of space overhead the stars, flowers of light, were also blossoming, one by one, as evening deepened. The music, the stars, the flowers, Mr. Browning and his child, all combined to entrance my wits."

Hawthorne, on his first visit, appears to have been chiefly impressed with the elfin appearance of the little boy, Robert, whom "they call Pennini for fondness." This cognomen, he was informed, was " a diminutive of Apennino, which was bestowed upon him at his first advent into the world because he was so very small, there being a statue in Florence of colossal size called Apennino. I never saw such a boy as this before," he says, "so slender, so fragile, and spirit-like—not as if he were actually in ill-health, but as if he had little or nothing to do with human flesh and blood. His face is very pretty and most intelligent, and exceedingly like his mother's. He is nine years old, and seems at once less childlike and less manly than would befit that age. I should not like to be the father of such a boy, and should fear to stake so much interest and affection on him as he cannot fail to inspire. I wonder what is to become of him — whether he will ever grow to be a man—whether it is desirable that he should. His parents ought to turn their whole attention to making him robust and earthly, and to giving him a thicker scabbard to sheathe his spirit in. He was born in Florence, and prides himself upon being a Florentine, and, indeed, is as un-English a production as if he were a native of another planet."

The romancist proceeds, in his characteristic style :— "Mrs. Browning met us at the door of the drawing-room, and greeted us most kindly—a pale, small person, scarcely embodied at all; at any rate, only substantial enough to put forth her slender fingers to be grasped, and to speak with a shrill, yet sweet tenuity of voice. Really, I do not see how Mr. Browning can suppose that he has an earthly wife any more than an earthly child; both are of the elfin race, and will flit away from him some day when he least thinks of it. She is a good and kind fairy, however, and sweetly disposed towards the human race, although only remotely akin to it. It is wonderful to see how small she is, how pale her cheek, how bright and dark her eyes. There is not such another figure in the world; and her black ringlets cluster down into her neck, and make her face look the whiter by their sable profusion. I could not form any judgment about her age; it may range anywhere within the limits of human life or elfin life. When I met her in London at Lord Houghton's breakfast-table, she did not impress me so singularly; for the morning light is more prosaic than the dim illumination of their great tapestried drawing-room; and besides, sitting next to her, she did not have occasion to raise her voice in speaking, and I was not sensible what a slender voice she has. It is marvellous to me how so extraordinary, so acute, so sensitive a creature can impress us, as she does, with the certainty of her benevolence. It seems to me there were a million chances to one that she would have been a miracle of acidity and bitterness."

Mrs. Hawthorne's account of their hostess is quite as representative as her husband's. She describes her as " very small, delicate, dark, and expressive. She looked like a spirit. A cloud of hair falls on each side her face in curls, so as partly to veil her features. But out of the veil look sweet, sad eyes, musing and far-seeing and weird. Her fairy fingers looked too airy to hold, and yet their pressure was very firm and strong. The smallest possible amount of substance encloses her soul, and every particle of it is infused with heart and intellect. I was never conscious of so little unredeemed, perishable dust in any human being. I gave her a branch of small pink roses, twelve on the stem, in various stages of bloom, which I had plucked from our terrace vine, and she fastened it in her black velvet dress with most lovely effect to her whole aspect. Such roses were fit emblems of her. We soon returned to the drawing-room—a lofty, spacious apartment, hung with Gobelin tapestry and pictures, and filled with carved' furniture and objects of *vertù*. Everything harmonized—poet, poetess, child, house, the rich air, and the starry night. Pennini was an Ariel, flitting about, gentle, tricksy, and intellectual."

What a picture does not this present to the mind's eye! The Hawthornes and the Brownings, gathered together in that weird old Florentine palace and conversing as only they could. How thoroughly one can sympathise with Mrs. Hawthorne when she exclaims, " It rather disturbed my dream! to have other guests come in. Eventually tea was brought and served on a long, narrow table, placed before a sofa, and Mrs. Browning presided. We all gathered at this table. Pennini handed about the cake, graceful as Ganymede."

" Little Pennini," says Hawthorne, who appears to have been much interested in young Browning, " sometimes helped the guests to cake and strawberries, joined in the conversation when he had anything to say, or sat down upon a couch to enjoy his own meditations. He has long curling hair, and has not yet emerged from his frock and short hose. It is funny to think of putting him into trousers. His likeness to his mother is strange to behold."

After alluding to there being other guests present, Hawthorne remarked that " Mr. Browning was very efficient in keeping up conversation with everybody, and seemed to be in all parts of the room and in every group at the same moment; a most vivid and quick-thoughted person, logical and common-sensible, as I presume poets generally are in their daily talk."

A pleasant evening was passed by that group of noteworthy persons, who have now nearly all escaped from the " coffin of their cares." The conversation was general, " the most interesting topic," récords Hawthorne, " being that disagreeable and now wearisome one of spiritual communications, as regards which Mrs. Browning is a believer, and her husband an infidel. . . . Browning and his wife had both been present at a spiritual session held by Mr. Hume, and had seen and felt the unearthly hands, one of which had placed a laurel wreath on Mrs. Browning's head. Browning, however, avowed his belief that these hands were affixed to the feet of Mr. Hume, who lay extended in his chair, with his legs stretched far under the table. The marvellousness of the fact, as I have read of it, and heard it from other eye-witnesses, melted strangely away in his hearty gripe, and at the sharp touch of his logic; while his wife, ever and anon, put in a little gentle word of expostu lation.

" I am rather surprised that Browning's conversation should be so clear and so much to the purpose at the moment, since his poetry can seldom proceed far without running into the high grass of latent meanings and obscure allusions."

Mrs. Browning's health was too delicate to permit late hours, so her visitors had to leave about ten. She expressed her regret that she should not see much of the Hawthornes for some time, as she was going with her husband to the seaside, but hoped to find them in Florence on her return.

Two days later, however, in response to Mrs. Browning's invitation, Mrs. Hawthorne called with her daughters at Casa Guidi. Mrs. Browning did not receive till eight in the evening, but as the younger child would have been in bed by that time Mrs. Hawthorne was asked to bring her at one in the day. "We rang a great while," says Mrs. Hawthorne, "and no one answered the bell; but presently a woman came up the staircase and admitted us, but she was surprised that we expected to see Mrs. Browning at such a time. I gave her my credentials, and so she invited us to follow her in. We found the wondrous lady in her drawing-room, very pale, and looking ill; yet she received us affectionately, and was deeply interesting as usual. She took R—— into her lap, and seemed to enjoy talking to and looking at her, as well as at Una. She said, 'Oh! how rich and happy you are to have two daughters, a son, and such a husband.' Her boy was gone to his music-master's, which I was very sorry for; but we saw two pictures of him. Mrs. Browning said he had a vocation for music, but did not like to apply to anything else any more than a butterfly, and the only way she could command his attention was to have him upon her knees, and hold his hands and feet. He knows German pretty well already, and Italian perfectly, being born a Florentine."

"I was afraid to stay long, or to have Mrs. Browning talk," comments the visitor, "because she looked so pale and seemed so much exhausted, and I perceived that the motion of R——'s fan distressed her. I do not understand how she can live long, or be at all restored while she does live. I ought rather to say that she lives so ardently that her delicate earthly vesture must soon be burnt up and destroyed by her soul of pure fire."

On the 25th of June, Mrs. Hawthorne records in her diary: "We spent this evening at Casa Guidi. I saw Mrs. Browning more satisfactorily, and she grows

lovelier on farther knowing.   Mr. Browning gave me
a pomegranate bud from *Casa Guidi Windows*, to press
in my memorial book. . . . The finest light gleams
from Mrs. Browning's arched eyes—for she has those
arched eyes so unusual, with an intellectual, spiritual
radiance in them.   They are sapphire, with dark
lashes, shining from out a bower of curling, very dark,
but, I think, not black hair.   It is sad to see such
deep pain furrowed into her face—such pain that the
great happiness of her life cannot smooth it away.   In
moments of rest from speaking her countenance re-
minds one of those mountain sides, ploughed deep with
spent water-torrents, there are traces in it of so much
grief, so much suffering.   The angelic spirit, triumph-
ing at moments, restores the even surface.   How has
anything so delicate braved the storms?   Her soul is
mighty, and a great love has kept her on earth a
season longer.   She is a seraph in her flaming worship
of heart, while a calm, cherubic knowledge sits en-
throned on her large brow.   How she remains visible
to us, with so little admixture of earth, is a mystery ;
but fortunate are the eyes that see her, and the ears
that hear her."

On the 2nd July the Brownings left Florence for
France, intending to spend the remainder of the sum-
mer in Normandy, and, pathetically exclaims Mrs.
Hawthorne, "there seems to be nobody in Florence
now for us !"

CHAPTER IX.

BEFORE CONGRESS.

FOR some months the records of Mrs. Browning's
story are nought but blank pages. Burning, heart-
burning questions, however, were coming to the fore,
thrilling her delicate frame and agitating her weary heart
with volcanic themes. Instead of the quietude and re-
pose her invalided constitution needed, she gave her-
self up with her usual ardency to the aspirations of
her Italian friends and neighbours. "To her," says
Mr. Story, "Italy was from the first a living fire."
Her joy and enthusiasm at the Italian uprising in 1848
was fervently sung in the early portion of *Casa Guidi
Windows*; the second part expresses her sorrow and
dejection at the abortive results of that revolution.
Still she hoped on, watching events from her Floren-
tine home, with a firm trust that the days of fulfil-
ment would arrive. She was angered with her native
land, or rather with its leaders, that they turned
their back upon the trials and struggles of her adopted
country, and scorned them for what she deemed their
insular view of the world.

Her hopes, however, were largely if not entirely

gratified. "It is a matter of great thankfulness," says Mr. Story, "that God permitted Mrs. Browning to witness the second Italian revolution. No patriot Italian gave greater sympathy to the aspirations of 1859 than Mrs. Browning. . . . Great was the moral courage of this frail woman, to publish the *Poems Before Congress* at a time when England was most suspicious of Napoleon. Greater was her conviction, when she abased England and exalted France for the cold neutrality of the one and the generous aid of the other in this War of Italian Independence. Bravely did she bear up against the angry criticisms excited by such anti-English sentiment."

During the uprising of the Italians in 1859, when, aided by the French, they were successful in driving their oppressors back from so large a portion of Italian soil, Mrs. Browning's pen and brain both worked hard for the cause she had so strong at heart. Her poems and her life at this period are part of Italian history. Above all did she exalt and glory in the ideal Emperor her imagination had portrayed. The hero she had already believed the Third Napoleon to be was now fully confirmed. Had he not sworn to free Italy from sea to sea, and was he not aiding her people to accomplish this great object by defeating and driving out the hated Tedeschi? With full faith in her Emperor she wrote her passionate lines on "Napoleon the Third in Italy."

July came, and with it the sudden and maddening Treaty of Peace. Mrs. Browning could not but mourn with Italy at the overthrow of hopes which had appeared so close on their realisation yet were so rudely crashed. In the first pangs of her grief, when stunned, if not crushed by the course of events, she addressed to her son those bitter lines "A Tale of Villafranca," beginning :—

> My little son, my Florentino,
>   Sit down beside my knee,
> And I will tell you why the sign
>   Of joy which flushed our Italy
> Has faded since but yesternight,
> And why your Florence of delight
>   Is mourning as you see.

Mr. Story avers that the news of the Imperial Treaty of Villafranca, following so fast upon the victories of Solferino and San Martino, almost killed Mrs. Browning. "That it hastened her into the grave," he says, " is beyond a doubt, as she never fully shook off the severe attack of illness occasioned by this check upon her life-hopes."

Notwithstanding, however, his failure to fulfil his promise to Italy; notwithstanding the annexation of Nice and Savoy, Mrs. Browning would not give up her faith in Napoleon the Third; as Savage Landor said of it, " If that woman put her faith in a man as good as Jesus, and he should become as wicked as Pontius Pilate, she would not change it." In language somewhat more to the purpose, Professor Dowden points out, in explanation of Mrs. Browning's belief of one whose political deeds were often so diametrically opposed to her own principles, " She saw a great work being worked out around her, and instinctively she believed that in the workers also there must be something great and god-like. Still," he proceeds, " the keenness of Mrs. Browning's Imperialism dated from the time of the Italian War. It is difficult to convey an idea to strangers of the intenseness of all her feelings about Italy. Hers was no

dilettante artistic love, but a deep personal attachment
for the land of her home and her affections.   All who
had written or spoken or worked in behalf of Italy were
as welcome to her as friends of long standing ; while
for those who had exerted their powers against Italy,
as open enemies or false friends, she felt as personal
an enmity as it was possible for that gentle nature to
feel against any living being.   One who knew her
towards the end of her life has told me that her last
words to him, at their parting, were to thank him,
with thanks that were little merited, because he had
done something for the cause of Italy.   Higher
thanks, however undeserved, she knew none to give.

"This being so, it would have been strange had she not
shared the common Italian feeling about the Emperor
of the French. . . . In this world men, after all, look
to the facts, not to motives, and . . . you cannot
escape the broad fact that, in the hour of Italy's need
(*before,* mind you, not *after* the victory) it was the
Emperor Napoleon alone who came forward to rescue
Italy, who overthrew the tyranny of Austria, and who,
willingly or unwillingly, thereby created the Italian
kingdom. . . . This is the one simple fact which the
Italians have not forgotten and cannot forget ; and of
this fact Mrs. Browning's mind took hold with all the
ardour of her love for Italy, and all the intensity of
her poet's feelings."

Sick at heart and bodily ill, Mrs. Browning spent a
weary, suffering summer.   In July she removed with
her husband to Siena, and spent the autumn there.
Both in Siena and in Florence, whither they returned
for a few days' rest before proceeding to Rome for the
winter, the Brownings were much interested in the
troubles and eccentricities of Walter Savage Landor.

But for the kindly care of Mr. Browning, it is hard to say what would have been the ultimate fate of the strange old genius. He saw to his immediate wants, and made such pecuniary arrangements with Landor's relatives as secured him from any further dread of downright poverty. Apartments were secured for him in the close vicinity of Casa Guidi, and Mrs. Browning's old servant, Wilson, was induced to devote herself to the care of him. Wilson, who had been a more than servant to her mistress, was most faithful in the discharge of her duties to the new master, and fully fulfilled the trust reposed in her by the Brownings, notwithstanding she had family ties of her own.

The winter was spent by the Brownings in Rome, where the mild climate seemed to have somewhat restored the invalid, for such the poetess was again. In the beginning of 1860 she collected her recent political pieces, and published them as *Poems Before Congress.* In her Preface, dated February, she says :—" These poems were written under the pressure of the events they indicate, after a residence in Italy of so many years, that the present triumph of great principles is heightened to the writer's feelings by the disastrous issue of the last movement, witnessed from *Casa Guidi Windows* in 1849."

"If the verses should appear to English readers," she explains, " too pungently rendered to admit of a patriotic respect to the English sense of things, I will not excuse myself on such, nor on the grounds of my attachment to the Italian people, and my admiration of their heroic constancy and union. What I have written has simply been because I love truth and justice—*quand même*—more than Plato and Plato's country, more than Dante and Dante's country, more even than Shakespeare and Shakespeare's country."

After urging that non-intervention in a neighbour's affairs may be carried too far, may only mean passing by on the other side when that neighbour has fallen among thieves, she earnestly entreats her countrymen to "put away the Little Pedlingtonism, unworthy of a great nation, and too prevalent among us. If the man who does not look beyond this natural life is of a somewhat narrow order," she argues, "what must be the man who does not look beyond his own frontier or his own sea ?"

"I confess," she exclaims, in language of real poetic grandeur, and with a visionary hope of what appears not yet very near unto realisation, "I confess that I dream of the day when an English statesman shall arise with a heart too large for England; having courage in the face of his countrymen to assert of some suggested policy, 'This is good for your trade; this is necessary for your domination; but it will vex a people hard by, it will hurt a people further off, it will profit nothing to the general humanity; therefore, away with it—it is not for you or for me.' When a British minister dares speak so, and when a British public applauds him speaking, then shall the nation be glorious, and her praise, instead of exploding from within from loud civic mouths, come to her from without, as all worthy praise must, from the alliances she has fostered, and the populations she has saved."

Some of the poems in the volume thus heralded certainly contained a few bitter allusions to England, and contrasted her conduct, and of course not to her advantage, with that of France. Yet, that there was very much in the book to arouse the wrath Mrs.

Browning believed she had aroused in her native country is preposterous. The asperity of a few reviews, such as that which Chorley deemed it his political duty to indulge in, could have had very little influence upon any class in England, however much the literary susceptibilities of the authoress may have magnified it. To an American friend Mrs. Browning said, " My book has had a very angry reception in my native country, as you probably observe; but I shall be forgiven one day; and meanwhile, forgiven or unforgiven, it is satisfactory to one's own soul to have spoken the truth as one apprehends the truth."

That England did sympathise very strongly with Italy in her struggles for independence, no one who reads the history of the time can doubt, and that her moral and political aid was of immense value to the Italian cause cannot be gainsaid; but English statesmen did not deem it for their country's welfare to interfere too actively, especially while the occult motives of Napoleon were to be taken into account, and this it was that stirred up Mrs. Browning's anger. She, whose heart and brain throbbed but for Italy, could not brook the reticence of England, the reluctance of Englishmen to join Napoleon in his adventurous, perhaps chivalrous, policy. During 1860 she continued to pour forth passionate poems on behalf of Italy, or inspired by Italian themes, but none of them, it must be confessed, equal in poetic value to some lines entitled " Little Mattie," which she published in the *Cornhill Magazine*. In this lyric she attained a higher standard of poetic excellence than she had done for some years past.

About this time, in viewing Rome's gift of swords to her heroes, Napoleon and Victor Emmanuel, she caught a severe cold, which is said to have affected her lungs. The autumn, also, saw her prostrated with sorrow at the news of her favourite sister's death. Again was Rome resorted to for the winter, and once more the balmy air seemed to revive her drooping form, so that she believed and wrote that she was " better in body and soul."

At intervals she continued to write short poems, but one entitled " The North and the South," written in May, in honour of Hans Christian Andersen's visit to Rome, was the last she ever wrote. During the same month the Brownings returned to Florence, and, although she had found the overland journey very fatiguing, her Florentine friends considered Mrs. Browning had never looked better than when in these early days of June she returned to Casa Guidi.

Mr. Story recounts that in the last but one conversation he had with Mrs. Browning after her return home, they discussed Motley's recently written letters on the American Crisis, and that she warmly approved of them. "Why," she said, referring to the attitude assumed by foreign nations towards America at that time, "why do you heed what others say? You are strong and can do without sympathy; and when you have triumphed your glory will be the greater."

Mrs. Browning had not returned to Florence more than a week or so before she caught another severe cold, and one of an even more threatening character than usual. Medical aid was obtained, but, although anxiety was naturally felt, there does not appear to have been any idea of imminent danger entertained until the third or fourth night, when, says Mr. Story, whose account must now be mainly followed, " those

who most loved her said they had never seen her
so ill."

The following morning, however, the poetess ap-
peared to be better, and for a day or two was sup-
posed to be recovering. She herself was of this belief,
and those about her had such confidence in her
vitality that the worst seemed to have been passed.
"So little did Mrs. Browning realise her critical con-
dition," says Mr. Story, "that until the last day she
did not consider herself sufficiently indisposed to re-
main in bed, and then the precaution was accidental.
So much encouraged did she feel with regard to her-
self that on this final evening an intimate female
friend was admitted to her bedside, and found her in
good spirits, ready at pleasantry and willing to con-
verse on all the old loved subjects. Her ruling passion
had prompted her to glance at the *Athenæum* and
Nazione; and when this friend repeated the opinions
she had heard expressed by an acquaintance of the
new Italian Premier, Ricasoli, to the effect that his
policy and Cavour's were identical, Mrs. Browning
'smiled like Italy,' and thankfully replied, 'I am
glad of it; I thought so.' Even then her thoughts
were not of self."

Little did this friend think, as she bade the poetess
"good-bye," that it was indeed a farewell she was
taking. Friends who called to inquire after her were
sent away cheered with the assurance that she was
better, and even her "own bright boy," says Mr.
Story, as he bade his mother good night, was sent to
bed consoled by her oft-repeated "I am better, dear,
much better."

One only watched her breathing through the night,
he who for fifteen years had ministered to her with all

the tenderness of a woman. It was a night devoid of suffering to her. As morning approached, and for two hours previous to the dread moment, she seemed to be in a partial ecstasy, and though not apparently conscious of the coming on of death, she gave her husband all those holy words of love, all the consolation of an oft-repeated blessing, whose value death has made priceless. Such moments are too sacred for the common pen, which pauses as the woman poet raises herself up to die in the arms of her poet husband. He knew not that death had robbed him of his treasure until the drooping form grew chill. . . . Her last words were: "It is beautiful!"

GRATEFUL FLORENCE.

Mrs. Browning died at half-past four in the morning of June 29th, 1861, in the fifty-third year of her age. She died of congestion of the lungs; and from the shattered condition of her lungs the physicians asserted that her existence could not have been prolonged, in any circumstance, many months.

From the grief of those dearest to her the veil may not be rudely torn. Suffice to say that on the evening of July 1st all that remained of England's great poetess was reverently borne to the lovely little Protestant cemetery, looking out towards Fiesole. The bier was surrounded by a sympathetic band of English, Americans, and Italians, whose intense sorrow dared hardly display itself in presence of the holy grief of the husband and the son of her whom they had loved so well.

There, amid the dust of illustrious fellow poets, and where tall cypresses wave over the graves, and the beautiful hills keep guard around, rises a stately marble cenotaph, designed by Sir Frederick Leighton, to the memory of the authoress of *Aurora Leigh*. Owing, however, to the removal of the old city walls

of Florence, the Protestant cemetery is now included
within the city limits, and further interments there
are forbidden by law; but the place is preserved by
the municipality.

As long as the language she wrote in lives, the
memory of Elizabeth Barrett Browning will exist; but
it is pleasant to know that the people among whom
she lived and laboured during the latter years of her
life, and whom she loved so well, were not forgetful
of her. Upon Casa Guidi the municipality of Florence
placed a white marble slab, and thereon, inscribed
in letters of gold, are these words written by
Tommaseo:—

QUI SCRISSE E MORÌ
ELIZABETH BARRETT BROWNING,
CHE IN CUORE DI DONNA SEPPE UNIRE
SAPIENZA DE DOTTO, E FACONDIA DI POETA,
FECE DEL SUO AUREO VERSO, ANELLO,
FRA ITALIA E INGHILTERRA.
POSE QUESTA MEMORIA
FIRENZE GRATA.
A.D. 1861.

which may be thus rendered in English:—

HERE WROTE AND DIED
ELIZABETH BARRETT BROWNING,
WHO IN HER WOMAN'S HEART UNITED
THE WISDOM OF THE SAGE AND THE ELOQUENCE OF THE POET;
WITH HER GOLDEN VERSE LINKING ITALY TO ENGLAND.
GRATEFUL FLORENCE PLACED
THIS MEMORIAL.
A.D. 1861.

APPENDIX.

BIRTH OF MRS. BROWNING.

THE date and place of Mrs. Browning's birth have
been variously stated. For some years biographers
wavered between London and Hope End, Hereford-
shire as her natal place. Quite recently Mrs. Richmond
Ritchie, authorised by Mr. Browning, declared Burn
Hall, Durham, the place, and March 6th, 1809, the
date of Mrs. Browning's birth. My researches have
enabled me to disprove these statements. In *The Tyne
Mercury*, for March 14th, 1809, is announced for
March 4th, "In London the wife of Edward M.
Barrett Esq., of a daughter."

Having published my *data*, their accuracy was chal-
lenged by Mr. Browning, who now asserted that his wife
was "born on March 6th, 1806, at Carlton Hall, Durham,
the residence of her father's brother." Carlton Hall
was not in Durham but in Yorkshire, and I am
authoritatively informed, did not become the residence

of Mr. S. Moulton Barrett until some time after 1810. Mr. Browning's latest suggestions cannot, therefore, be accepted.

All the obtainable evidence favours my statement. In 1806, Mr. E. Moulton Barrett, not yet twenty, is scarcely likely to have already had the two children assigned him. Most decidedly he had no children born by that date at either Burn Hall, Durham, or Carlton Hall, Yorkshire. A daughter was unquestionably born to his wife in London on March 4th, 1809. In 1840, Mrs. Browning referred to her childish epic, *The Battle of Marathon,* as written when she was ten, and, at a later period, spoke of it having been produced when she was about eleven : it was published in 1820. She also referred to her *Essay on Mind,* published in 1826, as " written when I was seventeen or eighteen."

Having these *data* before me it is difficult to assign any other date and place than those given in this work for the birth of Mrs. Browning.

JOHN H. INGRAM.

June 1888.

LONDON:

PRINTED BY W. H. ALLEN AND CO., 13 WATERLOO PLACE, S.W

THE
NATIONAL REVIEW.

MONTHLY, 2s. 6d.

Vols. I. to XII. already issued, 17s. each.

Cases for Binding, 2s.

THE
ILLUSTRATED NAVAL & MILITARY MAGAZINE.

A MONTHLY JOURNAL

Devoted to all subjects connected with H.M.
Land and Sea Forces.

2s. 6d.

Vols. I. to VIII. already issued, 18s. 6d. each.
Cases for Binding, 2s. 6d., Reading Covers, 3s. 6d.

COLBURN'S UNITED SERVICE MAGAZINE.

With which is incorporated

THE ARMY AND NAVY MAGAZINE.

A Monthly Service Review.

ONE SHILLING.

Vols. I. to XIV. already issued, 7s. 6d. each.
Cases for Binding, 1s. 6d.

LONDON:

W. H. ALLEN AND CO., 13, WATERLOO PLACE.

MESSRS. W. H. ALLEN & CO.'S CATALOGUE OF BOOKS, &c.

[All bound in cloth unless otherwise stated.]

ABERIGH-MACKAY, GEORGE
Twenty-one Days in India. Being the Tour of Sir Ali Baba, K.C.B. Post 8vo. 4s. An Illustrated Edition. Demy 8vo. 10s. 6d.

ABBOTT, Capt. JAMES.
Narrative of a Journey from Herat to Khiva, Moscow, and St. Petersburg, during the late Russian Invasion of Khiva. With some Account of the Court of Khiva and the Kingdom of Khaurism. With Map and Portrait. 2 vols. Demy 8vo. 24s.

Academy Sketches, including Various Exhibitions. Edited by Henry Blackburn, Editor of "Academy" and "Grosvenor" Notes. Sixth year, 1888, 200 Illustrations. Demy 8vo. 2s.

Academy Sketches, 1883, 1884, 1885, in One vol. 600 Illustrations. Demy 8vo. 6s.

Æsop, the Fables of, and other Eminent Mythologists. With Morals and Reflections. By Sir Roger L'Estrange, kt. A facsimile reprint of the Edition of 1669. Fcap. Folio, antique, sheep. 21s.

Akbar: An Eastern Romance. By Dr. P. A. S. Van Limburg-Brouwer. Translated from the Dutch by M. M. With Notes and Introductory Life of the Emperor Akbar, by Clements R. Markham, C.B., F.R.S. Cr. 8vo. 10s. 6d.

Alexander II., Emperor of all the Russias, Life of. By the Author of "Science, Art, and Literature in Russia," "Life and Times of Alexander I.," &c. Cr. 8vo. 10s. 6d.

ALFORD, HENRY, D.D., the late Dean of Canterbury.
The New Testament. After the Authorised Version. Newly compared with the original Greek, and Revised. Long Primer, Cr. 8vo., cloth, red edges, 6s.; Brevier, Fcap. 8vo., cloth, 3s. 6d.; Nonpareil, small 8vo., 1s. 6d., or in calf extra, red edges, 4s. 6d.

How to Study the New Testament. Vol. I. The Gospels and the Acts. Vol. II. The Epistles, Part 1. Vol. III. The Epistles, Part 2, and The Revelation. Three vols. Small 8vo. 3s. 6d. each.

ALGER, J. G.
The New Paris Sketch Book. Men, Manners, and Institutions. Crown 8vo. 6s.

AMEER ALI, SYED, MOULVI, M.A., LL.B., Barrister-at-Law.
The Personal Law of the Mahommedans (according to all The Schools). Together with a Comparative Sketch of the Law of Inheritance among the Sunnis and Shiahs. Demy 8vo. 15s.

ANDERSON, EDWARD L.
How to Ride and School a Horse. With a System of Horse Gymnastics. Cr. 8vo 2s. 6d.

A System of School Training for Horses. Cr. 8vo. 2s. 6d.

ANDERSON, THOMAS, *Parliamentary Reporter, &c.*
  History of Shorthand. With an analysis and review of its present condition and prospects in Europe and America. With Portraits. Cr. 8vo. 12s. 6d.
  Catechism of Shorthand; being a Critical Examination of the various Styles, with special reference to the question, Which is the best English System of Shorthand? Fcap. 8vo. 1s.

ANDREW, *Sir WILLIAM PATRICK, C.I E , M.R.A.S., F.R.G.S., F.S.A.*
  India and Her Neighbours. With Two Maps. Demy 8vo. 15s.
  Our Scientific Frontier. With Sketch-Map and Appendix Demy 8vo. 6s.
  Euphrates Valley Route, in connection with the Central Asian and Egyptian Questions. Lecture delivered at the National Club, 16th June 1882. Roy. 8vo., with 2 Maps. 5s.
  Through Booking of Goods between the Interior of India and the United Kingdom. Demy 8vo. 2s.
  Indian Railways as Connected with the British Empire in the East. Fourth Edition. With Map and Appendix. Demy 8vo. 10s. 6d.

ANDREW, W. R.
  Life of Sir Henry Raeburn, R.A. With Portait and Appendix. Demy 8vo. 10s. 6d.

ANGELL, H C., M.D.
  The Sight, and How to Preserve it. With Numerous Illustrations. Fifth Thousand. Fcap. 8vo. 1s. 6d.

ANSTED, *Professor DAVID THOMAS, M A., F.R.S., &c*
  Physical Geography. Fifth Edition. With Illustrative Maps. Post 8vo. 7s.
  Elements of Physiography. For the Use of Science Schools. Fcap. 8vo. 1s. 4d.
  The World We Live In. Or, First Lessons in Physical Geography. For the use of Schools and Students. Twenty-fifth Thousand, with Illustrations. Fcap. 8vo. 2s.
  The Earth's History. Or, First Lessons in Geology. For the use of Schools and Students. Third Thousand. Fcap. 8vo. 2s.
  Two Thousand Examination Questions in Physical Geography. pp. 180. Fcap. 8vo. 2s.
  Water, and Water Supply. Chiefly with reference to the British Islands. Part I.—Surface Waters. With Maps. Demy 8vo. 18s.
  The Applications of Geology to the Arts and Manufactures. Illustrated. Fcap. 8vo., cloth. 4s.

AQUARIUS.
  Books on Games at Cards. Piquet and Cribbage—New Games at Cards principally for Three Players—Tarocco and Tresillo—Norseman—New Games with Cards and Dice—Écarté and other Games—Imperial and other Games for Two Players—Round Games, English and Foreign. Crown 16mo. 1s. each.

ARCHER, *Capt. J. H. LAWRENCE, Bengal H. P.*
  Commentaries on the Punjaub Campaign—1848-49, including some additions to the History of the Second Sikh War, from original sources. Cr. 8vo. 8s.
  The Orders of Chivalry, from the Original Statutes of the various Orders of Knighthood and other sources of information. With 3 Portraits and 63 Plates. 4to. Coloured, £6 6s. Plain, £3 3s.

Army and Navy Calendar for the Financial Year 1888-89. Being a Compendium of General Information relating to the Army, Navy, Militia, and Volunteers, and containing Maps, Plans, Tabulated Statements, Abstracts, &c. Compiled from authentic sources. Published Annually. Demy 8vo. 2s. 6d.

Army and Navy Magazine. Vols. I. to XIV. are issued. Demy 8vo. 7s. 6d. each. Monthly, 1s.

BAGOT, A. G.
Shooting and Yachting in the Mediterranean. With some Practical Hints to Yachtsmen. Second Edition. Crown 8vo. 1s.

BAILDON, SAMUEL, *Author of "Tea in Assam."*
The Tea Industry in India. A Review of Finance and Labour, and a Guide for Capitalists and Assistants. Demy 8vo. 10s. 6d.

BARNARD, H.
Oral Training Lessons in Natural Science and General Knowledge: Embracing the subjects of Astronomy, Anatomy, Physiology, Chemistry, Mathematics and Geography. Cr. 8vo. 2s. 6d.

BAYLEY, Sir EDWARD CLIVE, K.C.S.I.
The Local Muhammadan Dynasties. GUJARAT. Forming a Sequel to Sir H. M. Elliot's "History of the Muhammadan Empire of India." Demy 8vo. 21s.

BAYLISS, WYKE.
The Higher Life in Art: with a Chapter on Hobgoblins, by the Great Masters. Illustrated. Second Edition Cr. 8vo. 6s.

BELLEW, *Captain.*
Memoirs of a Griffin; or, A Cadet's First Year in India. Illustrated from Designs by the Author. A New Edition. Cr. 8vo. 10s. 6d

BENTON, SAMUEL, L.R.C.P., &c.
Home Nursing, and How to Help in Cases of Accident. Illustrated with 19 Woodcuts. Cr. 8vo. 2s. 6d.

BERRINGTON, B. S.
Fortunes of Albert Travers. A Tale of the Eighteenth Century. Cr. 8vo. 6s.

BERRINGTON, JAS.
The Self-Tests Series: I.—French. Fcap. roan. 5s.

BIOGRAPHIES OF GREAT COMPOSERS.
Handel. By J. Cuthbert Hadden. With Portrait. Fcap. 1s. 6d.
Mendelssohn. By J. Cuthbert Hadden. (*In preparation.*)

BOILEAU, *Major-General J. T.*
A New and Complete Set of Traverse Tables, showing the Differences of Latitude and the Departures to every Minute of the Quadrant and to Five Places of Decimals. Together with a Table of the Lengths of each Degree of Latitude and corresponding Degree of Longitude from the Equator to the Poles; with other Tables useful to the Surveyor and Engineer. Fourth Edition, thoroughly revised and corrected by the Author. 1876. Roy. 8vo. 12s.

BOULGER, DEMETRIUS CHARLES, M.R.A.S.
History of China. Demy 8vo. Vol. I., with Portrait, 18s. Vol. II., 18s. Vol. III., with Portraits and Map, 28s.
England and Russia in Central Asia. With Appendices and Two Maps, one being the latest Russian Official Map of Central Asia. 2 vols. Demy 8vo. 36s.
Central Asian Portraits; or, The Celebrities of the Khanates and the Neighbouring States. Cr. 8vo. 7s. 6d.
The Life of Yakoob Beg, Athalik Ghazi and Badaulet, Ameer of Kashgar. With Map and Appendix. Demy 8vo. 16s.

BOWLES, THOMAS GIBSON, *Master Mariner.*
Flotsam and Jetsam. A Yachtsman's Experiences at Sea and Ashore. Cr. 8vo. 7s. 6d.

BOYD, R. NELSON, F.R.G.S., F.G.S., &c.
Chili and the Chilians, during the War 1879-80. Cloth, Illustrated. Cr. 8vo. 10s. 6d.
Coal Mines Inspection; Its History and Results. Demy 8vo. 14s.

BRADSHAW, JOHN, LL.D., Inspector of Schools, Madras.

The Poetical Works of John Milton, with Notes, explanatory and philological. New Edition. Post 8vo. 7s. 6d.

BRADSHAW, Mrs. J.

Gabrielle ; or, Worth the Winning. Crown 8vo. 5s.

BRAITHWAITE, R., M.D., F.L.S., &c.

The Sphagnaceae, or Peat Mosses of Europe and North America. Illustrated with 29 Plates, coloured by hand. Imp. 8vo. 25s.

BRANDE, Professor, D.C.L., F.R.S., &c , and Professor, A. S. TAYLOR, M.D., F.R.S., &c.

Chemistry, a Manual of. Fcap. 8vo. 900 pages. 12s. 6d.

BRANDIS, Dr., Inspector-General of Forests to the Government of India.

The Forest Flora of North-Western and Central India. Text Demy 8vo. and Plates Roy. 4to. £2 18s.

BRERETON, WILLIAM H., late of Hong Kong, Solicitor.

The Truth about Opium. Being the Substance of Three Lectures delivered at St. James's Hall. Demy 8vo. 7s. 6d. Cheap edition, sewed, Cr. 8vo., 1s.

BRIGHT, W., late Colour-Sergeant 19th Middlesex R.V.

Red Book for Sergeants. Sixth and Revised Edition, 1886. Interleaved. Fcap. 8vo., 1s.

BRISTOWE, J.S., M.D., F.R.C.P., Senior Physician and Joint Lecturer on Medicine, St. Thomas's Hospital.

The Physiological and Pathological Relations of the Voice and Speech. Illustrated. Demy 8vo. 7s. 6d.

British Pharmacopœia, Pocket Guide to the, Being an Explanatory Classification of its Drugs, Preparations, and Compounds. All essentials being comprised in a form and size adapted to the Practitioner's Note Book. 1s.

BROWNE, G. LATHOM.

Wellington ; or, the Public and Private Life of Arthur first Duke of Wellington, as told by himself, his Comrades, and intimate Friends. With Portrait, &c. Cr. 8vo. 6s.

BUCKLAND, C.T., F.Z.S.

Whist for Beginners. Second Edition. Cr. 16mo. 1s.
Sketches of Social Life in India. Cr. 8vo. 5s.

BUCKLE, the late Captain E., Assistant Adjutant-General, Bengal Artillery.

Bengal Artillery. A Memoir of the Services of the Bengal Artillery from the formation of the Corps. Edited by Sir J. W. Kaye. Demy 8vo. 10s.

BUCKLEY, ROBERT B., A.M.I.C.E., Executive Engineer to the Public Works Department of India.

The Irrigation Works of India, and their Financial Results. Being a brief History and Description of the Irrigation Works of India, and of the Profits and Losses they have caused to the State. With Map and Appendix. Demy 8vo. 9s.

BURBIDGE, F. W.

Cool Orchids, and How to Grow Them. With Descriptive List of all the best Species in Cultivation. Illustrated with numerous Woodcuts and Coloured Figures of 13 varieties. Cr. 8vo. 6s.

BURGESS, Captain F. Bengal Staff Corps.

Sporting Fire-arms for Bush and Jungle ; or, Hints to Intending Griffs and Colonists on the Purchase, Care, and Use of Fire-arms, with Useful Notes on Sporting Rifles, &c. Illustrated by the Author. Cr. 8vo. 5s.

BURKE, PETER, Serjeant-at-Law.

Celebrated Naval and Military Trials. Post 8vo. 10s. 6d

BURNLEY, JAMES, Author of "The Romance of Invention."
The Romance of Life Preservation. Cr. 8vo. 10s. 6d.

BURROWS, MONTAGU, Captain R.N., Retired List, Chichele Professor of Modern History in the University of Oxford.
Life of Edward Lord Hawke, Admiral of the Fleet, Vice-Admiral of Great Britain, and First Lord of the Admiralty from 1766 to 1771. Demy 8vo. 21s.

Byron Birthday Book, The. Compiled and edited by James Burrows. New Edition. 16mo. 2s. 6d.

CANNING, The Hon. ALBERT S. G., Author of "Macaulay, Essayist and Historian," &c.
Thoughts on Shakespeare's Historical Plays. Demy 8vo. 13s.
Revolted Ireland, 1798 to 1803. Crown 8vo. 3s. 6d.

CARLYLE, THOMAS.
Memoirs of the Life and Writings of, With Personal Reminiscences and Selections from his Private Letters to numerous Correspondents. Edited by Richard Herne Shepherd, Assisted by Charles N. Williamson. 2 vols. With Portrait and Illustrations. Cr. 8vo. 21s.

CARRINGTON B., M.D., F.R.S
British Hepaticæ. Containing Descriptions and Figures of the Native Species of Jungermannia, Marchantia, and Anthoceros. Imp. 8vo., sewed, Parts 1 to 4, each 2s. 6d. plain; 3s. 6d. coloured. To be completed in about 12 Parts.

CAVENAGH, Gen. Sir ORFEUR, K.C.S.I.
Reminiscences of an Indian Official. Cr. 8vo. 10s. 6d.

Challenge of Barletta, The. By Massimo D'Azeglio. Rendered into English by Lady Louisa Magenis. 2 vols., Cr. 8vo 21s.

CHAMISSO, ADALBERT VON.
Peter Schlemihl. Translated by Sir John Bowring, LL D., &c. Illustrations on India paper by George Cruikshank. Large paper, Cr. 4to., half-Roxburghe, 10s. 6d.

CHAYTOR, HENRY.
Secrets of National Finance. Demy 8vo. 3s. 6d.
Chesney, General F. R., Life of. By his Wife and Daughter. Edited by Stanley Lane-Poole. 8vo. 18s.
Civil Service Calendar. Official Regulations and Instructions for Candidates, &c., forming a Complete Handbook and Guide to the Civil Service. Edited by William Bussell. Issued Yearly. Cr. 8vo. 1s. 6d. Cloth 2s.
Collection Catalogue for Naturalists. A Ruled Book for keeping a Permanent Record of Objects in any branch of Natural History, with Appendix for recording interesting particulars, and lettered pages for general Index Strongly bound, 200 pages, 7s 6d ; 300 pages, 10s.; and 2s. 6d. extra for every additional 100 pages. Working Catalogues, 1s. 6d. each.

CLARKE, Captain H. W.
Longitude by Lunar Distances. Illustrated with examples worked out step by step, and with references to works on Practical Astronomy, &c. Royal 8vo. 7s. 6d.
The Sextant. Small 4to. 2s.

COLLINS, MABEL.
The Story of Helena Modjeska (Madame Chlapowska). Cr. 8vo. 7s. 6d.

COLOMB, Colonel.
Blue Stockings. A Comedy in Five Acts. Adapted from the French of Molière. Cr. 8vo. 3s. 6d.
Miss Crusoes. A Curious Story for Big and Little Children. Illustrated. Cr. 8vo. 3s. 6d.
Donnington Castle: a Royalist Story. Three Volumes. Crown 8vo. 31s. 6d.
For King and Kent: a True Story of the Great Rebellion. 10s. 6d.

COLQUHOUN, *Major J. A. S., R.A.*
With the Kurrum Force in the Caubul Campaign of 1878-79. With Illustrations from the Author's Drawings, and two Maps. Demy 8vo. 16s.

Companion to the Writing-Desk. How to Address Titled People, &c. Roy. 32mo. 1s.

CONDER, ALFRED.
The Discontent of Ireland: Its Origin and Cause. Crown 8vo. 6s.

COOKE, M. C., M A., LL.D.
The British Fungi: A Plain and Easy Account of. With Coloured Plates of 40 Species. Fifth Edition, Revised. Cr. 8vo. 6s.
British Hepaticæ. Sewed 8d.
Rust, Smut, Mildew, and Mould. An Introduction to the Study of Microscopic Fungi. Illustrated with 269 Coloured Figures by J. E. Sowerby. Fourth Edition, with Appendix of New Species. Cr. 8vo. 6s.
A Manual of Structural Botany. Revised Edition, with New Chemical Notation. Illustrated with 200 Woodcuts. Twenty-fifth Thousand. 32mo. 1s.
A Manual of Botanic Terms. New Edition, greatly Enlarged. Illustrated with over 300 Woodcuts Fcap. 8vo. 2s. 6d.

COOKE, M. C., M.A., A.L.S , et L. QUELET, M.D , O.A., Inst. et Sorb. laur.
Clavis Synoptica Hymenomycetum Europæorum. Fcap. 8vo. 7s. 6d.

Cooper's Hill Royal Indian Engineering College, Calendar of. Published (by Authority) in January each year. Demy 8vo. 5s.

COPLAND, JOHN
Walter Stanhope, a Man of varied Sympathies. Cr. 8vo. 6s.

CORBET, Mrs. M. E.
A Pleasure Trip to India, during the Visit of H.R.H. the Prince of Wales, and afterwards to Ceylon. Illustrated with Photos. Cr. 8vo. 7s. 6d.

COXWELL, HENRY
My Life and Balloon Experiences. Portrait. Crown 8vo. 3s. 6d.

CRESSWELL, C. N., of the Inner Temple.
Woman, and her Work in the World. Cr. 8vo. 3s. 6d.

CROSLAND, Mrs. NEWTON.
Stories of the City of London: Retold for Youthful Readers. With 10 Illustrations. Cr. 8vo. 6s.

Crown of Life, The. By M. Y. W. With elegantly illuminated borders from designs by Arthur Robertson, Fcap. 4to. 6s.

Cruise of H.M.S. "Galatea," Captain H.R.H. the Duke of Edinburgh, K G., in 1867-1868. By the Rev. John Milner, B.A, Chaplain; and Oswald W. Brierly. Illustrated by a Photograph of H.R.H. the Duke of Edinburgh; and by Chromo-lithographs and Graphotypes from Sketches taken on the spot by O. W. Brierly. Demy 8vo. 16s.

CUNNINGHAM, H. S., M A., one of the Judges of the High Court of Calcutta, and late Member of the Famine Commission.
British India, and its Rulers. Demy 8vo. 10s. 6d.

CUVIER, BARON.
The Animal Kingdom. With considerable Additions by W. B. Carpenter, M.D., F.R.S., and J O. Westwood, F.L.S. New Edition, Illustrated with 500 Engravings on Wood and 36 Coloured Plates. Imp. 8vo. 21s.

DALTON, C.
Memoir of Captain Dalton, H.E.I.C.S., Defender of Trichinopoly. With Portrait. Cr. 8vo. 6s.

DAMANT, MARY.
Peggy Thornhill. A Tale of the Irish Rebellion. Cr. 8vo. 7s. 6d.

DAUMAS, E., General of the Division Commanding at Bordeaux, Senator, &c. &c.
Horses of the Sahara, and the Manners of the Desert. With Commentaries by the Emir Abd-el-Kadir (Authorized Edition). Demy 8vo. 6s.

DAVIDSON, H. C.
    Mad or Married? A Manx Story. Cr. 8vo. 2s. 6d.

DAVIES, THOMAS.
    The Preparation and Mounting of Microscopic Objects. New Edition, greatly Enlarged and brought up to the Present Time by John Matthews, M.D., F.R.M.S., Vice-President of the Quekett Microscopical Club. Fcap. 8vo. 2s. 6d.

DAVIS, GEORGE E., F.R.M.S., F.C.S., F.I.C., &c.
    Practical Microscopy. Illustrated with 257 Woodcuts and a Coloured Frontispiece. Demy 8vo. 7s. 6d.

DICKENS, CHARLES.
    Plays and Poems, with a few Miscellanies in Prose. Now first collected. Edited, Prefaced, and Annotated by Richard Herne Shepherd. 2 vols. Demy 8vo. 21s.
        Edition de Luxe. 2 vols. Imp. 8vo. (Only 150 copies printed.)

DICKINS, FREDERICK V., Sc.B. of the Middle Temple, Barrister-at-law (translator).
    Chiushingura; or the Loyal League. A Japanese Romance. With Notes and an Appendix containing a Metrical Version of the Ballad of Takasako, and a specimen of the Original Text in Japanese character. Illustrated by numerous Engravings on Wood, drawn and executed by Japanese artists and printed on Japanese paper. Roy. 8vo. 10s. 6d.

Diplomatic Study on the Crimean War, 1852 to 1856. (Russian Official Publication.) 2 vols. Demy 8vo. 28s.

DOUGLAS, Mrs. MINNIE
    Countess Violet; or, What Grandmamma saw in the Fire. A Book for Girls. Illustrated. Cr. 8vo. 3s. 6d.
    Grandmother's Diamond Ring. A Tale for Girls. Cr. 8vo. 2s. 6d.

Dresden Gallery. Handbook of the Italian Schools. By C. J. Ff. With Illustrations. Cr. 8vo. 3s. 6d.

DRURY, Col. HEBER.
    The Useful Plants of India, with Notices of their chief value in Commerce, Medicine, and the Arts. Second Edition, with Additions and Corrections. Roy. 8vo. 16s.

DUKE, JOSHUA, F.R.A.S., Bengal Medical Service.
    Recollections of the Kabul Campaign 1879-1880. Illustrations and Map. Demy 8vo. 15s.

DURAND, HENRY MARION, C.S.I., Bengal Civil Service, Barrister-at-law.
    The Life of Major-General Sir Henry Marion Durand, K.C.S.I., C.B., of the Royal Engineers. With Portrait. 2 vols. Demy 8vo. 42s.

DURTNALL, ARTHUR A. (of the High Court of Justice in England).
    A Chronological and Historical Chart of India, showing, at one view, all the principal nations, governments, and empires which have existed in that country from the earliest times to the suppression of the Great Mutiny, A.D. 1858, with the date of each historical event according to the various eras used in India. Price, fully tinted, mounted on roller or in case, 20s. Size, about 40 in. by 5 in

DUTTON, Major the Hon. CHARLES.
    Life in India. Cr. 8vo. 2s. 6d.

DWIGHT, HENRY O.
    Turkish Life in War Time. Cr. 8vo. 12s.

DYER, The Rev. T. F. THISTLETON, M.A.
    English Folk-lore. Second Edition. Cr. 8vo. 5s.

EMINENT WOMEN SERIES. *Edited by JOHN H. INGRAM.* Cr. 8vo. 3s. 6d.

> BLIND, MATHILDE.
>> George Eliot.
>> Madame Roland.
>
> ROBINSON, A. MARY F.
>> Emily Bronte.
>> Margaret of Angoulême, Queen of Navarre.
>
> THOMAS, BERTHA.
>> George Sand.
>
> GILCHRIST, ANNE.
>> Mary Lamb.
>
> HOWE, JULIA WARD.
>> Margaret Fuller.
>
> ZIMMERN, HELEN.
>> Maria Edgeworth.
>
> PITMAN, Mrs. E. R.
>> Elizabeth Fry.
>
> LEE, VERNON.
>> Countess of Albany.
>
> MILLER, Mrs. FENWICK.
>> Harriet Martineau.
>
> PENNELL, ELIZABETH ROBINS.
>> Mary Wollstonecraft Godwin.
>
> KENNARD, Mrs. A.
>> Rachel.
>> Mrs. Siddons.
>
> CLARKE, ELIZA.
>> Susanna Wesley.
>
> DUFFY, BELLA.
>> Madame de Stael.
>
> CHARLOTTE M. YONGE.
>> Hannah More.
>
> JOHN H. INGRAM.
>> Elizabeth Barrett Browning.

ENSOR, F. SYDNEY, C.E.
Incidents of a Journey through Nubia to Darfoor. 10s. 6d.
The Queen's Speeches in Parliament, from Her Accession to the present time. A Compendium of the History of Her Majesty's Reign told from the Throne. Cr. 8vo. 7s. 6d.

EYRE, Major-General Sir V., K.C.S.I., C.B.
The Kabul Insurrection of 1841-42. Revised and corrected from Lieut. Eyre's Original Manuscript. Edited by Colonel G. B. Malleson, C.S.I. With Map and Illustrations. Cr. 8vo. 9s.

FINCH-HATTON, HON. HAROLD.
Advance Australia! An Account of Eight Years Work, Wandering, and Amusement in Queensland, New South Wales, and Victoria. Map and Plates. New edition. Crown 8vo. 7s. 6d.

FLEET, F. R.
Analysis of Wit and Humour. Second edition. Crown 8vo. 2s. 6d.

Following the Drum. Sketches of Soldier Life in Peace and War, Past and Present. The Verses selected and Illustrated by Richard Simkin. Small 4to. 1s.

FORBES, Capt. C. J. F. S., of the British Burma Commission.
Comparative Grammar of the Languages of Further India. A Fragment; and other Essays, being the Literary Remains of the Author. Demy 8vo. 6s.

Foreign Office, Diplomatic and Consular Sketches. Reprinted from "Vanity Fair." Cr. 8vo. 6s.

FOURNIER, ALFRED, *Professeur à la Faculté de Médecine de Paris, Médecin de l'Hôpital Saint Louis, Membre de l'Académie de Médecine.*

Syphilis and Marriage: Lectures delivered at the Hospital of St. Louis. Translated by Alfred Lingard. Cr. 8vo. 10s. 6d.

FRASER, *Lieut.-Col. G. T., formerly of 1st Bombay Fusiliers, and recently attached to the Staff of H.M. Indian Army.*

Records of Sport and Military Life in Western India. With an Introduction by Colonel G. B. Malleson, C.S.I. Cr. 8vo 7s. 6d

FRY, HERBERT.

London in 1888. Its Suburbs and Environs. Illustrated with 8 Bird's-eye Views of the Principal Streets, and a Map. Sixth year of publication. Revised and Enlarged Cr 8vo. 2s.

GALL, *Capt. H. R., late 5th Fusiliers*

Modern Tactics. Text and Plates. 2 vols. Demy 8vo. 10s. 6d.

Gazetteer of Southern India. With the Tenasserim Provinces and Singapore. Compiled from original and authentic sources. Accompanied by an Atlas, including plans of all the principal towns and cantonments. With 4to. Atlas. Roy. 8vo. £3 3s.

Geography of India. Comprising an account of British India and the various states enclosed and adjoining. pp. 250. Fcap 8vo. 2s

Geological Papers on Western India. Including Cutch, Scinde, and the south-east coast of Arabia To which is added a Summary of the Geology of India generally. Edited for the Government by Henry J. Carter, Assistant Surgeon, Bombay Army. With folio Atlas of Maps and Plates; half-bound. Roy. 8vo. £2 2s.

GIBNEY, *Major R. D., late Adj. 1st Wilts R.V.*

Earnest Madement; a Tale of Wiltshire Dedicated by permission to Lieut.-Gen. Sir Garnet Wolseley, G.C.B. Cr. 8vo. 6s.

Gibraltar (To) and Back. By One of the Crew. With Chart, Illustrations from Sketches by Barlow, Moore, and Photographs. Cr. 8vo. 6s.

GILLMORE, PARKER (UBIQUE).

Prairie and Forest. A description of the Game of North America, with Personal Adventures in its Pursuit. With 37 Illustrations Cr. 8vo. 7s. 6d.

GOLDSTUCKER, *Prof. THEODORE, The late.*

The Literary Remains of. With a Memoir. 2 vols. Demy 8vo. 21s.

GOULD, CHARLES, B.A., *late Geological Surveyor of Tasmania, &c.*

Mythical Monsters. Royal 8vo., with Coloured Frontispiece and Ninety-three Illustrations. 25s.

GRAHAM, ALEXANDER

Genealogical and Chronological Tables, illustrative of Indian History. Demy 4to. 5s.

GRANVILLE, J. MORTIMER, M.D.

The Care and Cure of the Insane. 2 vols. Demy 8vo. 36s.
Change as a Mental Restorative. Demy 8vo. 1s.
Nerves and Nerve Troubles. Fcap. 8vo. 1s.
Common Mind Troubles. Fcap. 8vo. 1s.
How to make the Best of Life. Fcap. 8vo. 1s.
Youth: Its Care and Culture. Post 8vo. 2s. 6d.
The Secret of a Clear Head. Fcap. 8vo. 1s.
The Secret of a Good Memory. Fcap. 8vo. 1s.
Sleep and Sleeplessness. Fcap. 8vo. 1s.

GRAY, MELVILLE.

A Life's Trouble: a Story of the Nineteenth Century. Crown 8vo. 5s
Una's Revenge. A Picture of Real Life in the Nineteenth Century. Crown 8vo. 3s. 6d.

GREENE, F. V., Lieut. U.S. Army, and lately Military Attaché to the U. S. Legation at St. Petersburg.

The Russian Army and its Campaigns in Turkey in 1877-1878. Second Edition. Roy 8vo. 32s.
Sketches of Army Life in Russia. Cr. 8vo. 9s.

GREG, PERCY.

History of the United States from the Foundation of Virginia to the Reconstruction of the Union. 2 vols. demy 8vo., with Maps. 32s.

GRIESINGER, THEODOR.

The Jesuits; a Complete History of their Open and Secret Proceedings from the Foundation of the Order to the Present Time. Translated by A. J. Scott, M.D. Illustrated. Second Edition. One Volume. Demy 8vo. 10s. 6d.

GRIFFIS, WILLIAM ELLIOT, late of the Imperial University of Tokio, Japan.
Corea, the Hermit Nation. Roy. 8vo. 18s.

Grove's System of Medical Book-keeping. The Complete Set, 4to., £4 14s. 6d.

HALL, E. HEPPLE, F.S.S.
Lands of Plenty for Health, Sport, and Profit. British North America. A Book for all Travellers and Settlers. With Maps. Cr. 8vo. 6s.

HALL, The Rev. T. G., M.A., Prof. of Mathematics in King's College, London.
The Elements of Plane and Spherical Trigonometry. With an Appendix, containing the solution of the Problems in Nautical Astronomy. For the use of Schools. 12mo. 2s.

Handbook of Reference to the Maps of India. Giving the Lat. and Long. of places of note Demy 18mo. 3s. 6d.

> *⁎* *This will be found a valuable Companion to Messrs. Allen & Co.'s Maps of India.*

HARCOURT-ROE, Mrs.
Whose Wife? Cr. 8vo. 6s.

Hardwicke's Elementary Books, paper covers: Chemistry, 6d. Mechanics, 2 parts, 4d.; Hydrostatics, 2d.; Hydraulics, 2d.; Pneumatics, 2d.

HARDWICKE, HERBERT JUNIUS, M.D., &c.
> **Health Resorts and Spas**; or, Climatic and Hygienic Treatment of Disease. Fcap. 8vo. 2s. 6d.

HARTING, JAMES EDMUND.
> **Sketches of Bird Life.** With numerous Illustrations. Demy 8vo 10s. 6d.

HAWEIS, Rev. H. R.
> **Music and Morals.** Thirteenth Edition. With Portraits. Cr. 8vo. 7s. 6d.
> **My Musical Life.** 2nd Edition. With Portraits. Cr. 8vo. 7s. 6d.

HAWEIS, Mrs.
> **Chaucer's Beads:** A Birthday Book, Diary, and Concordance of Chaucer's Proverbs or Sooth-saws. Cr. 8vo, vellum. 5s.; paper boards, 4s. 6d.

Health Primers. 1. Premature Death. 2. Alcohol. 3. Exercise and Training. 4. The House. 5. Personal Appearances. 6. Baths and Bathing. 7. The Skin. 8. The Heart. 9. The Nervous System. 10 Health in Schools. Demy 16mo. 1s. each.

HEINE, HEINRICH.
> **The Book of Songs.** Translated from the German by Stratheir. Cr. 8vo. 7s. 6d.

HELMS, LUDWIG VERNER.
> **Pioneering in the Far East,** and Journeys to California in 1849, and to the White Sea in 1878. With Illustrations from original Sketches and Photographs, and Maps. Demy 8vo. 18s.

HENNEBERT, Lieutenant-Colonel.
> **The English in Egypt**; England and the Mahdi—Arabi and the Suez Canal. Translated from the French (by permission) by Bernard Paunce-fote. 3 Maps. Cr. 8vo. 2s. 6d.

HENSMAN, HOWARD, Special Correspondent of the " Pioneer" (Allahabad), and the "Daily News" (London).
> **The Afghan War, 1879-80.** Being a complete Narrative of the Capture of Cabul, the Siege of Sherpur, the Battle of Ahmed Khel, the brilliant March to Candahar, and the Defeat of Ayub Khan, with the Operations on the Helmund, and the Settlement with Abdur Rahman Khan. With Maps. Demy 8vo. 21s.

HERRICK, SOPHIE BLEDSOE.
> **The Wonders of Plant Life under the Microscope.** With numerous Illustrations. Small 4to. 6s.

HERSCHEL, Sir JOHN F. W., Bt., K.H., &c., Member of the Institute of France, &c.
> **Popular Lectures on Scientific Subjects.** Cr. 8vo. 6s.

HILLAM, S. A.
> **Sheykh Hassan, the Spiritualist.** A View of the Supernatural. Cr. 8vo. 3s. 6d.

HODGSON, W. EARL.
> **Unrest**; or, The Newer Republic. Crown 8vo. 6s.

HOLDEN, EDWARD S., *United States Naval Observatory.*

Sir William Herschel: His Life and Works. Cr. 8vo. 6s.

Holland. Translated from the Italian of Edmondo Amicis, by Caroline Tilton. Cr. 8vo. 10s. 6d.

HOLMES, T. R. E.

A History of the Indian Mutiny, and of the Disturbances which accompanied it among the Civil Population. Third Edition. With Maps and Plans. Cr. 8vo. 7s. 6d.

HOOKER, Sir W. J., F.R.S., and J. G. BAKER, F.L S.

Synopsis Filicum; or, a Synopsis of all Known Ferns, including the Osmundaceæ, Schizæaceæ, Marratiaceæ, and Ophioglossaceæ (chiefly derived from the Kew Herbarium), accompanied by Figures representing the essential Characters of each Genus. Second Edition, brought up to the present time. Coloured Plates. Demy 8vo. £1 8s.

HOWDEN, PETER, V S.

Horse Warranty: a Plain and Comprehensive Guide to the various Points to be noted, showing which are essential and which are unimportant. With Forms of Warranty. Fcap. 8vo. 3s. 6d.

HUGHES, Rev. T. P.

Notes on Muhammadanism. Second Edition, revised and enlarged. Fcap. 8vo. 6s.

A Dictionary of Islam. Being a Cyclopædia of the Doctrines, Rites, Ceremonies, and Customs, together with the Technical and Theological Terms, of the Muhammadan Religion. With numerous Illustrations. Royal 8vo. £2 2s.

HUNT, Major S. LEIGH, Madras Army, and ALEX. S. KENNY, M.R.C.S.E., A.K.C., Senior Demonstrator of Anatomy at King's College, London.

On Duty under a Tropical Sun. Being some Practical Suggestions for the Maintenance of Health and Bodily Comfort, and the Treatment of Simple Diseases; with Remarks on Clothing and Equipment for the Guidance of Travellers in Tropical Countries. Second Edition. Cr. 8vo. 4s.

Tropical Trials. A Handbook for Women in the Tropics. Cr. 8vo. 7s. 6d

HUNTER, J., late Hon. Sec. of the British Bee-Keepers' Association.

A Manual of Bee-Keeping. Containing Practical Information for Rational and Profitable Methods of Bee Management. Full Instructions on Stimulative Feeding, Ligurianizing and Queen-raising, with descriptions of the American Comb Foundation, Sectional Supers, and the best Hives and Apiarian Appliances on all systems. With Illustrations. Fourth Edition. Cr. 8vo. 3s. 6d.

HUTTON, JAMES.

The Thugs and Dacoits of India. A Popular Account of the Thugs and Dacoits, the Hereditary Garotters and Gang Robbers of India. Post 8vo. 5s.

India Directory, The. For the Guidance of Commanders of Steamers and Sailing Vessels. Founded upon the Work of the late Captain James Horsburgh, F.R.S.

Part I.—The East Indies, and Interjacent Ports of Africa and South America. Revised, Extended, and Illustrated with Charts of Winds, Currents, Passages, Variation, and Tides. By Commander Alfred Dundas Taylor, F.R.G.S., Superintendent of Marine Surveys to the Government of India. Sup. roy. 8vo. £1 18s.

Part II.—The China Sea, with the Ports of Java, Australia, and Japan, and the Indian Archipelago Harbours, as well as those of New Zealand. Illustrated with Charts of the Winds, Currents, Passages, &c. By the same. (*In preparation.*)

INGRAM, JOHN H.

The Haunted Homes and Family Traditions of Great Britain. New and cheaper edition, in one vol. 6s.

In the Company's Service. A Reminiscence. Demy 8vo. 10s. 6d.

Ireland, Letters from, 1886. By the Special Correspondent of "The Times." Crown 8vo. 2s. 6d.

IRWIN, H. C., B.A., Oxon, Bengal Civil Service.

The Garden of India; or, Chapters on Oudh History and Affairs. Demy 8vo. 12s.

JACKSON, LOWIS D'A., A.M.I.C.E., Author of "Hydraulic Manual and Statistics," &c.

Canal and Culvert Tables. With Explanatory Text and Examples. New and corrected edition, with 40 pp. of additional Tables. Roy. 8vo. 28s.

Accented Four-Figure Logarithms, and other Tables. For purposes both of Ordinary and of Trigonometrical Calculation, and for the Correction of Altitudes and Lunar Distances. Cr 8vo. 9s.

Accented Five-Figure Logarithms of Numbers from 1 to 99999, without Differences. Roy. 8vo. 16s.

Units of Measurement for Scientific and Professional Men. Cr. 4to. 2s.

JAMES, Mrs. A. G. F. ELIOT.

Indian Industries. Cr. 8vo. 9s.

James' Naval History. Epitomised by Robert O'Byrne, F.R.G.S., &c. Cr. 8vo. 7s. 6d.

JEWITT, LLEWELLYN, F.S.A.

Half-Hours among English Antiquities. Contents: Arms, Armour, Pottery, Brasses, Coins, Church Bells, Glass, Tapestry, Ornaments, Flint Implements, &c. With 304 Illustrations. Second Edition. Cr. 8vo. 5s.

JOHNSON, R. LOCKE, L.R.C.P., L.R.C.I., L.S.A., &c.

Food Chart. Giving the Names, Classification, Composition, Elementary Value, Rates of Digestibility, Adulterations, Tests, &c., of the Alimentary Substances in General Use. In wrapper, 4to., 2s. 6d.; or on roller, varnished, 6s.

JONES, LUCY.

Puddings and Sweets. 365 Receipts approved by Experience. Fcap. 1s.

JOYNER, *Mrs. A. BATSON.*

Cyprus: Historical and Descriptive. Adapted from the German of Herr Franz von Loher. With much additional matter. With 2 Maps. Cr. 8vo. 10s. 6d.

KAYE, *Sir J. W.*

History of the War in Afghanistan. New Edition. 3 vols. Cr. 8vo. £1 6s.

The Sepoy War in India. A History of the Sepoy War in India 1857-1858. By Sir John William Kaye. Demy 8vo. Vol. I., 18s Vol. II., £1. Vol. III., £1.

(For continuation, *see* **History of the Indian Mutiny**, by Colonel G. B. Malleson, Vol. I. of which is contemporary with Vol. III. of Kaye's work.)

KEATINGE, *Mrs.*

English Homes in India. 2 vols. Post 8vo. 16s.

KEBBEL, *T. E.*

History of Toryism. From the Accession of Mr. Pitt to power in 1783, to the Death of Lord Beaconsfield in 1881. Demy 8vo. 16s
This work traces the progress of the Tory theory and the policy of successive Tory Governments during the hundred years which intervened between the rise of the Younger Pitt and the Death of Lord Beaconsfield.

The Agricultural Labourer. A Short Summary of his Position. A New Edition, brought down to date with fresh Chapters on Wages, &c Crown 8vo. 3s. 6d.

KEENE, *HENRY GEORGE, C.I.E., B.C.S., M.R.A.S., &c.*

A Sketch of the History of Hindustan. From the First Muslim Conquest to the Fall of the Mughol Empire. By H. G. Keene, C.I.E., M.R.A.S., Author of "The Turks in India," &c. 8vo. 18s.

The Fall of the Moghul Empire. From the Death of Aurungzeb to the overthrow of the Mahratta Power. A New Edition, with Corrections and Additions. With Map. Crown 8vo. 7s. 6d.

This Work fills up a blank between the ending of Elphinstone's and the commencement of Thornton's Histories.

Administration in India. Post 8vo. 5s.

Peepul Leaves. Poems written in India. Post 8vo. 5s.

Fifty-Seven. Some account of the Administration of Indian Districts during the Revolt of the Bengal Army. Demy 8vo. 6s.

The Turks in India. Historical Chapters on the Administration of Hindostan by the Chugtai Tartar, Babar, and his Descendants. Demy 8vo. 12s. 6d.

Verses. Translated and Original. Fcap. 8vo. 3s. 6d.

KEMPSON, *M., M.A.*

The Repentance of Nussooh. Translated from the original Hindustani tale, with an introduction by Sir Wm. Muir, K.C.S.I. Cr. 8vo. 3s. 6d.

KENNY, *ALEXANDER S., M.R.C.S. Edin., &c.*

The Tissues, and their Structure. Fcap. 8vo. 6s.

KENT, W. SAVILLE, F.L.S., F.Z.S., F.R.M.S., formerly Assistant in the Nat. Hist. Department, the British Museum.

A Manual of the Infusoria. Including a Description of the Flagellate, Ciliate, and Tentaculiferous Protozoa, British and Foreign, and an account of the Organization and Affinities of the Sponges. With numerous Illustrations. Super-roy. 8vo. £4 4s.

KINAHAN, G. H.

A Handy Book of Rock Names. Fcap. 8vo., cloth. 4s.

Knots, the Book of. Illustrated by 172 Examples, showing the manner of making every Knot, Tie, and Splice. By "Tom Bowling." Third Edition. Cr. 8vo. 2s. 6d.

LANE-POOLE, STANLEY, Laureat de l'Institut de France.

Studies in a Mosque. Demy 8vo. 12s.

LANKESTER, Mrs.

Talks about Health: A Book for Boys and Girls. Being an Explanation of all the Processes by which Life is sustained. Illustrated. Small 8vo. 1s.

British Ferns: Their Classification, Arrangement of Genera, Structures, and Functions, Directions for Out-door and Indoor Cultivation, &c. Illustrated with Coloured Figures of all the Species. New and Enlarged Edition. Cr. 8vo. 3s. 6d.

Wild Flowers Worth Notice: A Selection of some of our Native Plants which are most attractive for their Beauty, Uses, or Associations. With 108 Coloured Figures by J. E. Sowerby. New Edition. Cr. 8vo. 5s.

LANKESTER, E., M.D., F.R.S., F.L.S.

Our Food. Illustrated. New Edition. Cr. 8vo. 4s.

Half-hours with the Microscope. With 250 Illustrations. Seventeenth Thousand, enlarged. Fcap. 8vo., plain, 2s. 6d.; coloured, 4s.

Practical Physiology: A School Manual of Health. Numerous Woodcuts. Sixth Edition. Fcap. 8vo. 2s. 6d.

The Uses of Animals in Relation to the Industry of Man. Illustrated. New Edition. Cr. 8vo. 4s.

Sanitary Instructions: A Series of Handbills for General Distribution:—1. Management of Infants; 2. Scarlet Fever and the best Means of Preventing it; 3 Typhoid or Drain Fever, and its Prevention; 4. Small Pox, and its Prevention; 5. Cholera and Diarrhœa, and its Prevention; 6. Measles, and their Prevention. Each, 1d.; per dozen, 6d.; per 100, 4s.; per 1,000, 30s.

LAURIE, Col. W. F. B.

Sketches of some Distinguished Anglo-Indians. With Portrait of Sir John Kaye. Cr. 8vo. 7s. 6d.
             Second Series, with Portrait of Colonel G. B. Malleson. Cr. 8vo. 7s. 6d.

Burma, the Foremost Country: A Timely Discourse. To which is added, How the Frenchman sought to win an Empire in the East. With Notes on the probable effects of French success in Tonquin on British interests in Burma. Cr. 8vo. 2s.

Our Burmese Wars and Relations with Burma. With a Summary of Events from 1826 to 1879, including a Sketch of King Theebau's Progress. With Local, Statistical, andCommercial Information. **Second** Edition. With Plans and Map. Demy 8vo. 10s. 6d.

Ashe Pyee, the Superior Country; or the great attractions of Burma to British Enterprise and Commerce. Cr. 8vo. 5s.

LAW AND PROCEDURE, INDIAN CIVIL.

Mahommedan Law of Inheritance, &c. A Manual of the Mahommedan Law of Inheritance and Contract; comprising the Doctrine of Soonee and Sheea Schools, and based upon the text of Sir H. W. Macnaghten's Principles and Precedents, together with the Decisions of the Privy Council and High Courts of the Presidencies in India. For the use of Schools and Students. By Standish Grove Grady, Barrister-at-Law, Reader of Hindoo, Mahommedan, and Indian Law to the Inns of Court. Demy 8vo. 14s.

Hedaya, or Guide, a Commentary on the Mussulman Laws, translated by order of the Governor-General and Council of Bengal. By Charles Hamilton. Second Edition, with Preface and Index by Standish Grove Grady. Demy 8vo. £1 15s.

Institutes of Menu in English. The Institutes of Hindu Law or the Ordinances of Menu, according to Gloss of Collucca. Comprising the Indian System of Duties, Religious and Civil, verbally translated from the Original, with a Preface by Sir William Jones, and collated with the Sanscrit Text by Graves Chamney Haughton, M.A., F.B.S., Professor of Hindu Literature in the East India College. New Edition, with Preface and Index by Standish G. Grady, Barrister-at-Law, and Reader of Hindu, Mahommedan, and Indian Law to the Inns of Court. Demy 8vo. 12s.

Indian Code of Civil Procedure. Being Act X. of 1877. Demy 8vo. 6s.

Indian Code of Civil Procedure. In the form of Questions and Answers, with Explanatory and Illustrative Notes. By Angelo J. Lewis. Barrister-at-Law. Imp. 12mo. 12s. 6d.

Hindu Law. Defence of the Daya Bhaga. Notice of the Case on Prosoono Coomar Tajore's Will. Judgment of the Judicial Committee of the Privy Council. Examination of such Judgment. By John Cochrane, Barrister-at-Law. Roy. 8vo. 20s.

Law and Customs of Hindu Castes, within the Dekhan Provinces subject to the Presidency of Bombay, chiefly affecting Civil Suits. By Arthur Steele. Roy. 8vo. £1 1s.

Moohummudan Law of Inheritance, and Rights and Relations affecting it (Sunni Doctrine). By Almaric Rumsey. Demy 8vo. 12s.

A Chart of Hindu Family Inheritance. By Almaric Rumsey. Second Edition, much enlarged. Demy 8vo. 6s. 6d.

INDIAN CRIMINAL.

Including the Procedure in the High Courts, as well as that not in the Courts not established by Royal Charter; with Forms of Charges and Notes on Evidence, illustrated by a large number of English Cases, and Cases decided in the High Courts of India; and an Appendix of selected Acts passed by the Legislative Council relating to Criminal matters. By M. H. Starling, Esq., LL.B., and F. B. Constable, M.A. Third Edition. Medium 8vo. £2 2s.

Law and Procedure, Indian Criminal—*cont.*

Indian Code of Criminal Procedure. Being Act X. of 1872, Passed by the Governor-General of India in Council on the 25th of April 1872. Demy 8vo. 12s.

Indian Penal Code. In the form of Questions and Answers. With Explanatory and Illustrative Notes. By Angelo J. Lewis, Barrister-at-Law. Imp. 12mo 7s. 6d.

Indian Code of Criminal Procedure, Act of 1882. Roy. 8vo. cloth. 6s.

MILITARY.

Manual of Military Law. For all ranks of the Army, Militia, and Volunteer Services. By Colonel J. K. Pipon, Assistant Adjutant-General at Head-quarters, and J. F. Collier, Esq., of the Inner Temple, Barrister-at-Law. Third and Revised Edition. Pocket size. 5s.

Precedents in Military Law; including the Practice of Courts-Martial; the Mode of Conducting Trials; the Duties of Officers at Military Courts of Inquests, Courts of Inquiry, Courts of Requests, &c. &c. By Lieut.-Col. W. Hough, late Deputy Judge-Advocate-General, Bengal Army, and Author of several Works on Courts-Martial. One thick Demy 8vo. vol. 25s.

The Practice of Courts-Martial. By Hough and Long. Thick Demy 8vo. London, 1825. 26s.

Leaves from Memory's Log-Book, and Jottings from Old Journals. By An Ancient Mariner. Compiled and Edited by C. A. Montresor. Crown 8vo. 7s. 6d.

LEE, The Rev. F. G., D.D.

The Church under Queen Elizabeth. An Historical Sketch. · 2 vols. Cr. 8vo. 21s.

LETHBRIDGE, ROPER, C.I.E., M.A.

High Education in India. A Plea for the State Colleges. Cr. 8vo. 5s.

LEWIN, Col. T. H., Dep. Comm. of Hill Tracts.

Indian Frontier Life. A Fly on the Wheel, or How I helped to govern India. Map and Illustrations. Demy 8vo. 18s.

LLOYD, Mrs. JESSIE SALE.

Its Own Reward. Crown 8vo. Illustrated. 3s. 6d.

LOCKWOOD, EDWARD, B.S.C.

Natural History, Sport and Travel. With numerous Illustrations. Cr. 8vo. 9s.

LOVELL, The late Vice-Adm. WM. STANHOPE, R.N., K.H.

Personal Narrative of Events from 1799 to 1815. With Anecdotes. Second Edition. Fcap. 8vo. 4s.

LOW, CHARLES RATHBONE.

Major-General Sir Frederick S. Roberts, Bart., V.C., G.C.B., C.I.E., R.A.: a Memoir. With Portrait. Demy 8vo. 18s.

LUND, T. W. M., M.A., Chaplain to the School for the Blind, Liverpool.

Como and Italian Lake Land. With 3 Maps, and 11 Illustrations by Miss Jessie Macgregor.' Crown 8vo. 10s. 6d.

LUPTON, JAMES IRVINE, F.R.C.V.S.

The Horse, as he Was, as he Is, and as he Ought to Be. Illustrated. Cr. 8vo. 3s. 6d.

MACGREGOR, Col. C.M , C.S.I., C.I.E., Beng. Staff Corps.

Narrative of a Journey through the Province of Khorassan and on the N.W. Frontier of Afghanistan in 1875. With Map and Numerous Illustrations. 2 vols. 8vo. 30s.

Wanderings in Balochistan. With Illustrations and Map. Demy 8vo. 18s.

MACKAY, CHARLES, LL.D.

Through the Long Day: or, Memorials of a Literary Life during half, a century. 2 vols. With Portraits. Demy 8vo. 21s.

MACKENZIE, —

Educational Series; Commercial, Arithmetical and Miscellaneous TABLES, paper covers, 2d.; Arithmetic, 6d.; Murray's Grammar, 4d., paper covers, 2d.; Phrenology, paper covers, 2d.; Shorthand, 4d. Spelling, 2 parts, paper covers, 4d.

MALABARI, BEHRAMJI, M.

Gujerat and the Gujeratis. Pictures of Men and Manners taken from Life. Cr. 8vo. 6s.

MALLESON, Col. G. B., C.S.I.

Final French Struggles in India and on the Indian Seas. Including an Account of the Capture of the Isles of France and Bourbon, and Sketches of the most eminent Foreign Adventurers in India up to the Period of that Capture. With an Appendix containing an Account of the Expedition from India to Egypt in 1801. New Edition. Cr. 8vo. 6s.

History of the Indian Mutiny, 1857-1858, commencing from the close of the Second Volume of Sir John Kaye's History of the Sepoy War. Vol. I. With Map. Demy 8vo. 20s.—Vol. II. With 4 plans. Demy 8vo. 20s.—Vol. III. With plans. Demy 8vo. 20s.

History of Afghanistan, from the Earliest Period to the Outbreak of the War of 1878. Second Edition. With Map. Demy 8vo. 18s

The Decisive Battles of India, from 1746-1849. Third Edition. With a Portrait of the Author, a Map, and Four Plans. Cr. 8vo. 7s. 6d.

Herat: The Garden and Granary of Central Asia. With Map and Index. Demy 8vo. 8s.

Founders of the Indian Empire. Clive, Warren Hastings, and Wellesley. Vol. I.—LORD CLIVE. With Portraits and 4 Plans. Demy 8vo. 20s.

Captain Musafir's Rambles in Alpine Lands. Illustrated by G. Strangman Handcock. Cr. 4to. 10s. 6d.

Battle-fields of Germany. With Maps and Plan. Demy 8vo. 16s.

Ambushes and Surprises: Being a Description of some of the most famous Instances of the Leading into Ambush and the Surprise of Armies, from the Time of Hannibal to the Period of the Indian Mutiny. With a Portrait of General Lord Mark Kerr, K.C.B. Demy 8vo. 18s.

Metternich. (THE STATESMEN SERIES.) Cr. 8vo. 2s. 6d.

MALLOCK, W. H.

A Chart showing the Proportion borne by the Rental of the Landlords to the Gross Income of the People. Cr. 1s.

MANGNALL, Mrs.

Historical and Miscellaneous Questions (generally known as "Mangnall's Questions"). New and Improved Edition. 18mo. 1s.

MANNING, Mrs.

Ancient and Mediæval India. Being the History, Religion, Laws, Caste, Manners and Customs, Language, Literature, Poetry, Philosophy, Astronomy, Algebra, Medicine, Architecture, Manufactures, Commerce, &c. of the Hindus, taken from their Writings With Illustrations. 2 vols. Demy 8vo. 30s.

MARSHALL, ARTHUR, Architect, A.R.I.B.A., &c.

Specimens of Antique Carved Furniture and Woodwork. With 50 Plates from Drawings by the Author. Folio. £3.

MARVIN, CHARLES.

The Eye-Witnesses' Account of the Disastrous Russian Campaign against the Akhal Tekke Turcomans: Describing the March across the Burning Desert, the Storming of Dengeel Tepe, and the Disastrous Retreat to the Caspian. With numerous Maps and Plans. Demy 8vo. 18s.

The Russians at Merv and Herat, and their Power of invading India. With 24 Illustrations and 3 Maps. Demy 8vo. 24s.

Merv, the Queen of the World; and the Scourge of the Man-stealing Turcomans. With Portraits and Maps. Demy 8vo. 18s.

Colonel Grodekoff's Ride from Samarcand to Herat, through Balkh and the Uzbek States of Afghan Turkestan. With his own March-route from the Oxus to Herat. With Portrait Cr. 8vo. 8s

The Region of the Eternal Fire. An Account of a Journey to the Caspian Region in 1883. New Edition. Maps and Illustrations. Cr. 8vo. 7s. 6d.

MATEER, The Rev. SAMUEL, of the London Miss. Soc.

Native Life in Travancore. With Numerous Illustrations and Map. Demy 8vo. 18s.

MAYHEW, EDWARD, M.R.C.V.S.

Illustrated Horse Doctor. Being an Accurate and Detailed Account accompanied by more than 400 Pictorial Representations, characteristic of the various Diseases to which the Equine Race are subjected; together with the latest Mode of Treatment, and all the requisite Prescriptions written in Plain English. New and Cheaper Edition. Half-bound. Demy 8vo. 10s. 6d.

Illustrated Horse Management. Containing descriptive remarks upon Anatomy, Medicine, Shoeing, Teeth, Food, Vices, Stables; likewise a plain account of the situation, nature, and value of the various points; together with comments on grooms, dealers, breeders, breakers, and trainers; Embellished with more than 400 engravings from Original designs made expressly for this work. A new Edition, revised and improved by J. I. Lupton, M.R.C.V.S. New and Cheaper Edition. Half-bound. Demy 8vo. 7s. 6d.

McCARTHY, T. A.

An Easy System of Calisthenics and Drilling, including Light Dumb-Bell and Indian Club Exercises. Fcap. 8vo. 1s. 6d.

MENZIES, SUTHERLAND.

Turkey Old and New: Historical, Geographical, and Statistical. With Map and numerous Illustrations. Third Edition. Demy 8vo. 21s.

MICHOD, C. J.

Good Condition: A Guide to Athletic Training for Amateurs and Professionals. Small 8vo. 1s.

Microscope, How to Choose a. By a Demonstrator. With 90 Illustrations. Demy 8vo. 1s.

MILITARY WORKS.

Modern Tactics. By Captain H. E. Gall, late 5th Fusiliers. 2 vols. Text and Plates. Roy. 8vo. 10s. 6d.

A Treatise on Scales. By Major F. Hart-Dyke. 2s.

Red Book for Sergeants. By William Bright, Colour-Sergeant, 19th Middlesex R.V. Fcap. 8vo. 1s.

Volunteer Artillery Drill-Book. By Captain W. Brooke Hoggan, R.A., Adjutant 1st Shropshire and Staffordshire V.A. Square 16mo. 2s.

Position Artillery. Its History, Employment, Equipment, Volunteer Organization, Drills, &c. By Captain H. C. C. D. Simpson, R.A. Fcap 3s.

Principles of Gunnery. By John T. Hyde, M.A., late Professor of Fortification and Artillery, Royal Indian Military College, Addiscombe. Second Edition, revised and enlarged. With many Plates and Cuts, and Photograph of Armstrong Gun. Roy. 8vo. 14s.

Treatise on Fortification and Artillery. By Major Hector Straith. Revised and re-arranged by Thomas Cook, R.N., by John T. Hyde, M.A. Seventh Edition. Illustrated and 400 Plans, Cuts, &c. Roy. 8vo £2 2s.

Elementary Principles of Fortification. A Text-Book for Military Examinations. By J. T. Hyde, M.A. With numerous Plans and Illustrations. Roy. 8vo. 10s. 6d.

Military Surveying and Field Sketching. The Various Methods of Contouring, Levelling, Sketching without Instruments, Scale of Shade, Examples in Military Drawing, &c. &c. &c. As at present taught in the Military Colleges. By Major W. H. Richards, 55th Regiment, Chief Garrison Instructor in India, Late Instructor in Military Surveying, Royal Military College, Sandhurst. Second Edition, Revised and Corrected. Roy. 12s.

Celebrated Naval and Military Trials. By Peter Burke. Post 8vo. 10s. 6d.

Military Life of the Duke of Wellington. By Jackson and Scott. 2 vols. Maps, Plans, &c. Demy 8vo. 12s.

Single Stick Exercise of the Aldershot Gymnasium. Paper cover. Fcap. 8vo. 6d.

An Essay on the Principles and Construction of Military Bridges. By Sir Howard Douglas. Demy 8vo. 15s.

Military Works—*cont.*

Hand-book Dictionary for the Militia and Volunteer Ser vices, containing a variety of useful information, Alphabetically arranged. Pocket size, 3s. 6d.; by post, 3s. 8d.

Lectures on Tactics for Officers of the Army, Militia, and Volunteers. By Major F. H. Dyke, Garrison Instructor, E.D. Fcap. 4to. 4s.

Precedents in Military Law. By Lieut.-Col. W. Hough. Demy 8vo. 25s

The Practice of Courts-Martial. By Hough and Long. Demy 8vo. 26s.

Lectures on Tactics. By Lieut.-Col. F. H. Dyke. 4to. sewed. 4s.

The Military Encyclopædia; refer ing exclusively to the Military Sciences, Memoirs of distinguished Soldiers, and the Narratives of Remarkable Battles. By J. H. Stocqueler. Demy 8vo. 12s.

MILL, JAMES.

History of British India, With Notes and Continuation by H. H. Wilson. 9 vols. Cr. 8vo. £2 10s.

MITFORD, EDWARD L.

A Land March from England to Ceylon Forty Years Ago. With Map and numerous Illustrations. 2 vols. Demy 8vo. 24s.

MITFORD, Major R. C. W., 14th Bengal Lancers.

To Caubul with the Cavalry Brigade. A Narrative of Personal Experiences with the Force under General Sir F. S. Roberts, G.C. With Map and Illustrations from Sketches by the Author. Second Edition. Demy 8vo. 9s.

Orient and Occident. A Journey East from Lahore to Liverpool. Illustrated. Cr. 8vo. 8s. 6d.

MONTRESOR, C. A.

Some Hobby Horses, and How to Ride Them. Illustrated. Cr. 8vo. 5s.

MULLER, MAX.

Rig-Veda-Sanhita. The Sacred Hymns of the Brahmins; together with the Commentary of Sayanacharya. Published under the Patronage of the Right Honourable the Secretary of State for India in Council. Demy 4to. 6 vols. £2 10s. per volume.

Napoleon and his Detractors. By H.I.H. Prince Napoleon. Translated, With Biographical Sketch, two Portraits, and Autograph. By Raphael L. de Beaufort. Demy 8vo. 16s.

National Review. Vols. I. to XII. Royal 8vo. 17s. each.

Nation in Arms (The). From the German of Lieut.-Col. Baron von der Goltz. Translated by Philip A. Ashworth. Demy 8vo. 15s.

Naval Reform. From the French of the late M. Gabriel Charmes. Translated by J. E. Gordon-Cumming. Demy 8vo. 12s.

NAVE, JOHANN.

The Collector's Handy-Book of Algæ, Diatoms, Desmids, Fungi, Lichens, Mosses, &c. Translated and Edited by the Rev. W. W. Spicer, M.A. Illustrated with 114 Woodcuts. Fcap. 8vo. 2s. 6d.

NEWMAN, The Late EDWARD, F.Z.S.

British Butterflies and Moths. With over 800 Illustrations. Super-roy. 8vo., cloth gilt. 25s.
The above Work may also be had in Two Volumes, sold separately. Vol. I., Butterflies, 7s. 6d.; Vol. II., Moths, 20s.

NICHOLSON, Capt. H. WHALLEY.

From Sword to Share; or, a Fortune in Five Years at Hawaii. With Map and Photographs. Cr. 8vo. 12s. 6d.

Nirgis and Bismillah. NIRGIS; a Tale of the Indian Mutiny, from the Diary of a Slave Girl: and BISMILLAH; or, Happy Days in Cashmere. By Hafiz Allard. Post 8vo. 10s. 6d.

NORMAN, Captain C. B.

Colonial France: Its History, Administration, and Commerce. Maps. Demy 8vo. 15s.

NORRIS-NEWMAN, CHARLES L., Special Correspondent of the London "Standard."

With the Boers in the Transvaal and Orange Free State in 1880-81. With Maps. Demy 8vo. 14s.

Notes on Collecting and Preserving Natural History Objects. Edited by J. E. Taylor, F.L.S., F.G.S., Editor of "Science Gossip." With numerous Illustrations. Cr. 8vo. 3s. 6d.

O'DONOGHUE, Mrs. POWER.

Ladies on Horseback. Learning, Park Riding, and Hunting. With Notes upon Costume, and numerous Anecdotes. With Portrait. Second Edition. Cr. 8vo. 5s.

OLDFIELD, The Late HENRY ARMSTRONG, M.D., H.M. Indian Army.

Sketches from Nipal, Historical and Descriptive; with Anecdotes of the Court Life and Wild Sports of the Country in the time of Maharaja Jung Bahadur, G.C.B.; to which is added an Essay on Nipalese Buddhism, and Illustrations of Religious Monuments, Architecture, and Scenery, from the Author's own Drawings. 2 vols. Demy 8vo. 36s.

O'MEARA, Miss K.

Life of Thomas Grant, First Bishop of Southwark. Second Crown 8vo. 7s. 6d.

OSBORNE, Mrs. WILLOUGHBY.

A Pilgrimage to Mecca. By the Nawab Sikandar Begum of Bhopal. Translated from the original Urdu by Mrs. Willoughby Osborne. Followed by a Sketch of the History of Bhopal by Colonel Willoughby Osborne, C.B. With Photographs. Dedicated, by permission, to Her Majesty Queen Victoria. Post 8vo. £1 1s.

O'SHEA, JOHN AUGUSTUS.

Military Mosaics. A Set of Tales and Sketches on Soldierly Themes. Cr. 8vo. 5s.

OSWALD, FELIX S.

Zoological Sketches: a Contribution to the Out-door Study of Natural History. With 36 Illustrations by Hermann Faber. Cr. 8vo. 7s. 6d.

OXENHAM, Rev. HENRY NUTCOMBE, M.A.

Catholic Eschatology and Universalism. An Essay on the Doctrine of Future Retribution. Second Edition, revised and enlarged. Cr. 8vo. 7s. 6d.

Catholic Doctrine of the Atonement. An Historical Inquiry into its Development in the Church, with an Introduction on the Principle of Theological Development. Third Edition and enlarged. 8vo. 14s.

The First Age of Christianity and the Church. By John Ignatius Dollinger, D.D., Professor of Ecclesiastical History in the University of Munich, &c. &c. Translated from the German by H. N. Oxenham, M.A. Third Edition. 2 vols., Cr 8vo. 18s.

PANTON, J. E.

Country Sketches in Black and White. Cr. 8vo. 6s.

PAYNE, JOHN.

Lautrec. A Poem. New Edition. Paper cover. Fcap. 8vo. 2s. 6d.
Intaglios. New Edition. Fcap 8vo. 3s. 6d.
Songs of Life and Death. New Edition. Cr. 8vo. 5s.
Masque of Shadows. New Edition. Cr. 8vo. 5s.
New Poems. New Edition. Cr. 8vo. 7s. 6d.

PELLY, Colonel Sir LEWIS, K.C.B., K.C.S.I., &c.

The Miracle Play of Hasan and Husain. Collected from Oral Tradition by Colonel Sir Lewis Pelly, K.C.B., K.C.S.I. Revised, with Explanatory Notes, by Arthur N. Wollaston, H.M. Indian (Home) Service, Translator of Anwar-i-Suhaili, &c. 2 vols., Roy. 8vo. 32s.

Pen and Ink Sketches of Military Subjects. By "Ignotus." Reprinted, by permission, from the "Saturday Review." Cr. 8vo. 5s.

PINCOTT, FREDERIC, M.R.A.S.

Analytical Index to Sir John Kaye's History of the Sepoy War, and Colonel G. B. Malleson's History of the Indian Mutiny. (Combined in one volume.) Demy 8vo. 10s. 6d.

PITTENGER, Rev. W.

Capturing a Locomotive. A History of Secret Service in the late American War. With 13 Illustrations. Cr. 8vo. 6s.

Plutarch, Our Young Folks'. Edited by Rosalie Kaufmann. With Maps and Illustrations. Small 4to. 10s. 6d.

POPE, Rev. G. U., D.D., Fellow of Madras University.

Text-Book of Indian History; with Geographical Notes, Genealogical Tables, Examination Questions, and Chronological, Biographical, Geographical, and General Indexes. For the use of Schools, Colleges, and Private Students. Third Edition, thoroughly revised. Fcap. 4to. 12s.

PRATTEN, MARY A.

My Hundred Swiss Flowers. With a Short Account of Swiss Ferns. With 60 Illustrations. Crown 8vo. 12s. 6d.; coloured, 25s.

PRICHARD, I. I.

The Chronicles of Budgepore, &c ; or, Sketches of Life in Upper India. 2 vols., Fcap. 8vo. 12s.

Private Theatricals. Being a Practical Guide to the Home Stage, both Before and Behind the Curtain. By an Old Stager. Illustrated with Suggestions for Scenes after designs by Shirley Hodson. Cr. 8vo. 3s. 6d.

PROCTOR, RICHARD A., B.A., F.R.A.S.

Half-Hours with the Stars. Demy 4to. 3s. 6d.

Half-Hours with the Telescope. Illustrated. Fcap. 8vo. 2s. 6d.

Other Suns than Ours. A Series of Essays on Suns, Old, Young and Dead, with other Science Gleanings, &c. Crown 8vo. 7s. 6d.

Watched by the Dead. A Loving Story of Dickens' Half-Told Tale. Boards, 1s. ; Cloth, 1s. 6d.

PROCTER, WILLIAM, Stud Groom.

The Management and Treatment of the Horse in the Stable, Field, and on the Road. New and revised edition. Cr. 8vo. 6s.

Puffs from the Engine of War. By "An Officer of the Line." Cr. 8vo. 1s.

RALFE, CHARLES H., M.A., M.D. Cantab.; F.R.C.P. Lond.; late Teacher of Physiological Chemistry, St. George's Hospital, &c.

Demonstrations in Physiological and Pathological Chemistry. Arranged to meet the requirements for the Practical Examination in these subjects at the Royal College of Physicians and College of Surgeons. Fcap. 8vo. 5s.

RAMANN, Fraulein L.

Franz Liszt, Artist and Man. Translated from the German by Miss E. Cowdery. 2 vols., Cr. 8vo. 21s.

Ranche Life in California, from the Home Correspondence of E. M. H. Fcap. Illustrated. 2s. 6d.

Ranche Life in Montana (a Lady's). By I. R. Fcap. 2s. 6d.

RANSOME, A. H.

Sunday Thoughts for the Little Ones. 24mo. 1s. 6d.

RICE, WILLIAM, Major-General (Retired) Indian Army.

Indian Game: from Quail to Tiger. With 12 Coloured Plates. Imp. 8vo. 21s.

RIDLEY, MARIAN S.

A Pocket Guide to British Ferns. Fcap. 8vo. 2s. 6d.

RIMMER, R., F.L.S.

The Land and Fresh Water Shells of the British Isles. Illustrated with Photographs and 3 Lithographs, containing figures of all the principal Species. Cr. 8vo. 10s. 6d.

Ristori (Adelaide). Studies and Memoirs. With Portrait. Cr. 8vo. 5s.

ROBERTS, SIR RANDAL H.

The Silver Trout, and other Stories.. Crown 8vo. 3s. 6d.

Rural Rambles. Twelve Sketches in Colour on Pictorial Easel Stand for the Table. The Sketches from Drawings by Alfred Woodruff and S. P. Cargill. 2s.

SACHAU, Dr. C. EDWARD, Professor Royal University of Berlin.

The Chronology of Ancient Nations. An English Version of the Arabic Text of the Athar-ut-Bâkiya of Albirûni, or "Vestiges of the Past." Collected and reduced to writing by the Author in A.H. 390-1, A.D. 1000. Translated and Edited, with Notes and Index. Roy. 8vo. 42s.

SANDERSON, G. P., Officer in Charge of the Government Elephant Keddahs at Mysore.

Thirteen Years among the Wild Beasts of India; their Haunts and Habits, from Personal Observation. With an account of the Modes of Capturing and Taming Wild Elephants. With 21 full-page Illustrations and 3 Maps. Second Edition. Fcap. 4to. £1 5s.

SCHAIBLE, CHARLES II., M.D., Ph.D.

First Help in Accidents: Being a Surgical Guide in the absence, or before the arrival of medical assistance. Fully Illustrated. 32mo. 1s.

SCHLEIDEN, J. M., M.D.

The Principles of Scientific Botany. Translated by Dr. Lankester. Numerous Woodcuts and Six Steel Plates. Demy 8vo. 10s. 6d.

SECCOMBE, Lieut.-Col. T. S.

Comic Sketches from English History. For Children of various Ages. With Descriptive Rhymes. With 12 full-page Illustrations and numerous Woodcuts. Oblong 4to. 6s.

Service Afloat; or, the Naval Career of Sir William Hoste. Portrait. Crown 8vo. 7s. 6d.

SEWELL, ROBERT, Madras Civil Service.

Analytical History of India. From the earliest times to the Abolition of the East India Company in 1858. Post 8vo. 8s.

SHERER, J. W., C.S.I.

The Conjuror's Daughter. A Tale. With Illustrations by Alf. T. Elwes and J. Jellicoe. Cr. 8vo. 6s.

Who is Mary? A Cabinet Novel, in one volume. Cr. 8vo. 10s. 6d.

At Home and in India. A Volume of Miscellanies. With Frontispiece. Cr. 8vo. 5s.

Worldly Tales. Inscribed to Edmund Yates. Cr. 8vo. Bds. 1s Cloth, 1s. 6d.

SHERIFF, DANIEL.

An Improved Principle of Single Entry Book-keeping. Roy. 8vo. 3s. 6d.

The Whole Science of Double Entry Book-keeping. Third Edition. 8vo. 4s.

Signor Monaldini's Niece. A Novel of Italian Life. By the Author of "The Jewel in the Lotus." Cr. 8vo. 6s.

SKENE, F. M. F.

The Lesters. A Family Record. 2 vols. Crown 8vo. 11s.

SMALL, *Rev. G., Interpreter to the Strangers' Home for Asiatics.*

A Dictionary of Naval Terms, English and Hindustani. For the use of Nautical Men trading to India, &c. Cr. 8vo. 2s. 6d.

SMITH, J., A.L.S.

Ferns: British and Foreign. Fourth Edition, revised and greatly enlarged, with New Figures, &c. Cr 8vo. 7s. 6d.

SMITH, WORTHINGTON, F.L.S.

Mushrooms and Toadstools: How to Distinguish easily the Difference between Edible and Poisonous Fungi. Two large Sheets, containing Figures of 29 Edible and 31 Poisonous Species, drawn the natural size, and Coloured from Living Specimens. With descriptive letterpress, 6s. ; on canvas, in cloth case for pocket, 10s. 6d. ; on canvas, on rollers and varnished, 10s. 6d. The letterpress may be had separately, with key-plates of figures, 1s.

STANHOPE, WALTER.

A Martyr to Pride. Cr 8vo. 6s.

STATESMEN SERIES. *Edited by* LLOYD C. SANDERS.

Beaconsfield. By T. E. Kebbel, author of "History of Toryism," &c. Cr 8vo. 2s. 6d.

Palmerston. By L. C. Sanders.

O'Connell. By J A Hamilton.

Metternich. By Col. G B. Malleson.

Peel. By F. C. Montague.

STEINMETZ, A.

The Smoker's Guide, Philosopher, and Friend: What to Smoke —What to Smoke with—and the whole "What's What" of Tobacco, Historical, Botanical, Manufactural, Anecdotal, Social, Medical, &c. Roy. 32mo. 1s.

STOTHARD, ROBERT T., F.S.A.

The A B C of Art. Being a system of delineating forms and objects in nature necessary for the attainments of a draughtsman. Fcap. 8vo. 1s.

STUART, ESMÉ.

In his Grasp. A Psychological Romance. Crown 8vo. 5s.

SYMONDS, *Rev. W. S., Rector of Pendock.*

Old Bones; or, Notes for Young Naturalists. With References to the Typical Specimens in the British Museum. Second Edition, much improved and enlarged. Numerous Illustrations. Fcap. 8vo. 2s. 6d.

SWINNERTON, *Rev. C. Chaplain in the Field with the First Division, Peshawur Valley Field Force.*

The Afghan War. Gough's Action at Futtehabad. With Frontispiece and 2 Plans. Cr. 8vo. 5s.

"Taken In." A Sketch of New Zealand Life. By Hopeful. Fcap. 2s. 6d.

TAUNTON, ALFRED GEORGE.

The Family Register. A Key to such Official Entries of Births, Marriages, and Deaths at the Registrar-General's Office as may refer to any particular family. Half bound. Demy folio. 21s.

TAYLER, WILLIAM, Retired B.C.S., late Commissioner of Patna.

Thirty-eight Years in India, from Juganath to the Himalaya Mountains. 200 Illustrations from Original Sketches. 2 vols. Demy 8vo. 25s. each.

The Patna Crisis; or, Three Months at Patna during the Insurrection of 1857. Third Edition. Fcap. 8vo. 2s.

TAYLOR, J. E., F.L.S., F.G.S., &c.

The Aquarium : Its Inhabitants, Structure, and Management. With 238 Woodcuts. Second Edition. Cr. 8vo. 3s. 6d.

Flowers : Their Origin, Shapes, Perfumes, and Colours. Illustrated with 32 Coloured Figures by Sowerby, and 161 Woodcuts. Second Edition. Cr. 8vo. 7s. 6d.

Geological Stories. Numerous Illustrations. Fourth Edition. Cr. 8vo. 2s. 6d.

Nature's Bye-paths : A Series of Recreative Papers in Natural History. Cr. 8vo. 3s. 6d.

Half-Hours at the Sea-side. Illustrated with 250 Woodcuts. Fourth Edition. Cr. 8vo. 2s. 6d.

Half-Hours in the Green Lanes. Illustrated with 300 Woodcuts. Fifth Edition. Cr. 8vo. 2s. 6d.

TEMPLE, Sir RICHARD, Bart., M.P., G.C.S.I., &c.

Journals in Hyderabad, Kashmir, Sikkim, and Nepal. Edited, with Introductions, by his Son, Captain R. C. Temple, Bengal Staff Corps, &c. 2 vols., with Chromo-lithographs, Maps, and other Illustrations. 32s.

Palestine Illustrated. With 32 Coloured Plates, reproduced by chromo-lithography from the Author's Original Paintings. Imperial 8vo. 31s. 6d.

THOMS, JOHN ALEXANDER.

A Complete Concordance to the Revised Version of the New Testament, embracing the Marginal Readings of the English Revisers as well as those of the American Committee. Roy. 8vo. 6s.

THOMSON, DAVID.

Lunar and Horary Tables. For New and Concise Methods of Performing the Calculations necessary for ascertaining the Longitude by Lunar Observations, or Chronometers; with directions for acquiring a knowledge of the Principal Fixed Stars and finding the Latitude of them. Sixty-fifth Edition. Roy. 8vo. 10s.

THORNTON, EDWARD.

The History of the British Empire in India. Containing a Copious Glossary of Indian Terms, and a Complete Chronological Index of Events, to aid the Aspirant for Public Examinations. Third Edition. With Map. 1 vol. Demy 8vo. 12s.

    ** The Library Edition of the above in 6 volumes, 8vo., may be had, price £2 8s.

A Gazetteer of the Territories under the Government of the Viceroy of India. Revised and Edited by Sir Roper Lethbridge, C.I.E., formerly Press Commissioner in India, &c., and Arthur N. Wollaston, C.I.E., of H.M.'s Indian (Home) Civil Service, Translator of the "Anvár-i-Sahaili." Demy 8vo. 28s.

Gazetteer of the Punjaub, Affghanistan, &c. Gazetteer of the Countries adjacent to India, on the north-west, including Scinde, Affghanistan, Beloochistan, the Punjaub, and the neighbouring States. 2 vols. Demy 8vo. £1 5s

THORNTON, PERCY M.

Foreign Secretaries of the Nineteenth Century. Lord Grenville, Lord Hawkesbury, Lord Harrowby Lord Mulgrave, C. J. Fox, Lord Howick, George Canning, Lord Bathurst, Lord Wellesley together with estimate of his Indian Rule by Col. G. B. Malleson, C.S.I.), Lord Castlereagh, Lord Dudley, Lord Aberdeen, and Lord Palmerston. Also, Extracts from Lord Bexley's Papers, including lithographed letters of Lords Castlereagh and Canning, bearing on important points of public policy; never before published. With Ten Portraits, and a View showing Interior of the old House of Lords. Second Edition. 2 vols. Demy 8vo. 32s. 6d.
   Vol. III. Second Edition. With Portraits. Demy 8vo. 18s.
Harrow School and its Surroundings. Maps and Plates. Demy 8vo. 15s.

THORNTON, T.

East India Calculator. Demy 8vo. 10s.
History of the Punjaub, and Present Condition of the Sikhs. 2 vols. Cr. 8vo. 8s.

TORRIANO, W. H.

William the Third. Fcap. 2s. 6d.

Treasury of Choice Quotations: Selections from more than 300 Eminent Authors. With a complete Index. Cr. 8vo. 3s. 6d.

TRIMEN, H., M.B. (Lond.), F L.S., and DYER, W. T, B.A.

The Flora of Middlesex: A Topographical and Historical Account of the Plants found in the County. With Sketches of its Physical Geography and Climate, and of the Progress of Middlesex Botany during the last Three Centuries. With a Map of Botanical Districts. Cr. 8vo. 12s. 6d.

TRIMEN, Capt. R., late 35th Regiment.

Regiments of the British Army, Chronologically arranged. Showing their History, Services, Uniform, &c. Demy 8vo. 10s. 6d.

TROTTER, Capt. LIONEL JAMES, late Beng. Fusiliers.

India under Victoria from 1836 to 1880. 2 vols. Demy 8vo. 30s.
History of India. The History of the British Empire in India, from the Appointment of Lord Hardinge to the Death of Lord Canning (1844 to 1862). 2 vols. Demy 8vo. 16s. each.
Lord Lawrence. A Sketch of his Career. Fcap. 8vo. 1s. 6d.
Warren Hastings, a Biography. Cr. 8vo. 9s.

TROTTER, M. E.

A Method of Teaching Plain Needlework in Schools. Illustrated with Diagrams and Samplers. New Edition, revised and arranged according to Standards. Demy 8vo. 2s. 6d.

Turkish Cookery. A collection of Receipts, compiled by Turabi Effendi from the best Turkish authorities. Second Edition. Fcap. 2s. 6d

TYRWHITT, W. S. S.
The New Chum in New Zealand. Cr. 8vo. 2s. 6d.

UNDERWOOD, ARTHUR S., M.R.C.S, L.D.S.E., Assistant-Surgeon to the Dental Hospital of London.
Surgery for Dental Students. Cr. 8vo. 5s.

VALBEZEN, E. DE, late Consul-General at Calcutta, Minister Plenipotentiary.
The English and India. New Sketches. Translated from the French (with the Author's permission) by a Diplomate. Demy 8vo. 18s.

VAMBERY, ARMENIUS.
Sketches of Central Asia. Additional Chapters on My Travels and Adventures, and of the Ethnology of Central Asia. Demy 8vo. 16s.

VAN GELDER, Mrs. JANE.
The Storehouses of the King; or the Pyramids of Egypt, what they are and who built them. Gilt. Demy 8vo. 21s.

VIBART, Major H.M., Royal (late Madras) Engineers.
The Military History of the Madras Engineers and Pioneers. 2 vols. With numerous Maps and Plans. Demy 8vo. 32s. each.

VICARY, J. FULFORD.
An American in Norway. Cr. 8vo. 7s. 6d.
Olav the King and Olav King and Martyr. Cr. 8vo. 5s.

Victoria Cross (The), An Official Chronicle of Deeds of Personal Valour achieved in the presence of the Enemy during the Crimean and Baltic Campaigns, and the Indian, Chinese, New Zealand, and African Wars, from the Institution of the Order in 1856 to 1880. Edited by Robert W. O'Byrne. With Plate. Cr. 8vo. 5s.

WALFORD, M.A., &c. &c.
Holidays in Home Counties. With numerous Illustrations. Cr. 8vo. 5s.
Pleasant Days in Pleasant Places. Illustrated with numerous Woodcuts. Second Edition. Cr. 8vo. 5s.

WALL, A. J., M.D , F.R.C.S., Med. Staff H.M.'s Indian Army.
Indian Snake Poisons, their Nature and Effects. Cr. 8vo. 6s.

WATSON, Dr. J. FORBES, and JOHN WILLIAM KAYE.
Races and Tribes of Hindostan, A series of Photographic Illustrations of ; prepared under the Authority of the Government of India containing about 450 Photographs on mounts, in Eight Volumes, super royal 4to. £2 5s. per volume.

WEBB, Dr. ALLAN, B M.S.
Pathologia Indica. Based [upon [Morbid Specimens from all parts of the Indian Empire. Second Edition. Demy 8vo. 14s.

Wellesley's Despatches. The Despatches, Minutes, and Correspondence of the Marquis Wellesley, K.G., during his Administration in India. 5 vols. With Portrait, Map, &c. Demy 8vo. £6 10s.

Wellington in India. Military History of the Duke of Wellington in India. Cr. 8vo. 1s.

WELLS, J. W., *Author of " Three Thousand Miles through Brazil."*
The Voice of Urbano. Cr. 8vo. 6s.

"Where Chinese Drive." English Student-Life at Peking. By a Student Interpreter. With Examples of Chinese Block-printing and other Illustrations. Demy 8vo. 12s.

WHINYATES, Col. F. A, late R.H.A, formerly commanding the Battery.
From Coruna to Sevastopol. The History of "C" Battery, "A" Brigade, late "C" Troop, Royal Horse Artillery. With succession of officers from its formation to the present time. With 3 maps. Demy 8vo. 14s.

WILLIAMS, C. R.
The Defence of Kahun. A Forgotten Episode of the First Afghan War. With Frontispiece. Cr. 8vo. 3s 6d.

WILLIAMS, FOLKESTONE.
Lives of the English Cardinals, from Nicholas Breakspeare (Pope Adrien IV.) to Thomas Wolsey, Cardinal Legate   With Historical Notices of the Papal Court. 2 vols. Demy 8vo. 14s.
Life, &c. of Bishop Atterbury. The Memoir and Correspondence of Francis Atterbury, Bishop of Rochester, with his distinguished contemporaries. Compiled chiefly from the Atterbury and Stuart Papers. 2 vols Demy 8vo. 14s.

WILLIAMS, S. WELLS, LL.D. Professor of the Chinese Language and Literature at Yale College.
The Middle Kingdom. A Survey of the Geography, Government, Literature, Social Life, Arts, and History of the Chinese Empire and Its Inhabitants. Revised Edition, with 74 Illustrations and a New Map of the Empire. 2 vols. Demy 8vo. 42s.

WILSON, H. H.
Glossary of Judicial and Revenue Terms, and of useful Words occurring in Official Documents relating to the Administration of the Government of British India. From the Arabic, Persian, Hindustani, Sanskrit, Hindi, Bengali, Uriya, Marathi, Guzarathi, Telugu, Karnata, Tamil, Malayalam, and other Languages. Compiled and published under the authority of the Hon the Court of Directors of the E. I. Company   Demy 4to. £1 10s.

WOLFF, Captain M. P., F.S S., Author of "Food for the Million," &c.
The Rational Alimentation of the Labouring Classes. With an Alimentation Table. Crown 8vo. 1s.

WOLLASTON, ARTHUR N, C.I.E,
Anwari Suhaili, or Lights of Canopus. Commonly known as Kalilah and Damnah, being an adaptation of the Fables of Bidpai. Translated from the Persian. Royal 8vo., 42s.; also with illuminated borders, designed specially for the work, cloth, extra gilt. Roy. 4to. £3 13s. 6d.

Half-Hours with Muhammad. Being a Popular Account of the Prophet of Arabia, and of his more immediate Followers; together with a short Synopsis of the Religion he founded. Crown 8vo., cloth, with Map and Nineteen Illustrations. 6s.

WORDSWORTH, W.

Poems for the Young. With 50 Illustrations by John Macwhirter and John Pettie, and a Vignette by J. E. Millais, R.A. Demy 16mo. 1s. 6d.

YOUNG, Prof. J. R.

Course of Mathematics. A Course of Elementary Mathematics for the use of candidates for admission into either of the Military Colleges ; of applicants for appointments in the Home or Indian Civil Services ; and of mathematical students generally. In one closely-printed volume pp. 648. Demy 8vo. 12s.

YOUNG, MINNIE, and TRENT, RACHEL.

A Home Ruler. A Story for Girls. Illustrated by C. P. Colnaghi. Cr. 8vo. 3s. 6d.

WOOD, WALTER.

The Book of Patience ; or, Cards for a Single Player. With full-page Illustrations. Crown 8vo. 2s. 6d.

YOUNGHUSBAND, Lieut. G. J., Queen's Own Corps of Guides

Eighteen Hundred Miles in a Burmese Tat, through Burmah, Siam, and the Eastern Shan States. Illustrated. Cr. 8vo. 5s.

A Selection from Messrs. ALLEN'S Catalogue of Books in the Eastern Languages, &c.

HINDUSTANI, HINDI, &c.

Dr. Forbes's Works are used as Class Books in the Colleges and Schools in India.

ABDOOLAH, SYED.

Singhasan Battisi. Translated into Hindi from the Sanscrit. A New Edition. Revised, Corrected, and Accompanied with Copius Notes. Roy. 8vo. 12s. 6d.

Akhlaki Hindi, translated into Urdu, with an Introduction and Notes. Roy. 8vo. 12s. 6d.

BALLANTYNE, JAMES R.

Hindustani Selections, with a Vocabulary of the Words. Second Edition. 1845. 5s.

Principles of Persian Caligraphy. Illustrated by Lithographic Plates of the Ta"lik Character, the one usually employed in writing the Persian and the Hindustani Prepared for the use of the Scottish Naval and Military Academy. Second Edition. 4to. 3s. 6d.

EASTWICK, EDWARD B.

The Bagh-o-Bahar—literally translated into English, with copious explanatory notes. 8vo. 10s. 6d.

Hindostani Grammar. Post 8vo. 5s.

Prem Sagar. Demy 4to. £2 2s.

FORBES, DUNCAN, LL D.

Hindustani-English Dictionary, in the Persian Character, with the Hindi words in Nagari also; and an English-Hindustani Dictionary the English Character; both in one volume. Roy. 8vo. 42s.

Hindustani-English and English-Hindustani Dictionary, in the English Character. Roy. 8vo. 36s.

Smaller Dictionary, Hindustani and English, in the English Character. 12s.

Hindustani Grammar, with Specimens of Writing in the Persian and Nagari Characters, Reading Lessons, and Vocabulary. 8vo 10s. 6d.

Hindustani Manual, containing a Compendious Grammar, Exercises for Translation, Dialogues, and Vocabulary, in the Roman Character. New Edition, entirely revised. By J. T. Platts. 18mo. 3s. 6d.

Bagh o Bahar, in the Persian Character, with a complete Vocabulary. Roy. 8vo. 12s. 6d.

Bagh o Bahar, in English, with Explanatory Notes, illustrative of Eastern Character. 8vo. 8s.

Bagh o Bahar, with Vocabulary. English Character. 5s.

Tota Kahani; or, "Tales of a Parrot," in the Persian Character, with a complete Vocabulary. Roy. 8vo. 8s.

Baital Pachisi; or, "Twenty-five Tales of a Demon," in the Nagari Character, with a complete Vocabulary. Roy. 8vo. 9s.

Forbes, Duncan, LL.D.—*cont.*

Ikhwanu-s-Safa; or, "Brothers of Purity," in the Persian Character. Roy. 8vo. 12s. 6d.

KEMPSON, M., *Director of Public Instruction in N.W. Provinces,* 1862–78.

Taubatu-n-Nusah (Repentance of Nussooh) of Moulvi Haji Hâfiz Nazir Ahmed of Delhi. Edited, with Notes and Index. Demy 8vo. 12s. 6d.

MULVIHILL, P.

A Vocabulary for the Lower Standard in Hindustani. Containing the meanings of every word and idiomatic expression in "Jarrett's Hindu Period," and in "Selections from the Bagh o Bahar." Fcap. 3s. 6d.

PINCOTT, FREDERIC, M.R.A.S., &c. &c.

Sakuntala in Hindi. Translated from the Bengali recension of the Sanskrit. Critically edited, with grammatical, idiomatical, and exegetical notes. 4to. 12s. 6d.

Alf Laila ba-Zuban-i-Urdu (The Arabian Nights in Hindustani). Roman Character. Cr. 8vo 10s. 6d.

Hindi Manual. Comprising a Grammar of the Hindi Language both Literary and Provincial; a complete Syntax, Exercises in various styles of Hindi composition; Dialogues on several subjects; and a complete Vocabulary. Fcap. 6s.

PLATTS, J. T.

Hindustani Dictionary. Dictionary of Urdú and Classical Hindí. Super Roy. 8vo. £3 3s.

Grammar of the Urdu or Hindustani Language. 8vo. 12s.

Baital Pachisi; translated into English 8vo 8s.

Ikhwanu-s-Safa; translated into English. 8vo. 10s. 6d.

ROGERS, E. H.

How to Speak Hindustani. Roy 12mo. 1s.

SMALL, Rev. G.

Tota Kahani; or, "Tales of a Parrot" Translated into English. 8vo. 8s.

Dictionary of Naval Terms, English and Hindustani. For the use of Nautical Men Trading to India, &c. Fcap. 2s. 6d.

SANSCRIT.

COWELL, E. B

Translation of the Vikramorvasi. 8vo. 3s. 6d.

GOUGH, A. E.

Key to the Exercises in Williams's Sanscrit Manual. 18mo. 4s.

HAUGHTON, —.

Sanscrit and Bengali Dictionary, in the Bengali Character, with Index, serving as a reversed dictionary. 4to. 30s.

Menu, with English Translation. 2 vols. 4to. 24s.

Hitopadesa, with Bengali and English Translations. 10s. 6d.

JOHNSON, Prof. F.

Hitopadesa, with Vocabulary. 15s.

PINCOTT, FREDERIC, M.R.A.S., &c., &c.

Hitopadesa. A new literal Translation from the Sanskrit Text of Pro F. Johnson. For the use of Students. 6s.

THOMPSON, J. C.
  Bhagavat Gita. Sanscrit Text. 5s.
WILLIAMS, —.
  English-Sanscrit Dictionary. 4to., cloth. £3 3s
  Sanscrit-English Dictionary. 4to. £4 14s. 6d
WILLIAMS, MONIER.
  Sanscrit Grammar. 8vo. 15s
  Sanscrit Manual; to which is added, a Vocabulary, by A. E Gough. 18mo. 7s. 6d.
  Sakuntala, with Literal English Translation of all the Metrical Passages, Schemes of the Metres, and copious Critical and Explanatory Notes. Roy. 8vo. 21s
  Sakuntala. Translated into English Prose and Verse Fourth Edition. 8s.
  Vikramorvasi. The Text 8vo 5s
WILKIN, Sir CHARLES
  Sanscrit Grammar. 4to. 15s.
WILSON —
  Megha Duta, with Translation into English Verse, Notes, Illustrations and a Vocabulary. Roy. 8vo. 6s.

PERSIAN.

BARETTO, —
  Persian Dictionary. 2 vols. 8vo | |12s.
CLARKE, Captain H WILBERFORCE, R.E
  The Persian Manual. A Pocket Companion.
  Part I.—A Concise Grammar of the Language, with Exercises on its more Prominent Peculiarities, together with a Selection of Useful Phrases, Dialogues, and Subjects for Translation into Persian.
  Part II.—A Vocabulary of Useful Words, English, and Persian, showing at the same time the Difference of idiom between the two Languages. 18mo. 7s. 6d.
  The Bustan. By Shaikh Muslihu-d-Dín Sa'di Shírází. Translated for the first time into Prose, with Explanatory Notes and Index. With Portrait. 8vo. 30s
  The Sikandar Nama,e Bara, or, Book of Alexander the Great. Written, A.D. 1200, by Abu Muhammad Bin Yusuf Bin Mu'ayyid-l-Nizámu-d-Dín Translated for the first time out of the Persian into Prose, with Critical and Explanatory Remarks, and an Introductory Preface, and a Life of the Author, collected from various Persian sources. Roy. 8vo. 42s
FORBES, DUNCAN, LL.D.
  Persian Grammar, Reading Lessons, and Vocabulary. Roy. 8vo. 12s. 6d.
IBRAHEEM, —.
  Persian Grammar, Dialogues, &c. Roy. 8vo. 12s. 6d.
KEENE, Rev. H. G.
  First Book of The Anwari Soheili. Persian Text. 8vo 5s.
  Akhlaki Mushini. Translated into English 8vo. 3s. 6d.
OUSELEY, Col.
  Anwari Soheili. 4to. 42s.
  Akhlaki Mushini. Persian Text. 8vo. 5s.

W. H. ALLEN & Co.,

PLATTS, J. T.
  Gulistan. Carefully collated with the original MS., with a full Vocabulary. Roy. 8vo. 12s. 6d.
  Gulistan. Translated from a revised Text, with copious Notes. 8vo. 12s. 6d.
RICHARDSON,—.
  Persian, Arabic, and English Dictionary. Edition of 1852. By F. Johnson. 4to £4.
TOLBORT, T. W. H., Bengal Civil Service.
  A Translation of Robinson Crusoe into the Persian Language. Roman Character. Cr. 8vo. 7s.
WOLLASTON, ARTHUR N., C.I.E.
  Translation of the Anvari Soheili. Roy. 8vo. £2 2s.
  English-Persian Dictionary. Compiled from Original Sources 8vo. 25s.

BENGALI.

BATEI, —.
  Singhasan. Demy 8vo. 5s.
FORBES, DUNCAN, LL.D.
  Bengali Grammar, with Phrases and Dialogues. Roy. 8vo. 12
  Bengali Reader, with a Translation and Vocabulary. Roy. 8vo.
HAUGHTON, —.
  Bengali, Sanscrit, and English Dictionary, adapted for Students in either language; to which is added an Index, serving as a reverse dictionary. 4to. 30s.
Nabo Nari. Anecdotes of the Nine Famous Women of India. [Text-book for examinations in Bengali.] 12mo. 7s.
Tota Itihas. The Tales of a Parrot. Demy 8vo. 5s

ARABIC.
FORBES, DUNCAN, LL.D.
  Arabic Grammar, intended more especially for the use of young men preparing for the East India Civil Service, and also for the use of self-instructing students in general. Royal 8vo., cloth. 18s.
  Arabic Reading Lessons, consisting of Easy Extracts from the best Authors, with Vocabulary. Roy. 8vo., cloth. 15s.
KAYAT, ASSAAD YAKOOB.
  The Eastern Traveller's Interpreter; or, Arabic Without a Teacher. Oblong. 5s.
PALMER, Prof. E. H., M.A., &c.
  Arabic Grammar. On the principles of the best Native Grammarians. 8vo. 18s.
  The Arabic Manual. Comprising a condensed Grammar of both Classical and Modern Arabic; Reading Lessons and Exercises, with Analyses and a Vocabulary of useful Words. Fcap. 7s. 6d.
RICHARDSON, —.
  Arabic, Persian, and English Dictionary. Edition of 1852. By F. Johnson. 4to., cloth. £4.
STEINGASS, Dr. F.
  Students' Arabic-English Dictionary. Demy 8vo. 50s.
  English-Arabic Dictionary. Demy 8vo. 28s.

TIEN, Rev. ANTON, PhD., M.R.A.S.

Egyptian, Syrian, and North-African Handbook. A Simple Phrase-Book in English and Arabic for the use of the British Forces, Civilians, and Residents in Egypt. Fcap. 4s.

Manual of Colloquial Arabic. Comprising Practical Rules for learning the Language, Vocabulary, Dialogues, Letters and Idioms, &c., in English and Arabic. Fcap. 7s. 6d.

TELOOGOO.

BROWN, —.

Dictionary, reversed; with a Dictionary of the Mixed Dialects used in Teloogoo. 3 vols. in 2. Roy. 8vo. £5.

Reader. 8vo. 2 vols. 14s.

Dialogues, Teloogoo and English. 8vo. 5s. 6d.

CAMPBELL, —.

Dictionary. Roy. 8vo. 30s.

Pancha Tantra. 8s.

PERCIVAL, —.

English-Teloogoo Dictionary. 10s. 6d.

TAMIL.

BABINGTON, —.

Grammar (High Dialect). 4to. 12s.

Gooroo Paramatan. Demy 4to. 8s.

PERCIVAL, —.

Tamil Dictionary. 2 vols. 10s. 6d.

POPE, Rev. G. U.

Tamil Handbook. In Three Parts. 12s. 6d. each. Part I. Introduction—Grammatical Lessons—General Index. Part II. Appendices—Notes on the Study of the "Kurral"—Key to the Exercises. Part III. Dictionaries: I. Tamil-English—II English-Tamil.

"Sacred" Kurral of Tiruvallura-Nâyanâr. With Introduction, Grammar, Translation, Notes, Lexicon, and Concordance. Demy 8vo. 24s.

ROTTLER, —.

Dictionary, Tamil and English 4to. 42s.

GUZRATTEE.

MAVOR, —.

Spelling, Guzrattee and English. 7s. 6d.

SHAPUAJI EDALJI.

Dictionary, Guzrattee and English. 21s.

MAHRATTA.

BALLANTYNE, JAMES R., of the Scottish Naval and Military Academy.

A Grammar of the Mahratta Language. For the use of the East India College at Hayleybury. 4to. 5s.

Æsop's Fables. 12mo. 2s. 6d.

MOLESWORTH, —.

Dictionary, Mahratta and English. 4to. 42s.

Dictionary, English and Mahratta. 4to. 42s.

MALAY.

BIKKERS, Dr. A. J. W.

Malay, Achinese, French, and English Vocabulary. Alphabetically arranged under each of the four languages. With a concise Malay Grammar. Post 8vo. 7s. 6d.

MARSDEN, —.

Grammar. 4to. £1 1s.

CHINESE.

MARSHMAN, —.
Clavis Sinica. A Chinese Grammar. 4to. £2 2s.

MORRISON, —.
Dictionary. 6 vols., 4to. £6 6s.

View of China, for Philological Purposes. Containing a Sketch of Chinese Chronology, Geography, Government, Religion, and Customs, designed for those who study the Chinese language. 4to. 6s.

PUSHTO.

RAVERTY, Major H. G., Bombay Infantry (Retired), Author of the Pus'hto Grammar, Dictionary, Selections Prose and Poetical, Selections from the Poetry of the Afghāns (English Translation), Æsop's Fables, &c. &c.

The Pushto Manual. Comprising a Concise Grammar; Exercises and Dialogues; Familiar Phrases, Proverbs, and Vocabulary. Fcap. 5s.

HUGHES, Rev. T. P
Ganj-i-Pukto, or Pukto Treasury. Being the Government Text-Book for the Lower Standard of Examination in Pukto, the Language of the Afghans. With Glossary of Words Post 8vo. 10s. 6d

MISCELLANEOUS.

COLLETT, —.
Malayalam Reader. 8vo. 12s. 6d.

Æsop's Fables in Carnatica. 8vo, bound. 12s. 6d.

MACKENZIE, Captain C. F., late of H.M's Consular Service.
A Turkish Manual. Comprising a Condensed Grammar with Idiomatic Phrases, Exercises and Dialogues, and Vocabulary 6s.

Oriental Penmanship : comprising Specimens of Persian Handwriting. Illustrated with Facsimiles from Originals in the South Kensington Museum, to which are added Illustrations of the Nagari Character. By the late Professor Palmer and Frederic Pincott. 4to. 12s

REEVE, —.
English-Carnatica and Carnatica-English Dictionary. (Very slightly damaged.) £8.

SCHNURMANN, J. NESTOR.
Russian Manual. 6s. (For details see next page.)
Aid to Russian Composition.

TIEN, REV. ANTON, M.R.A S.
Egyptian, Syrian, and North African Handbook. 4s.

PORTMAN, M. V., M.R.A.S.
Manual of the Andamanese Languages. 10s. 6d.

REEDS for Oriental Writing may be obtained from Messrs. W. H. Allen & Co. Price 6d.

W. H. ALLEN & Co.'s Oriental Manuals.

CLARKE, Captain H. W., R.E.
The Persian Manual. Containing a Concise Grammar, with Exercises, Useful Phrases, Dialogues, and Subjects for Translation into Persian; also a Vocabulary of Useful Words, English and Persian. 18mo. 7s. 6d.

GOUGH, A. E.
Key to the Exercises in Williams's Sanscrit Manual. 18mo. 4s.

MACKENZIE, Captain C. F.
A Turkish Manual. Comprising a Condensed Grammar with Idiomatic Phrases, Exercises and Dialogues, and Vocabulary. Fcap. 6s.

PALMER, Professor E. H., M.A.
The Arabic Manual. Comprising a Condensed Grammar of both Classical and Modern Arabic; Reading Lessons and Exercises, with Analyses and a Vocabulary of Useful Words Fcap. 7s. 6d.

PINCOTT, FREDERIC, M.R.A.S.
The Hindi Manual. Comprising a Grammar of the Hindi Language both Literary and Provincial; a Complete Syntax; Exercises in various styles of Hindi Composition; Dialogues on several subjects; and a Complete Vocabulary. Fcap. 6s.

PLATTS, J. T.
Forbes's Hindustani Manual, Containing a Compendious Grammar, Exercises for Translation, Dialogues, and Vocabulary, in the Roman Character. New Edition, entirely revised. 18mo. 3s 6d.

PORTMAN, M. V., M.R.A.S.
A Manual of the Andamanese Languages. 18mo. 10s. 6d.

RAVERTY, Major H. G.
The Pushto Manual. Comprising a Concise Grammar Exercises and Dialogues; Familiar Phrases, Proverbs, and Vocabulary Fcap. 5s.

SCHNURMANN, J. NESTOR.
The Russian Manual. Comprising a Condensed Grammar, Exercises with Analyses, Useful Dialogues, Reading Lessons, Tables of Coins, Weights and Measures, and a Collection of Idioms and Proverbs, alphabetically arranged. Fcap. 7s. 6d.

Aid to Russian Composition. Containing Exercises, Vocabularies, Syntactical Rules, and Specimens of Russian Manuscript. Fcap. 7s. 6d.

TIEN, Rev. ANTON, Ph.D., M R.A.S.
Egyptian, Syrian, and North-African Handbook. A Simple Phrase-Book in English and Arabic for the use of the British Forces, Civilians, and Residents in Egypt. Fcap. 4s.

Manual of Colloquial Arabic. Comprising Practical Rules for learning the Language, Vocabulary, Dialogues, Letters and Idioms, &c. in English and Arabic. Fcap. 7s. 6d.

Neo-Hellenic Manual. Comprising Practical Rules for Learning the Languages, Vocabulary, Dialogues, Letters, Idioms, &c. Fcap. 5s.

WILLIAMS, MONIER.
Sanscrit Manual. To which is added a Vocabulary, by A. E. Gough. 18mo. 7s. 6d.

Maps of India, &c.

A Diocesan Map of India and Ceylon, 1885. Drawn, and Compiled from the latest Authorities by the Rev. Donald J. Mackey, M.A., F.S.S., &c., Canon and Precentor of S. Ninian's Cathedral, Perth; Author of Diocesan Maps of England, Scotland, and Ireland. In cloth case, or on roller varnished. Dedicated to the Metropolitan and Bishops of India £1 11s. 6d.

A General Map of India. Corrected to 1884. Compiled chiefly from Surveys executed by order of the Government of India. On six sheets —size, 5ft. 3in. wide, 5ft. 4in. high, £2; or on cloth, in case, £2 12s. 6d. or rollers, varnished, £3 3s.

A Relievo Map of India. By Henry F. Brion. In frame. 21s.

District Map of India. Corrected to 1885. Divided into Collectorates with the Telegraphs and Railways from Government Surveys. On six sheets—size, 5ft. 6in. high, 5ft. 8in. wide, £2; in a case, £2 12s. 6d.; or rollers, varnished, £3 3s.

Handbook of Reference to the Maps of India. Giving the Latitude and Longitude of places of note. 18mo. 3s. 6d.

Map of India. Corrected to 1876. From the most recent authorities. On two sheets—size, 2ft. 10in. wide, 3ft. 3in. high, 16s.; or on cloth, in a case, £1 1s.

Map of the Routes in India. Corrected to 1874. With Tables of Distances between the principal Towns and Military Stations. On one sheet—size, 2ft. 3in. wide, 2ft. 9in. high, 9s.; or on cloth, in a case, 12s.

Map of the Western Provinces of Hindoostan—the Punjab, Cabool, Scinde, Bhawulpore, &c.—including all the States between Candahar and Allahabad. On four sheets—size, 4ft. 4in. wide, 4ft. 2in. high, 30s.; or in case, £2; rollers, varnished, £2 10s.

Map of India and China, Burmah, Siam, the Malay Peninsula, and the Empire of Anam. On two sheets—size, 4ft. 3in. wide, 3ft. 4in. high, 16s.; or on cloth, in a case, £1 5s.

Map of the Steam Communication and Overland Routes between England, India, China, and Australia. In a case, 14s.; on rollers and varnished, 18s.

Map of China. From the most authentic sources of information. One large sheet—size, 2ft. 7in. wide, 2ft. 2in. high, 6s.; or on cloth, in case, 8s.

Map of the World. On Mercator's Projection, showing the Tracts of the Early Navigators, the Currents of the Ocean, the Principal Lines of great Circle Sailing, and the most recent discoveries. On four sheets— size, 6ft. 2in. wide, 4ft. 3in. high, £2; on cloth, in a case, £2 10s.; or with rollers, and varnished, £3.

Russian Official Map of Central Asia. Compiled in Accordance with the Discoveries and Surveys of Russian Staff Officers up to the close of the year 1877. In two sheets. 10s. 6d.; or in cloth case, 4s.

New Books in the Press.

ILLUSTRATED BOOKS.

Fifty Years of a Showman's Life; or, The Life and Travels of Van Hare. By Himself. Crown 8vo. 10s. 6d.

The Falcon on the Baltic; a Voyage from London to Copenhagen in a Three Tonner. By E. F. KNIGHT, Author of "The Cruise of the Falcon." With 10 Full-page Illustrations. Crown 8vo. 6s.

The Enchanted Island. By WYKE BAYLISS, F.S.A., President of the Royal Society of British Artists, Author of "The Witness of Art," &c Crown 8vo. 5s.

Sketches of a Yachting Cruise. By Major E. GAMBIER PARRY, Author of "Life of Reynell Taylor." Demy 8vo. 9s.

Ad Orientem. By A. D. FREDERICKSON. Numerous Coloured Illustrations. Demy 8vo. 16s.

EDUCATIONAL BOOKS.

Students' Plane Trigonometry. By THOMAS RONEY Imperial 8vo

INCE AND GILBERT SERIES.

Outlines of English History. Revised and re-written in part by ARTHUR HASSALL, Student of Christ Church. Fcap. 8vo. Paper cover, 1s.; cloth, 1s. 6d.

Outlines of French History. Re-written by ARTHUR HASSALL, Student of Christ Church. Fcap. 8vo. Paper cover, 1s.; cloth, 1s. 6d.

NEW ORIENTAL MANUALS.

A Manual of Anglicised Colloquial Burmese. By F. A. DAVIDSON. Fcap 8vo 5s.

Chinese Manual. By Professor R. K. DOUGLAS. Fcap. 8vo.

An Arabic Reading Book. By ALAN B. BIRDWOOD. Fcap. 8vo.

EMINENT WOMEN SERIES.
EDITED BY JOHN H. INGRAM
TWO NEW VOLUMES.

Elizabeth Barrett Browning. By JOHN H. INGRAM

Jane Austen. By Mrs. MALDEN.

POPULAR EDITION, One Shilling and Sixpence each.
In limp cloth binding.

George Eliot. By MATHILDE BLIND.

BIOGRAPHIES OF GREAT COMPOSERS.
NEW VOLUME. Fcap. 8vo.

Mendelssohn. By J. CUTHBERT HADDEN.

LONDON:
W. H. ALLEN & CO., 13 WATERLOO PLACE. S.W.

New Books in the Press.

TO BE PUBLISHED AT INTERVALS, IN SIX CROWN 8vo. VOLUMES.
SIX SHILLINGS EACH.

KAYE'S SEPOY WAR AND MALLESON'S INDIAN MUTINY.
EDITED BY COLONEL G. B. MALLESON, C.S.I.

KAYE'S SEPOY WAR.   Vol. I.   [*October.*

Lives of Indian Officers. By Sir J. W. Kaye. (Originally published in 3 vols.) In 2 vols Crown 8vo. With Portrait.

Haydn's Book of Dignities. Revised and Enlarged by Horace Ockerby. Demy 8vo. 28s.

The Romance of Industry. By James Burnley.

Le Comte de Paris. By the Marquis de Flers. Translated by Constance Majendie. Illustrated with Six Portraits and Autograph.

The Dairy Farm. By James Long, Author of "Poultry for Prizes and Profit." Illustrated. Crown 8vo.

The Diseases and Disorders of the Ox. By George Gresswell, B.A., Oxford, recently Lecturer in Physical Science at the Diocesan College, Cape Town. With a few Notes by James B Gresswell, Fellow of the Royal College of Veterinary Surgeons.

First Wilts Rifle Volunteers. By Major R. D Gibney, late Adjutant 1st Battalion Wiltshire Volunteers. Crown 8vo. Paper cover. 1s.

With the Harrises. By the Author of "The Subaltern," "The Chronicles of Waltham," &c. &c. 6s.

History of the London Stage. By H. Barton Baker. 2 vols. Crown 8vo. 12s.

Home-Made Wines. By Clements. Crown 8vo. Paper cover.

The Cultivated Oranges and Lemons of India. By Dr. G. Bonavia. Demy 8vo. With Atlas of 250 Plates. 31s. 6d.

Old Madras Days; or, The Folk Lore of Southern India. Collected by Mrs. Howard Kingscote and Pandit Natesa Sastri. Crown 8vo.

In Anarchy's Net. By S. J. Baxter. Second Edition. Crown 8vo.

Hints to Travellers in India. By An Anglo-Indian. 1s.

Roaring in Horses : an Experimental Research. By R. H. Clarke, M.A., M.B., Cantab., M.R.C.S. With Numerous Illustrations by F. S. Sheldon. Demy 8vo.

Compensation: The Publican's Case. By C. Cagney. Demy 8vo.

The Floral King : a Life of Linnæus. Translated from the Swedish by A. Alberg.

Life and Balloon Experiences. Part II. By H. Coxwell. With Special Chapters on Military Ballooning. Crown 8vo.

An Account of the Chapel of Marlborough College. By the Rev. Newton Mant, B.A., Vicar of Sledmere, York. With Illustrations by H. C. Brewer. Crown 8vo.

BOOKS, &c.,

ISSUED BY

MESSRS. W. H. ALLEN & Co.,

𝕻ublishers & 𝕷iterary 𝕬gents to the 𝕴ndia 𝕺ffice

COMPRISING

MISCELLANEOUS PUBLICATIONS IN GENERAL LITERATURE.

INDIAN AND MILITARY LAW.

MAPS OF INDIA, &c.

LONDON:

W. H. ALLEN & CO., 13 WATERLOO PLACE,
PALL MALL, S.W.

Works issued from the India Office, and sold by
W. H. ALLEN & Co.

Illustrations of Ancient Buildings in Kashmir.
Prepared at the Indian Museum under the authority of the Secretary of State for India in Council. From Photographs, Plans, and Drawings taken by Order of the Government of India. By Henry Hardy Cole, Lieut. R.E., Superintendent Archæological Survey of India, North-West Provinces. In 1 vol.; half-bound, Quarto. 58 Plates. £3 10s.
The Illustrations in this work have been produced in Carbon from the original negatives, and are therefore permanent.

Pharmacopœia of India.
Prepared under the Authority of the Secretary of State for India. By Edward John Waring. M.D. Assisted by a Committee appointed for the Purpose. 8vo. 6s.

The Stupa of Bharhut. A Buddhist Monument.
Ornamented with numerous Sculptures illustrative of Buddhist Legend and History in the Third Century B.C. By Alexander Cunningham, C.S.I., C.I.E., Major-General, Royal Engineers (Bengal Retired); Director-General Archæological Survey of India. 4to. 57 Plates. Cloth gilt. £3 3s.

Archæological Survey of Western India.
Report of the First Season's Operations in the Belgâm and Kaladgi Districts. January to May 1874. Prepared at the India Museum and Published under the Authority of the Secretary of State for India in Council. By James Burgess, Author of the "Rock Temples of Elephanta," &c. &c., and Editor of "The Indian Antiquary." Half-bound. Quarto. 58 Plates and Woodcuts. £2 2s.

Archæological Survey of Western India. Vol. II.
Report on the Antiquities of Kâthiâwâd and Kachh, being the result of the Second Season's Operations of the Archæological Survey of Western India. 1874-1875. By James Burgess, F.R.G.S., M R A S., &c., Archæological Surveyor and Reporter to Government, Western India. 1876. Half-bound. Quarto. 74 Plates and Woodcuts. £3 3s.

Archæological Survey of Western India. Vol. III.
Report on the Antiquities in the Bidar and Aurungabad Districts in the Territory of H.H. the Nizam of Haidarabad, being the result of the Third Season's Operations of the Archæological Survey of Western India. 1875-1876. By James Burgess, F.R G.S., M R A.S., etc. Half-bound. Quarto. 66 Plates and Woodcuts. £2 2s.

Illustrations of Buildings near Muttra and Agra.
Showing the Mixed Hindu-Mahomedan Style of Upper India. Prepared at the India Museum under the Authority of the Secretary of State for India in Council, from Photographs, Plans, and Drawings taken by Order of the Government of India. By Henry Hardy Cole, Lieut. R.E., Superintendent Archæological Survey of India, North-West Provinces. 4to. With Photographs and Plates. £3 10s.

The Cave Temples of India.
By James Ferguson, D.C.L., F.R.A.S., V.P.R.A.S., and James Burgess, F.R.G.S., M.R.A.S., &c. Printed and Published by Order of Her Majesty's Secretary of State, &c. Roy. 8vo. With Photographs and Woodcuts. £2 2s.

Published on the arrival of each overland Mail from India. Subscription 26s. per annum. Specimen copy, 6d.

ALLEN'S INDIAN MAIL,

AND

Official Gazette

FROM

INDIA, CHINA, AND ALL PARTS OF THE EAST.

ALLEN'S INDIAN MAIL contains the fullest and most authentic Reports of all important Occurrences in the Countries to which it is devoted, compiled chiefly from private and exclusive sources. It has been pronounced by the Press in general to be *indispensable* to all who have Friends or Relatives in the East, as affording the only *correct* information regarding the Services, Movements of Troops, Shipping, and all events of Domestic and Individual interest.

The subjoined list of the usual Contents will show the importance and variety of the information concentrated in ALLEN'S INDIAN MAIL.

Summary and Review of Eastern News.

Precis of Public Intelligence	Shipping—Arrival of Ships
Selections from the Indian Press	,, ,, Passengers
Movements of Troops	,, Departure of Ships
The Government Gazette	,, ,, Passengers
Courts Martial	Commercial—State of the Markets
Domestic Intelligence—Births	,, Indian Securities
,, ,, Marriages	,, Freights
,, ,, Deaths	&c. &c. &c.

Home Intelligence relating to India, &c.

Original Articles	Arrivals reported in England
Miscellaneous Information	Departures ,, ,,
Appointments, Extensions of	Shipping—Arrival of Ships
Furloughs, &c., &c.	,, ,, Passengers
,, Civil	, Departure of Ships
,, Military	,, ,, Passengers
,, Ecclesiastical and	,, Vessel spoken with
,, Marine	&c. &c. &c.

Review of Works on the East, and Notices of all affairs connected with India and the Services.

Throughout the Paper one uniform system of arrangement prevails, and at the conclusion of each year an INDEX is furnished, to enable Subscribers to bind up the Volume, which forms a complete

ASIATIC ANNUAL REGISTER AND LIBRARY OF REFERENCE.

LONDON: W. H. ALLEN & Co., 13, WATERLOO PLACE, S.W

(PUBLISHERS TO THE INDIA OFFICE),

To whom communications for the Editor, and Advertisements, are requested to be addressed.

Eminent Women Series.

Edited by John H. Ingram.

VOLUMES ALREADY ISSUED:—

GEORGE ELIOT.	By Mathilde Blind.
EMILY BRONTË.	,, A. Mary F. Robinson.
GEORGE SAND.	,, Bertha Thomas.
MARY LAMB.	,. Anne Gilchrist.
MARIA EDGEWORTH.	., Helen Zimmern.
MARGARET FULLER.	,, Julia Ward Howe.
ELIZABETH FRY.	,, Mrs. E. R. Pitman.
COUNTESS OF ALBANY.	,, Vernon Lee.
HARRIET MARTINEAU.	., Mrs. Fenwick Miller
MARY WOLLSTONECRAFT GODWIN.	,, Elizabeth Robins Pennell.
RACHEL.	,, Mrs. A. Kennard.
MADAME ROLAND.	,. Mathilde Blind.
SUSANNA WESLEY.	,, Eliza Clarke.
MARGARET OF NAVARRE.	,, Mary A. Robinson.
MRS. SIDDONS.	,, Mrs. A. Kennard.
MADAME DE STAËL.	., Bella Duffy.
HANNAH MORE.	,, Charlotte M. Yonge.
ELIZABETH BARRETT BROWNING.	,, John H. Ingram.

POPULAR EDITION.

In Limp Cloth. Price 1s. 6d.

FIRST VOLUME.

GEORGE ELIOT. By Mathilde Blind.

W. H. ALLEN & CO., 13 Waterloo Place, S.W.